Library of
Davidson College
VOID

Library of
Davidson College

Twentieth-Century
Epic Novels

Twentieth-Century Epic Novels

Theodore L. Steinberg

Newark: University of Delaware Press

©2005 by Rosemont Publishing & Printing Corp.

All rights reserved. Authorization to photocopy items for internal or personal use, or the internal or personal use of specific clients, is granted by the copyright owner, provided that a base fee of $10.00, plus eight cents per page, per copy is paid directly to the Copyright Clearance Center, 222 Rosewood Drive, Danvers, Massachusetts 01923.[0-87413-889-2/05 $10.00 + 8¢ pp, pc.]

Other than as indicated in the foregoing, this book may not be reproduced, in whole or in part, in any form (except as permitted by Sections 107 and 108 of the U.S. Copyright Law, and except for brief quotes appearing in reviews in the public press).

Associated University Presses
2010 Eastpark Boulevard
Cranbury, NJ 08512

The paper used in this publication meets the requirements of the American National Standard for Permanence of Paper for Printed Library Materials Z39.48-1984.

Library of Congress Cataloging-in-Publication Data

Steinberg, Theodore L. (Theodore Louis), 1947-
  Twentieth-century epic novels / Theodore L. Steinberg.
    p. cm.
Includes bibliographical references and index.
ISBN 0-87413-889-2 (alk. paper)
1. English fiction—20th century—History and criticism. 2. Epic literature—History and criticism. 3. Asch, Sholem, 1880-1957—Criticism and interpretation. 4. Manning, Olivia—Criticism and interpretation. 5. Whittemore, Edward. Jerusalem quartet. 6. Durrell, Lawrence. Alexandria quartet. 7. Scott, Paul, 1920- Raj quartet. I. Title.

PR888.E6S74 2005
823'.9109—dc22

2004021652

PRINTED IN THE UNITED STATES OF AMERICA

For Phyllis

Contents

Preface	9
Acknowledgments	13
Abbreviations	15
1. Approaching the Epic	19
2. Sholem Asch's *Three Cities*	55
3. Olivia Manning's *Fortunes of War*	89
4. Paul Scott's *Raj Quartet*	121
5. Edward Whittemore's *Jerusalem Quartet*	157
6. Lawrence Durrell's *Alexandria Quartet*	190
Notes	221
Works Cited	231
Index	241

Preface

With very few exceptions, epics are long. A person who does not want to read thousands of pages of text would be well-advised to study the aphorism or haiku. Nevertheless, for those who persist, there are many rewards to working on epic: an encounter with some of the greatest literature that has ever been produced, constant challenges, and the necessity to move among cultures and eras to observe the numerous variations on the way epic has been conceived. This book is about some of those variations as they appear in twentieth-century epic novels.

By epic novels I mean, quite simply, novels that employ certain elements that have been characterized as epic through the centuries. As I explain in the introductory chapter, the definition of "epic" is often either taken for granted or is based on formal elements that are more properly thought of as optional ornamentation: particular verse forms, particular kinds of heroic behavior, the involvement of deities, and the like. These elements do appear in many epics, but they do not define the genre. In that introductory chapter, I try to provide a more substantial description of the elements that do characterize epic.

I should point out from the very beginning that my view of epic does not depend on any particular theoretical position, though I use theoretical insights whenever they are appropriate. Instead, I have read, over a number of years, many works that are traditionally considered to be epics, looking for the significant elements that they have in common. These elements, which characterize epic, are described in the introduction and they necessitate some reclassification of well-known works. I occasionally employ the unfashionable term "essence," by which I imply that there is a commonality among epics that justifies the use of the generic term.

Some readers may understandably look askance at the project I have undertaken, and I hope that my reasoning will justify my procedure. As I argue, genres matter; and if they matter, then understanding them and using them as a means of classification also matters. A lyric poem is not a novel, and neither is a play—despite what my students may tell me—and we do works a disservice if we do not correctly identify the families to which they belong. My approach to epic is descriptive rather than prescriptive.

I also attempt in the introduction to provide a brief description of the evolution of epic. This part of the argument may be particularly important to those readers who feel that "twentieth-century epic" is oxymoronic, that epic died with Milton. It does often seem that the world of literature has been taken over by novels, much as that world was dominated before the eighteenth century by poetry. Just as there are varieties of poetry—elegy, sonnet, ballad—so there are varieties of novels, and among their number is the epic novel. The matter of the novel, so to speak, has, in such cases, merged with the form of the epic; and that fusion did not leave epic untouched. It had to undergo change, but not such drastic change that it was no longer epic. It is simply a different kind of epic, just as the *Aeneid* is a different kind of epic than the *Iliad*, or *Paradise Lost* is a different kind of epic than either of those earlier works. One kind of epic novel is overtly based on classical models, as Fielding's *Amelia* is based on the *Aeneid*. Such novels are not the subject of this study. Rather, the following chapters examine works that move beyond imitation of classical models.

It might well be asked why I have chosen the particular works that I study, works by Sholem Asch, Olivia Manning, Paul Scott, Edward Whittemore, and Lawrence Durrell. I can offer three answers. In the first place, these works clearly fit the model that I try to establish in the introduction; and because epic has always been a rather exclusive genre, there are not all that many works to choose from. Still, there are other epic novels, so why these? One reason, a consequence of choosing to work with epic, concerns language. I could not discuss in proper depth a work whose original language I do not know. Consequently, I refer to a work like Mikhail Sholokhov's *Quiet Flows the Don*, but I would consider it improper to devote a chapter to that novel. I have, therefore, chosen works that I can read in the original languages. And finally, I have chosen works with what Jerome Dees has called a missionary impulse. These are wonderful, enriching novels, almost all of which are seldom read. I suspect that they are seldom read for two reasons: they are all fairly long, and their epicness differentiates them from other, more familiar sorts of novels. They feel, therefore, simultaneously familiar and unfamiliar. One of my hopes is that by identifying them as epics, thereby explaining and expunging their unfamiliarity, I might help to increase their readership.

One final point that I should make concerns something else that an early reader of the manuscript drew to my attention, the existence of what seems to be a "Jewish thread" in the book. Naturally, as I indicate in the chapter on Sholem Asch, his Yiddish novel is written from a Jewish point of view, just as Sholokhov's presents the Cossack point of view. Even so, the other works also contain significant references to Jews and Judaism. Perhaps I am especially attuned to such references. At the same time, those references do, it seems to me, help to broaden the scope of the works in which they appear; and by broadening the scope, they contribute to the epicness of the novels. In a similar fashion, I try to pay special attention to female characters in these epics. Traditionally epics have been thought to deal with "male" concerns and to relegate women to a subordinate status. As I argue in the introduction and as I try to indicate in each of the subsequent chapters, those perceptions are either mistaken or incomplete. The women, like the Jews, add essential elements to the epic themes of these works.

I would like to thank the following friends and scholars for their invaluable assistance: Minda Rae Amiran, Jerome Dees, Wayne Erickson, Karen Mills-Courts, Malcolm Nelson, John Stinson, and Clark Zlotchew. Do I dare to say that their help has been of epic proportions? I would also like to thank my children, Gillian, Daniel, and Miriam, and to acknowledge the constant support of my wife, Phyllis K. Steinberg.

Acknowledgments

Permission to reprint excerpts from the following is gratefully acknowledged:

Extracts from THREE CITIES by permissions of the Sholem Asch Literary Estate.

Extracts from JUSTINE by Lawrence Durrell, copyright © 1957, renewed ©1985 by Lawrence George Durrell. Used by permissions of Dutton, a division of Penguin Group (USA) and by permission of Faber & Faber Ltd.

Extracts from BALTHAZAR by Lawrence Durrell, copyright © 1958, renewed ©1986 by Lawrence Durrell. Used by permission of Viking Penguin, a division of Penguin Group (USA) Inc., and also reproduced with permission of Curtis Brown Ltd., London, on behalf of the estate of Lawrence Durrell.

Extracts from MOUNTOLIVE by Lawrence Durrell, copyright © 1958. Renewed ©1986 by Lawrence Durrell. Used by permissions of Dutton, a division of Penguin Group (USA) Inc., and also reproduced with permission of Curtis Brown Ltd., London, on behalf of the estate of Lawrence Durrell.

Extracts from CLEA by Lawrence Durrell, copyright © 1960, renewed ©1988 by Lawrence Durrell. Used by permissions of Dutton, a division of Penguin Group (USA) Inc., and also reproduced with permission of Curtis Brown Ltd., London, on behalf of the estate of Lawrence Durrell.

Extracts from THE ILIAD by Homer, translated by Richmond Lattimore. Used by permission of the University of Chicago Press.

Extracts from THE BALKAN TRILOGY by Olivia Manning, published by Heinemann. Used by permission of The Random House Group Limited.

Extracts from THE LEVANT TRILOGY by Olivia Manning, used by permission from Weidenfeld & Nicolson, a division of The Orion Publishing Group.

Extracts from THE RAJ QUARTET by Paul Scott. Reprinted by permission of Harold Ober Associates Incorporated. Copyright 1976.

Extracts from ON WRITING AND THE NOVEL by Paul Scott. Reprinted by permission of Harold Ober Associates Incorporated. Copyright 1987.

Extracts from WAR AND PEACE by Leo Tolstoy, translated by Rosemary Edmunds. Used by permission of the Penguin Group.

Extracts from THE JERUSALEM QUARTET by Edward Whittemore, by permission of Thomas Wallace.

Thanks to *Deus Loci: The Lawrence Durrell Journal* for permission to include material originally published in the essay: "Lawrence Durrell's Postmodern Epic" (NS7 1999–2000): 58–69.

Abbreviations

B	*Balthazar*
BT	*The Balkan Trilogy*
C	*Clea*
D	*A Division of the Spoils*
J	*Justine*
JE	*The Jewel in the Crown*
JM	*Jericho Mosaic*
JP	*Jerusalem Poker*
LT	*The Levant Trilogy*
M	*Mountolive*
NS	*Nile Shadows*
S	*The Day of the Scorpion*
ST	*Sinai Tapestry*
T	*The Towers of Silence*
W	*On Writing and the Novel*

Twentieth-Century
Epic Novels

1
Approaching the Epic

Why Bother with Genre?

A friend of mine recently attended a pot luck dinner. After she had placed her contribution to the meal on the table, an acquaintance approached and began talking to her, at the same time taking a morsel out of the plate she had just set down. His taste of that morsel was followed by a horrible grimace, and he spat out the barely chewed food, saying, "That's the worst brownie I ever tasted." My friend, nonplused and offended, explained, "That's not a brownie. It's a stuffed mushroom," to which the offender shamefacedly replied, "Oh, for a stuffed mushroom it's pretty good."

I have used that story elsewhere in order to illustrate the importance of genre, and I will undoubtedly use it again, because it illustrates graphically an important point, a point that Northrop Frye made in a more sophisticated manner when he wrote, "In nearly every period of literature there are many romances, confessions and anatomies that are neglected only because the categories to which they belong are unrecognized."[1] Generic classifications, that is, raise certain expectations in the knowledgeable reader, and those expectations themselves become important aspects of a literary work. Lesser writers, who become familiar with generic conventions, include them in their works, thereby declaring their affiliation with a particular tradition. The greatest writers are also familiar with those conventions, but they do not simply include them. Instead they use them, manipulate them, and play with them; ultimately they create something new with them. That new creation, as we will see, may still belong to the genre that gave birth to the conventions, but it has taken the genre in new directions. To borrow a term from Gérard Genette, those new creations are like palimpsests, works written over older works, allowing both works to be read.

Rosalie Colie quite correctly points out that we tend to regard "forms" as restrictive, and she regrets that New Criticism "excoriated the idea of genre."[2] Such an attitude toward genre is a modern development. In the Renaissance, which was a fertile period in the development of the epic, genres served as signposts that told the audience what to expect.[3] Jacques Derrida makes a similar point when he says at the beginning of an essay, "As soon as the word 'genre' is sounded . . . a limit is drawn. And when a limit is established, norms and interdictions are not far behind: 'Do,' 'Do not' says 'genre,' the word 'genre,' the figure, the voice, or law of genre" and then concludes, "The genre has always in all genres been able to play the role of order's principle: resemblance, analogy, identity, and difference, taxonomic classification, organization and genealogical tree, order of reason, order of reasons, sense of sense, truth of truth, natural light and sense of history."[4] For a variety of reasons, some better than others, it mattered to people whether *Orlando Furioso* was an epic, a romance, or some other kind of work. If it was an epic, it meant one thing and belonged with other epic works; if it was a romance, it meant something quite different and belonged with other works. And if, heaven forfend, it tried to combine those two distinct genres, the consequences were, for some critics, unthinkable, as though such a thing as a pure epic could be conceived.

As we examine the Renaissance controversies over such questions, we might allow ourselves to be amused. They do, after all, often sound like the kind of scholastic arguments that led to the end of medieval Aristotelianism. On the other hand, we ought to consider what was so vital about generic classifications that they aroused such strong passions. If genres served as signposts to Renaissance readers, do they still serve as signposts to us? Does it matter to us that we get a stuffed mushroom when we expect a brownie, or do we approach eating without expectations, allowing ourselves to be surprised with each new bite? Of course we have expectations before we eat something, and so should we as we read. At the same time, our expectations must not be too narrow. A mushroom may be stuffed with a variety of fillings, and an author may use a genre in a variety of ways.

Elsewhere I have explored Edmund Spenser's use of the elegy in his poem "Astrophel," which was written some years after the death of Sir Philip Sidney.[5] After Sidney's death in 1586, scores of elegies were written, and almost all of them relied on the standard elegiac conventions: mourning for the deceased, sadness for the living, and the hope that the deceased continues to live in a better place. Such poems may have been heartfelt, but they are easily forgotten. Spenser's "Astrophel," however, extends generic expectations. Spenser does employ those conventions, but he uses them to express his feeling that Sidney's death was an unnecessary waste, that Sidney's military derring-do was an abandonment of his poetic calling. Spenser's poem mourns as sincerely as any of the other elegies on Sidney, but it uses the conventions of elegy rather than being used by them. "Astrophel" helped lead to "Lycidas," which in turn led to "Adonais," and so on into the future. The greatest writers manipulate genre, and so it behooves us to pay attention to what constitutes those genres.

Alastair Fowler adds another dimension to the subject when he points to the significance of generic groupings. If we relate Thomas Pynchon's *The Crying of Lot 49* to Menippean satire, we see one thing; but if we group it with *Gravity's Rainbow* and Vonnegut's *Slaughterhouse-Five* as apocalyptic satire, "its significance is bound to alter in consequence of this new generic affiliation."[6] The implications of this observation are vital. In the past, generic classifications tended more to the absolute: a work belonged to a particular genre. It may have been a good example or a poor example of that genre, but the genre was clear. More recently we seem willing to consider works from multiple generic viewpoints. *The Tempest* may fulfill the conventions of a comedy, a romance, an apology for colonialism, or other generic classifications, and our understanding of the play increases as we grasp each possibility; but unless we understand at least some of those possibilities, we stand to miss a great deal.

Genre, then, helps us to understand what we read, but we must also be cautious about it, especially about the tendency to absolutize genres, as so many Aristotelian critics did. To choose just one example out of thousands, Le Bossu, basing himself on the *Poetics*, dictates that "the space of a Year is to the *Epick Narration*, what the space of a Day is to *Tragedy*; and that the Winter is as improper for this great Work, as the Night is for *Theatre*; since both being void of Action, make a vicious Interval."[7] Such strictures seem foolish to us, probably because they actually are foolish. As Voltaire pointed out, Homer and Virgil did not follow Le Bossu's rules. Genre is important, then, but it cannot be treated rigidly. Genres evolve, and individual works not only may but must partake of more than one genre. There can hardly be such a thing as a pure example of a genre.[8]

A major problem in genre study, however, involves deciding what constitutes a particular genre. Colie illustrates the basic conflict when she asks what kind of work Castiglione's *Courtier* is: "Is it chiefly a dialogue? If I say it is, I throw myself in with the Alexandrian librarians . . . who classify by formal means. Is it an *Institutio*, a blueprint for education? If this is what it is, then I must insist . . . that subject governs genre."[9] The conflict is between those who emphasize the formal elements of a genre, whether they be conventional elements such as meter and the invocation of a muse or conventional episodes, such as a journey, and those who emphasize its central characteristics. This conflict is further complicated by the division between those who view generic classifications as prescriptive (as Le Bossu does) and those who view them as descriptive (as Voltaire does). Thus David Maskell says of sixteenth- and seventeenth-century French critics, "There was little attempt to extract and recreate the essence of epic—whatever the essence of epic might be—for though the theorists did make some effort to define the purpose of epic, it was never suggested that this purpose could be achieved otherwise than in accordance with the precepts concerning externals which formed the main bulk of their treatises."[10]

Through much of history, the formalists have triumphed. Even now, students tend to be taught that epics are long poems, focusing on a hero whose powers either are or verge on the supernatural, involving a journey, incorporating the gods, and having both national and cosmic significance. It may be true that many of these characteristics do appear in many epics, but such formal elements do not define the epic. If they did, and if we took that concept to its ultimate end, we might have to agree with Georg Lukács that "strictly speaking," only Homer's works are epics, a wonderful example of *reductio ad absurdum*.[11] There are, however, scholars who believe that epic has disappeared as a living genre, that the last true epic was *Paradise Lost*. Thus David Quint says that "the classically modeled epic poem gave way to the 'modern' romance and the novel" after the Renaissance, a situation that he explains by asserting that Virgilian ideology, which he uses to define epic, no longer fit the social structure.[12] This argument seems somewhat backward. Quint, like Lukács, defines the genre in such a limited way that its obsolescence becomes part of the definition. Such an attitude not only renders the epic obsolete by denying its continuing evolution, but it also prevents readers from fully appreciating those post-Miltonic works that share the central characteristics, if not all the formal elements, that constitute epic. The formal elements are important, but we can note that in the eighteenth century, when a great deal of theoretical attention was paid to them, no epic worth mentioning was produced that relied on those elements. The nearest anyone came was Pope, with *The Rape of the Lock* and *The Dunciad*, two mock epics, much of whose humor derives from his incongruous use of those elements. But even so, epic was not dead. Rather it was evolving. As Thomas Maresca says, "Fielding, by discarding the petrified *forms* of epic and rediscovering the human nature of the epic hero, managed to restore epic to the culturally central position that, under the guise of the novel, it has not lost since."[13] Fielding knew those forms, but he transformed them.

His work, as we will see, formed a step in the evolution of the epic, an evolution that both preserves the essence of the genre and demonstrates the primacy of that essence.

This notion of evolution in genre, especially in the case of epic, requires attention. As I shall argue, every age and every people that have produced epic have produced their own kind of epic. There are essential elements that bind all such works together, that create a genre, but there are also significant differences among them. Our task is to identify those central characteristics. And our investigation should not be confined only to the Western tradition, to the descendents of Homer and Virgil. Epics from other parts of the world also share those central characteristics and deserve a place in our understanding of the genre's evolutionary development.

Epic has only stultified when writers felt that they had to follow specific patterns. Poets like Ronsard and Petrarch, who felt constrained to follow a simplistically rendered Virgilian model, were failures as epicists. As Greene notes, they were not writing for their own times. Rather, they were trying to be Augustan in most un-Augustan times.[14] Even some Renaissance critics were aware of the evolutionary nature of the genre. Giovambattista Giraldi Cinthio, a major voice in the Italian debates about epic and romance, denied that Aristotle's and Horace's principles were unchanging, arguing that the genre "changes as customs and tastes themselves change over time."[15] And again Voltaire, in his wonderful treatise on epic, said, "There are not more Revolutions in Governments, than in Arts. They are shifting and gliding away from our Pursuit, when we endeavour to fix them by our Rules and Definitions."[16] Scholars create rules; artists manipulate them. The conditions for certain types of epic no longer exist, so other types of epic, retaining the essence of epic, have come into being to reflect contemporary conditions.

It may be argued, alternatively, that the time for epic has passed, that epic simply can no longer be written. This argument derives from a partial view of what epic is, a view based largely on Homer, Virgil, and several other acknowledged epicists. Nikos Kazantzakis, however, has written, "So far as I am concerned, there has been no age more epical than ours. It is in such ages which come between two cultures—when one Myth dissolves and another struggles to be born—that epic poems are created."[17]

Milton also acknowledged the evolutionary nature of epic and the fitness of his own time for the creation of a new kind of epic, as he announces at the beginning of Book IX of *Paradise Lost*:

> Since first this Subject for Heroic Song
> Pleas'd me long choosing, beginning late;

> Not sedulous by Nature to indite
> Warrs, hitherto the onely Argument
> Heroic deem'd, chief maistrie to dissect
> With long and tedious havoc fabl'd Knights
> In Battels feign'd; the better fortitude
> Of Patience and Heroic Martyrdom
> Unsung; or to describe Races and Games,
> Or tilting Furniture, emblazon'd Shields,
> Impreses quaint, Caparisons and Steeds;
> Bases and tinsel Trappings, gorgious Knights
> At Joust and Torneament; the marshal'd Feast
> Serv'd up in Hall with Sewers, and Seneschals;
> The skill of Artifice or Office mean,
> Not that which justly gives Heroic name
> To Person or to Poem.
>
> (9.25–41)

In these lines, Milton declares that he is trying something new, that he is writing an epic, or Heroic (the word will be discussed shortly) poem that differs from its predecessors. His poem will not be about war (though it includes the memorable battle in heaven in which fighters on neither side can be injured!) or knights, and it will not rely on traditional epic machinery. Nevertheless, the poem is "Not less but more Heroic then the wrauth / Of stern *Achilles.*" (9.14–15). Milton adapts epic to his own time, and *Paradise Lost* becomes not only a poem about, in Milton's view, the universal condition of human beings but also an expression of the seventeenth century. Similarly, epic works since Milton, to the extent that they do not simply try to repeat the accomplishments of earlier works, are expressions of their own time and simultaneously part of the epic tradition. Like *Paradise Lost,* they take new views of the heroic and of the hero, among other things, but they preserve the essence of the genre.

Moving toward a Definition

The greatest age for discussions of epic was undoubtedly the late Renaissance, particularly in Italy. The immediate cause of these discussions was the publication of Ariosto's *Orlando Furioso* (final version, 1532), a poem that had many of the qualities that readers associated with epic but that had enough chivalric, or romance, features that many of those readers could not consider it a true epic. Today we may be content to call it an epic-romance, but in its own time such a hybrid was considered unnatural, a bastard form, akin to a man-woman. Either it was an epic, in which case all of its features had to be made to accord with accepted strictures about epic, or it was not, in which case it probably was not worth reading. The problem that faced critics who took this position was that the poem was enormously popular, as opposed to something like Trissino's neoclassic epic *Italia liberata dai goti*, which, like Petrarch's *Africa* and Ronsard's *Franciad*, was a popular failure.[18] How could this contrast, this violation of decorum, be explained? According to Javitch, epic theorizing began as a way to deny epic status to *Orlando Furioso*. After all, if it was not an epic, then its popularity represented just another example of the debasement of taste, the closing, so to speak, of the Italian mind.

A key figure in these discussions, of course, was Aristotle.[19] For the Italian theorists, the rules governing such things as the construction of an epic were derived not so much from reading epics as from reading the *Poetics*; but the *Poetics*, in truth, has little to say about epic, so the theorists used that little and then interpolated more based on what Aristotle had said about tragedy. A good example is the passage from Le Bossu quoted earlier, in which Le Bossu says that if a tragedy should cover no more time than a day, then an epic should cover no more than a year. Aristotle would certainly have been surprised. Nevertheless, the discussions became quite ferocious, though their ferocity did little to prevent the creation of more epic-romances, most notably Spenser's *Faerie Queene*, which borrows liberally from both *Orlando Furioso* and Tasso's *Gerusalemme Liberata*.[20] In fact, the case of Tasso is instructive. Poor Tasso, not wanting his poem to be tarred with the same brush as *Orlando Furioso*, emphasized the epic aspects, but it is the romance aspects that have helped his poem retain its popularity.

At the base of these Renaissance discussions of epic was a very simple and common problem, the desire for power and prestige. From early on in literary history, genres had been arranged in a hierarchy, and in the Western tradition the career of Virgil had given life to that hierarchy. Epic perched at the top of the hierarchy, though there was considerable debate over the relative places of epic and tragedy. In any case, epic was the highest of the narrative forms, and as such, the class of epics had to remain small. If any long narrative poem could be considered an epic, there would have been less point in preserving the hierarchy and in preserving the prestige of those scholars who were intimately involved in studying the epic. The handy cliché that academic arguments are so fierce because there tends to be so little at stake clearly applies to the argument over epic. The theorists who were involved in that argument were arguing over epic, certainly; but even more they fought over their own positions in relation to the culture around them, even though the surrounding culture did not seem to care.[21]

The same point may be made about this study of epic. Some of the works to be studied have attained a certain popularity, though in some cases that popularity resulted from the novels having been made into televised miniseries. Surely few readers and even fewer viewers care whether these works are epics or not. Nevertheless, determining whether they are may be valuable for those of us who study literature and may even have the effect of helping us appreciate them more. Such judgments aid in classification, and classification aids in understanding.

Modern discussions of epic often simply assume that readers know what an epic is. A recent collection of essays on the medieval epic includes studies of *Waltharius* and *Ruodlieb, Reinaert,* Icelandic sagas, the German *Prosa-Lancelot,* Hartman's *Armer Heinrich,* Ulrich von Lichtenstein's *Frauendienst,* and Wittenwiler's comic epic Der Ring, but it offers not a word about what makes any of these works an epic.[22] Somewhat more helpfully, Elaine Safer says that her study "focuses on the comic use of epic patterns in selected contemporary American novels of John Barth, Thomas Pynchon, William Gaddis, and Ken Kesey. A number of postmodern novels of these writers are encyclopedic in scope, allude to grand themes in history, and often employ epic devices such as epithets, similes, catalogues, and multiple cross-references.[23] Apparently, then, epics are encyclopedic, allude to grand themes, and use the epic conventions.[24] These assertions may be accurate, but they do little to tell us what epic is: why is epic encyclopedic? what is a "grand theme"? and how necessary are those epic conventions? These are not necessarily easy questions to answer, but if the word "epic" is to have any meaning, they must be answered. John McWilliams rightly says, "Although so loaded a term demands definition, securing a workable definition that is not idiosyncratic proves exasperating. A genre commonly considered to include *Gilgamesh*, Homer, Virgil, Lucan, *Beowulf,* Tasso, Milton, *The Prelude, Leaves of Grass, Ulysses* and *Paterson* is not a genre easily defined with precision."[25] Perhaps the problem McWilliams points to lies in the phrase "commonly considered." He may be correct that these works have all been called epics, but we must ask whether they actually are. They and other works—*Piers Plowman, A Dance to the Music of Time,* the *Kalevala*—are commonly considered epics largely because they are long narratives, but length is not a determining factor in this matter. The novel sequences of Zola and Balzac are also long narratives, as are *The Canterbury Tales,* Gower's *Confessio Amantis,* and *The Romance of the Rose,* but they are not consequently epics. Furthermore, neither *Gilgamesh* nor *Beowulf* is particularly long. In modern parlance, anything long—a novel, a movie, or a visit to the doctor—is called "epic," a situation that has led to the debasement of the term.

Other definitions are equally unhelpful. James Sheridan says that "Traditionally an epic is an account of the exploits of a hero, a man idealized in different ways according to the outlook of the poet and his times."[26] The word "traditionally" is a nice touch, since it seems to lend some backing to the definition, but Arthurian romances, Greek romances, the biblical book of Daniel, and thousands of novels give accounts of the exploits of heroes without being epics. On a similar note, A. M. Keith says that "The Homeric poet in his own voice . . . defines the subject of epic song as the 'famous exploits of men' (κλέα ανδρων. *Il.* 9.189, 524, *Od.* 8.73)."[27] A close look at those references, however, indicates otherwise. At *Iliad* 9.189, the emissaries have come from Agamemnon to try to persuade Achilleus to reenter the battle. They find him near his ships, holding a lyre: "With this he was pleasuring his heart, and singing of men's fame." Achilleus is indeed singing of the "famous exploits of men," but there is no indication here that he is singing an epic. Similarly, at 9.524, we read

> Thus it was in the old days also, the deeds that we hear of
> from the great men, when the swelling anger descended upon them.

These words are spoken by Phoinix, not in the poet's voice, and again there is no evidence that they refer specifically to epic. And, finally, the lines from the *Odyssey* tell us

> the Muse stirred the singer to sing the famous actions
> of men on that venture, whose fame goes up into the wide heaven,
> the quarrel between Odysseus and Peleus' son, Achilleus . . .

Demodokos' song concerns a particular episode, the quarrel between Odysseus and Achilleus. There is no indication that the bard here sings an epic. Thus, while many epics certainly do address the "famous exploits of men," those exploits do not, as Milton made clear, define the subject of epic.

Maurice Bowra also assumes that there exists a traditional definition of the epic: "An epic poem is by common consent a narrative of some length and deals with events which have a certain grandeur and importance and come from a life of action, especially of violent action such as war."[28] As I hope to demonstrate, much of what Bowra, Sheridan, and Keith assert can be properly applied to epic, but these elements do not in themselves define the genre. They are, more accurately, elements that flow from the central characteristics of epic.

As we try to define a term like epic, we must keep in mind that the study of literature is not a science, that while a good deal of literary study requires close reading and logical analysis, intuition and feeling also play major roles. One person's epic is another person's chivalric romance:

> Even if we know very little about literature we know that the *Iliad*, the *Odyssey*, the *Aeneid*, the *Divine Comedy* and *Paradise Lost* are epic poems, and once this is established we can make other definitions. *The Rape of the Lock* is a mock epic poem. *War and Peace* and *Ulysses* are novels with an epic quality, the *Book of Job* and *Gilgamesh* are near epics. It is fairly easy to reject other candidates as unworthy of being called epics; an epic is not just a long poem dealing with a philosophical subject like *The Prelude*, or a long poem dealing with adventure and chivalry like *Idylls of the King*.[29]

What Winnifrith implies in this passage is that we know an epic when we see one, an attitude toward which I am sympathetic, except that I would approach his list quite differently. For reasons that will become clear, I would remove the *Odyssey* from his list, I would say that *War and Peace* is an epic, and I would not mention Job at all in a discussion of epic. Other readers, with other intuitions, would certainly include *The Prelude* as an epic.[30]

While I am sympathetic to Winnifrith's approach, then, I still believe that it is a good idea to try to develop a more precise definition of epic, a definition that will characterize a class of literary works without being unnecessarily restrictive and without, if possible, being too absolute.[31] We have already seen some definitions that try to identify particular traits as fundamental to epic, all of which have been interesting but inadequate. Perhaps we should consider a few more that rely on less imprecise criteria. Our old friend Le Bossu offers a definition that modern readers would reject but that was typical of Renaissance approaches: "a Discourse invented by Art, to form the Manners by such Instructions as are disguis'd under the Allegories of some one important Action, which is related in Verse, after a probable, diverting, and surprising Manner."[32] The epic, that is, is a conduct book in the guise of a narrative poem, though whether we would want our children to grow up like Achilleus may be debatable.

One factor on which many critics agree is the special aura of epic. Voltaire says that the action of epic "should be *great*, to strike us with Awe," and Paul Merchant says that epic "is not a matter of length or size, but of weight," though he would include as epics not only *War and Peace* but *Anna Karenina* and *Crime and Punishment*.[33] These ideas of greatness and weight, however, have appeal. They bring us back to the "grandeur and importance" that Bowra mentioned, before he went on to add that epic "gives a special pleasure because its events and persons enhance our belief in the worth of human achievement and in the dignity and nobility of man."[34] More recently, Masaki Mori has identified three sources of epic grandeur: "The hero's attitude toward his mortality, his relation to the community, and the dual dimension of time and space."[35] That sense of weight, of grandeur, is essential for the epic, particularly in light of the first of Mori's sources, that involving the hero's mortality. As Greene says, "The most important recognition scenes in epic are not between two people but between the hero and his mortality."[36] This perceptive point brings us to the verge of a definition, for all that we need to add is the context in which that recognition takes place, for there are many works other than epics in which the recognition of human mortality is a major theme. Keats used a sonnet to explore his feelings "When I have fears that I may cease to be," and the elegies that were mentioned earlier all have human mortality as a theme.

What, then, distinguishes the epic? The epic is a narrative that focuses simultaneously on the lives of its characters and on a pivotal moment in the history of a community, whether that community be a nation or a people or the whole of humanity. That pivotal moment may be the founding of a civilization, the collapse of a civilization, or any other major event, such as an invasion or another sort of threat. The narrative deals with both the pivotal moment and with the individual characters as they live through that moment.[37] Because the action of the epic is so crucial to a whole civilization, it is often viewed as having cosmic significance, which means that whatever cosmic or divine powers inform the poet's world may also be included. It also means that the epic must have some sort of grandeur, however vague that term may be; and it also must have a huge scope in order to put the pivotal moment in perspective. That scope is often translated into length, because the length allows the writer to establish the historical situation and the ramifications of the pivotal moment; but poems like *Beowulf* or *Sundiata* manage to provide scope without length.

Implications

Much that previous critics have said about the epic flows from this way of regarding it. For instance, from Aristotle onward, there has been a general agreement that the epic must be based on an actual historical event, however much that event may be transformed in the literary work. There really were, for instance, a Troy and a Trojan War. It may have been a minor trade war that, unlike a multitude of minor conflicts, became a center for the growth of legends that over a span of hundreds of years were transformed into the

Iliad, a poem that uses the fall of the city to explore fundamental issues of human mortality, of war, and of heroism. The battle of Troy, augmented by the legends that grew around it, was viewed as having significance not only for the Trojans but for the poet's own time (or the poets' own times) and for the universe. And we must remember that whoever gave the poem the name by which it has been known for almost three thousand years called it the *Iliad*, not the *Achilleid*, recognizing that the poem focuses more centrally on the fall of Troy and the implications of that fall than it does on the wrath of Achilleus. (The *Odyssey*, of course, is indeed named after its hero. As I shall argue later, however, that wonderful poem is not an epic.)

Another element that may be clarified by my definition is the confusion between the epic and the heroic. Occasionally those terms are used interchangeably. Earlier in history, as we see in book 9 of *Paradise Lost* or in Philip Sidney's *Apology for Poetry*, they meant nearly the same thing, possibly because so many epics were heroic. Thus John Adams, who was hardly the archetype of a warrior, wrote in 1785, "I should hope to live to see our young America in Possession of an Heroick Poem, equal to those the most esteemed in any Country."[38] He knew, whether instinctively or as the result of a classical education, that many epics are about the founding of a new society, and he hoped that the recently founded United States might soon have its own epic.

In our time, however, it would be a good idea to separate the heroic from the epic, because while epic poetry is almost always heroic, heroic poetry is not necessarily epic.[39] The reason for this distinction is obvious. A pivotal moment often requires what we usually think of as heroic deeds, that is, military prowess, death-defying courage, actions that are (and this point will be addressed below) "manly." Consequently, epic tends to be at least in part heroic. Heroic poetry, on the other hand, has only to include heroic deeds.[40] Those heroic accomplishments do not have to be related to a pivotal moment in a community. Examples of such heroic poetry can be found in the Icelandic sagas. These are wonderful stories that are full of action, much of it admirable and much of it deplorable. Most of the sagas were apparently based on actual historical events, but those events were not pivotal for Icelandic civilization. In one of the best-known sagas, for instance, *Njal's Saga*, the action is moving and includes many heroic deeds, but the deaths of Njal and his family do nothing to change the course of Icelandic society. The society neither falls nor becomes stronger. The laws undergo no changes, and the society remains as it was before Njal's death, except that Njal and his family are no longer there. So *Njal's Saga* is a saga, "heroic prose," as Bowra puts it, but it is not an epic.[41]

An even further distinction may be made here. Many heroic works show a great delight in the actions of their heroes. Military prowess, after all, formed an important element in the societies that produced heroic literature. Epics, however, tend to look critically at the heroic code. Even the *Iliad*, which Simone Weil called "The Poem of Force," actually questions the heroic code that governs its characters' lives. We tend to assume that works like the *Iliad* glorify fighting and mayhem. We talk about heroic codes and we think about warriors sitting around the fire hearing these stories in order to fortify themselves for their next battle. We recall the story that Alexander the Great carried a copy of Homer with him on his expeditions. This approach to the literature encourages the glorification of such values as ferocity, ruthlessness, and even bloodthirstiness. On a somewhat more sophisticated level, it might be said that the *Iliad* is about the heroic code and Hektor is a hero because of his adherence to that code despite the odds against him. Such a reading, though it may have been prevalent since the poem was composed, is quite incorrect.

Certainly some kind of heroic code existed when the poem was composed, just as, for many people, such a code still exists. In fact, that code, so much of which involves the preservation of honor and the pursuit of glory, has not changed much over the past three thousand years. But one of the functions of literature is to challenge the accepted values of a society, and the *Iliad* challenges those values at almost every point. Let us consider just one of the many deaths that Homer describes. This one is in book 13, when Asios and Idomeneus meet:

> He was striving in all his fury
> to strike Idomeneus, but he, too quick with a spearcast
> struck him in the gorge underneath the chin, and drove the bronze
>   clean through.
> He fell, as when an oak goes down or a white poplar
> or like a towering pine tree which in the mountains the carpenters
> have hewn down with their whetted axes to make a ship timber.
> So he lay there felled in front of his horses and chariot,
> roaring, and clawed with his hands at the bloody dust.
>
> (13.386–93)

This passage surely describes the reality of war: it is cruel, it is painful, it transforms human beings into objects. Asios, as he dies, has less value even than a tree, which at least can be made into a ship timber. Asios can only scream and claw at the dust onto which his blood is spilling. This picture offers far less glory than horror. And later on, when Homer describes how

> before Aineias and Hektor the young Achaian warriors
> went, screaming terror, all delight of battle forgotten
> (17.758–59)

surely he is commenting sadly on our image of war as a glorious enterprise.

But the *Iliad* is more than simply a poem that describes the horrors of war. It explores the behavior of extraordinary human beings, male and female, in a world that is characterized by this war. The poem explores what it means to be a human being in a world where such wars, such shame, such mortality exist. Given the fact of human mortality—and the fact that we are so often in such haste to hurry it along—how do we, and how should we, continue to live in this world? Homer asks such questions, and he addresses them throughout the poem

Perhaps the best way to begin looking at Homer's questions, and his answers, is by considering two scenes from book 6. The first of these scenes actually illustrates at least two important points. The first has to do with the question of realism. In many ways, the *Iliad* is quite realistic, that is, it gives us a feeling for what the events must have been like, as we saw in the description of Asios' death. But the *Iliad,* like other epics, is not a work of representational realism; it does not pretend to portray everyday actualities. Later in the poem there will be a scene when Achilleus appears to be covered by a divine fire and when he sends the entire Trojan army running with just a shout. And earlier in the poem, Helen appears on the ramparts and Priam asks her to identify all of the Achaian heroes who are arrayed against the Trojans, a scene that might indeed seem realistic, except that the war has reached its tenth year, and it hardly seems likely that Priam has just gotten around to asking who his enemies are. There are, of course, explanations for each of these scenes, but the main point here is that we must not expect Homer to be realistic in the most common sense of the term. What the poem tells us about human existence is real, but the events of the poem are not necessarily realistic.

Such is the case in book 6. When the book opens, the Achaians and the Trojans are engaged in a major battle. Anyone who has never been in such a battle probably cannot imagine what it is truly like, but we must try to picture the tumult of hand-to-hand combat, with spears and arrows flying through the air, armor plates banging against each other, men shouting battle cries and other men, like Asios, screaming in pain. The picture has to be one of nearly total chaos. In the midst of this chaos, two soldiers, Diomedes and Glaukos, encounter each other. It is customary in Homeric battles—and it may have been the case in real battles—that when two warriors meet, they speak to each other, perhaps to issue a challenge or to offer insults or to boast about their prowess. (We can see this custom today in sporting events, where it is known as talking trash. Some things do not change.) As Glaukos and Diomedes approach each other, amid the tumult of the battle, Diomedes asks his opponent who he is. Diomedes assures Glaukos that if he is one of the gods, he will not fight with him, and he explains why in a story that takes up sixteen lines. Glaukos responds by giving his own family background and, in over sixty lines, tells stories about his ancestors. We must recognize that such pedigrees were very important to ancient people. A warrior had to establish his nobility, and family background was one of the criteria; but we also must remember that this lengthy exchange takes place against the noise and chaos of the fighting. Furthermore, when Diomedes learns who Glaukos is, he realizes that in days long past, his grandfather and Glaukos' grandfather had been allies, so he drives his spear into the ground and proposes that they vow never to fight against each other. Both warriors jump from their horses, shake hands, and, as a sign of their agreement, exchange armor, which means, obviously, that right there on the battlefield they each remove their armor. Even those of us who have never been in a battle would have to agree that removing one's armor in the midst of battle is not a recommended procedure, but the narrator's only comment is that Glaukos got the worse end of the deal, since his armor was more valuable than Diomedes'.

What is going on in this strange episode? Homer has a point to make here that transcends representational realism. In the midst of battle, surrounded by the dead and dying, two great warriors meet, intending to kill each other, and yet, in their brief encounter, they discover their human connections. No longer are they faceless enemies bent on mutual destruction. They learn to see each other as human beings, each with an identity, united by events in the distant past and by their common struggle against human mortality. We can see this point when Glaukos first responds to Diomedes:

> "High-hearted son of Tydeus, why ask of my generation?
> As is the generation of leaves, so is that of humanity.
> The wind scatters the leaves on the ground, but the live timber
> burgeons with leaves again in the season of spring returning.
> So one generation of men will grow while another dies."
>
> (6.145–50)

This philosophical and highly poetic response, based on an extended metaphor, hardly seems appropriate to a battlefield conversation; but if we forget about realism, it turns out to be amazingly appropriate. The battlefield is the site of death on a massive scale, and Glaukos' words address human mortality. The comparison of human life to the short life of plants is hardly novel, but Homer goes further than that. Individual human beings are like the leaves, which after a short existence will fall and be scattered by the wind; but the tree itself will continue to create new leaves, just as human beings will continue to flourish, even though individual generations will die off.

Glaukos' words here, however, are insufficient. He is responding to Diomedes' challenge and so he downplays the worth of the individual in relation to the whole of humanity. The subsequent action, though, shows also the value of the individual. Through such values, as evidenced by their grandfathers, these two warriors find and extend the link between them and acknowledge that they, too, as individuals are vitally important. That acknowledgement explains why the narrator's closing comment on the scene, when he remarks that Glaukos lost out on the exchange of armor, is a test for the audience. Does the audience think that the value of the armor matters? Its financial value has become irrelevant. What matters is that amidst the dead and dying, vivid reminders of human mortality, Glaukos and Diomedes have managed to come together and somehow affirm life rather than death. This triumph, unfortunately, is a small one, since death and battle will continue, but even minor triumphs are triumphs.

The other instructive episode of book 6 involves Hektor. As the battle rages, Hektor's brother Helenos advises him to return to the city and ask the women of the city to offer a sacrifice to Athena so that the goddess might help the Trojans. The audience of course, knows the futility of such a sacrifice because of Athena's hostility toward the city; but even beyond that tragic irony is the irony of sending the Trojans' best warrior away from the battle on such an errand. It would be like asking Babe Ruth to leave a World Series game in order to get coffee for the team. It makes no logical sense and it would never happen. On the other hand, as the action of the book develops, it makes a great deal of sense, because what happens to Hektor in Troy underscores the themes of the poem, so that the sacrifice of realism becomes a minor, and easily overlooked, inconsistency.

When Hektor arrives at Troy, he meets his mother and his brother, then goes to find his wife Andromache. When he finds her, husband and wife have one of the central and most revealing conversations in the poem. To get the full import of this conversation, we must remember that Hektor, hero though he may be, is a young man, the husband of a young, loving wife. He is widely respected, and even Helen says that he alone has been consistently kind to her. He has been the Trojan leader in this awful war, loyal to his city even though he has doubts about the rightness of the city's cause regarding

Helen's status, though by this point the war has taken on a life of its own and Helen's status barely seems to be an issue any longer.

When Hektor approaches Andromache, she weeps and pleads with him to stop putting himself in so much danger. She suggests that he pull his troops inside the city walls and concentrate them at the weakest spot, where the greatest attacks might be expected. Her plan would protect the city and the warriors, and it makes strategic sense. She strengthens her argument by telling him something that he already knows but that the audience does not know, that she has only Hektor and their son in the whole world, since her father, her mother, and her seven brothers have all perished at the hands of Achilleus. With some justice, she fears that Hektor will suffer the same fate, and she knows that her life as a widow in a conquered city will be hellish. What she has done, then, because she loves him and needs him, because she is a woman in a society that did not greatly value women, is to put Hektor in the position of having to make a clear choice, which he certainly does. His response to her pleas is revealing:

> Then tall Hektor of the shining helm answered her: "All these
> things are in my mind also, lady; yet I would feel deep shame
> before the Trojans and the Trojan women with trailing garments,
> if like a coward I were to shrink aside from the fighting;
> and the spirit will not let me, since I have learned to be valiant
> and to fight always among the foremost ranks of the Trojans,
> winning for my own self great glory, and for my father.
> For I know this thing well in my heart, and my mind knows it:
> there will come a day when sacred Ilion shall perish,
> and Priam, and the people of Priam of the strong ash spear.
> But it is not so much the pain to come of the Trojans
> that troubles me . . .
> as troubles me the thought of you, when some bronze-armoured
> Achaian leads you off, taking away your day of liberty
> in tears . . .
> But may I be dead and the piled earth hide me under before I
> hear you crying and know by this that they drag you captive."
>
> (6.440–65)

Hektor knows that if the Trojans continue to pursue the course they have been following, he will be killed and they will be conquered and destroyed. About the ultimate fate of Troy there can be no question (and we must remember that we have only recently heard Glaukos' words about human mortality). Furthermore, Hektor knows what will happen to his beloved

Andromache when he is dead and the city is conquered. Nevertheless, he sees no way to implement her plan, because he has to win glory for himself. If he did what Andromache suggests, he would feel shame, not simply because he would be following a woman's advice but because he is trapped by the heroic code, which dictates that the only way to win glory is through battle, through "manly" behavior. He could, conceivably, prevent his own death and the enslavement of his wife and son, but he refuses to do so entirely on the basis of pride

If we juxtapose Hektor's words here with Glaukos' words earlier in the book, as well as with the actions of Glaukos and Diomedes, we can see Homer building a pattern that will continue to develop throughout the epic. This scene, however, offers a particularly tragic part of the pattern, for Hektor knows that what Andromache fears will come true, yet he feels constrained to abandon his beloved wife and infant son for the sake of a pride that has little value. He knows from his earlier meeting with Paris and Helen that Paris is unworthy and that Helen despises her lover. He knows that his city will be destroyed. But none of those factors matters as much as his pride, as his need to lead the fighting in a cause that is both futile and wrong. Although this approach seems to impose twenty-first-century values on the poem, the evidence of the poem justifies it. Homer presents the heroic code as the source of avoidable tragedy. He emphasizes his tragic view of the so-called heroic code by having the fighting grow fiercer and more brutal as the poem continues, culminating in the terrible slaughter that accompanies Achilleus in his return to battle and in his sacrifice of Trojan warriors at Patroklos' funeral. It is no coincidence that the *Iliad* concludes with a series of laments.

Other epics show similar doubts about the value of traditional heroic behavior. *Beowulf* is a good example. Beowulf, the great hero, displays the requisite courage and fighting skill in his battles with Grendel, with Grendel's mother, and with the dragon, but those heroic activities are not enough to save either the Danes or the Geats. The monsters do indeed trouble those peoples, but it is not the monsters who destroy them. They are destroyed from within, by their reliance on a heroic code that values revenge, fighting, and war over civilization. Herein lies the relationship between the three monster stories and the poem's numerous digressions. In one sense, they are the same story: Grendel tries to destroy Heorot and threatens Hroþgar's reign, while Ingeld does destroy Heorot and Hroþulf does end the reign of Hroþgar's son. The only difference is that Grendel, who does not succeeed, exudes evil, while Ingeld and Hroþulf, who do succeed, conceal their evil. This pattern is repeated throughout the poem. Grendel, Grendel's mother, and the dragon all pose threats to human society, but they are all obviously evil and therefore can be opposed and destroyed by Beowulf's heroic behavior. The more dangerous threats to society, however, have human sources and frequently involve deception or some other human failing. Anyone looking at the monsters would recognize them immediately as evil, but how can we tell what evil lurks in the hearts of men? The monsters, then, provide most of the poem's excitement, but their major role is to contrast one form of evil, open, obvious, and opposable through the heroic code, with another form of evil, subtle, deceptive, and difficult to recognize, let alone combat.

Virtually every one of the subplots that are woven into the fabric of *Beowulf* has this relationship to the main story, even if those subplots operate in different ways. For example, when Beowulf arrives at the Danish court and announces his intention to fight Grendel, he is challenged by Unferð. Unferð, like the Danish warriors, has been afraid to stay in Heorot at night to challenge Grendel, but, motivated by his pride, he resents Beowulf's attempt and tries to shame the young warrior. During Beowulf's eloquent defense of himself against Unferð's accusations, he mentions that Unferð had killed his own brother; and the poet brings home to us that Grendel is not the only descendant of Cain in the poem.

Beowulf, then, operates according to the ideals of a heroic code, which means that he tries to protect his people, the Geats, and even another people, the Danes; but his heroism is impotent in the face of the failings he encounters in other human beings. Most of the male characters, Unferð, Ingeld, Hygelac, and the others, operate according to the usual kind of heroic code, which means that they are driven by pride, a lust for power, greed, revenge—basic human flaws. Like Grendel, they are descendants of Cain, and the heroic code is inadequate to control their behavior or to save the communities they represent. Beowulf is certainly a great hero, but if we focus on his exploits rather than seeing those exploits in the context of the digressions, which narrate the collapse of societies, we miss the point of the poem.

There are, of course, some excellent heroic poems, and calling a work heroic rather than epic does not put it on a lower level. Still, works like the medieval *Waltharius* or *The Poem of my Cid* and later compilations like the Finnish *Kalevala* or the Armenian *David of Sassoun* are more properly heroic than they are epic. They focus on and take delight in the heroic feats of their heroes, but they are not much concerned with a pivotal moment in the history of their nation. That history may be in the background, but it is far from central. *The Poem of my Cid*, for example, focuses entirely and always on Ruy Díaz. The military campaign to reconquer Spain is there, but it is never explored. The purpose of the poem is to glorify "my Cid," not to deal with history. Similarly, the *chansons de geste* concerning William of Orange are more like episodes from the extraordinary adventures of William than they are an exploration of historical forces or of the fate of a community. These are all fine poems, enjoyable to read and exploring important themes; but they are heroic poems. They are not epics.

It does seem to be the case that some epics, like the *Iliad* or *Beowulf*, began as heroic poems; but as the poems developed, those heroic characteristics were scrutinized and found wanting. In the *Iliad* no one wins, and in *Beowulf* everyone loses. Both poets, however, offer alternatives. In the description of Achilleus' shield in book 18, we see two cities. The first is a city at peace, where marriages and festivals are celebrated, symbols of life and continuity. This is a real city, however, populated by real people, and so there are disagreements and potential strife in the city as well. Two men argue over the blood price to be paid for a man who has been killed: they negotiate the value of the man's life so that proper restitution can be paid. How the narrator knows these details simply from looking at the shield is unexplained (and inexplicable), but the scene itself is certainly real enough. In the world of the *Iliad*, the solution would lie in violence: the families of the killed and of the killer would settle the issue by fighting, just as the Achaians and Trojans are attempting to settle their quarrel through war. In the world of the shield, however, the disputants attempt arbitration; and when the family of the deceased refuses the initial offer, they seek further arbitration with a prize being given not to the best warrior in the city but to the person who devises the best peaceful resolution. No wonder there are festivals and marriages in this city—the city operates on the basis of law and intelligence, not on the law of the jungle.

The other city depicted on the shield is quite different. This city, with its citadel like the citadel of Troy is, like Troy, under siege; and the warriors' wives and children populate the ramparts. This city is characterized by ambushes and treachery, by Hate and Confusion and Death. This is, in short, a city that embodies all the horrors of Troy, and it stands in sharp contrast to the other, ideal city. Thus the shield of Achilleus depicts the natural world as a world of harmony, but it describes two possibilities for the world of human beings. One of those possibilities offers peace and harmony, but the other offers war and destruction. The choice, Homer seems to say, is ours, though clearly the Achaians and the Trojans have made their choice, which will lead to tragedy for almost everyone.

Similarly *Beowulf* at least hints of another course that people might take. Hroþgar emphasizes to Beowulf the vicissitudes of human existence, the transitoriness of human happiness, and he urges Beowulf to pay attention to those things that have real and lasting value. Here and elsewhere the poem depicts a vision of civilization, of cooperation, and of individual and group responsibility which stand in clear contrast to the heroic code as it is too often understood. This heroic code, with its destructive implications, is constantly being examined in these earlier epics. As S. J. Harrison says in discussing K. Quinn's *Virgil's Aeneid*, "Its first chapter gives an interesting view of the heroism of Aeneas, which (he holds) indicates that the traditional Homeric heroic code is shown up as inadequate in the world of the *Aeneid*."[42] Quinn's judgment seems to be correct except that it does not go far enough. The traditional Homeric heroic code is shown up as inadequate even in the world of the *Iliad*.

Nor is this view only a Western phenomenon. In the *Mahabharata*, while martial prowess is clearly cultivated, peace is viewed as more valuable than war. The Pandavas do all they can to avoid clashes, especially the climactic battle, but to no avail; and that failure to avoid battle and its concomitant destruction is regarded as a failure by most of the warriors on both sides. Duryodhana's reliance on violence marks him as an inferior character.

Herein lies a problem for anyone who wants to write an epic in a less heroic time, that is, a time that already rejects the traditional martial heroic code, a time like the twentieth century, for instance, when war had ceased to be a matter of single combat, a mode that became more appropriate for the athletic field than it was for everyday life. John Newman points out that there is little taste for epic poetry in the contemporary world, but there is still a desire for heroic action in films and novels, as the popularity of writers like Robert Ludlum indicates.[43] In such circumstances, can there be epic? Several centuries ago, Milton seemed to think so, as he rejected the heroical and wrote a whole new kind of epic, one that focused on a pivotal moment not in an isolated society but in the history of humanity.

In the twentieth century, heroic epic would be either an anachronism or a matter of fantasy, as Joyce recognized in *Ulysses*. Leopold Bloom is hardly the traditional hero; and his combat with the Citizen in the Cyclops chapter parodies traditional heroic behavior, as does so much else in the novel. On the other hand, Wagner's *Ring*, which does rely on traditional notions of the heroic, is an unintentional parody. Siegfried, the heroic protagonist, is surely the stupidest epic hero ever devised. The *Ring* contains wonderful music, but the fact that it was viewed as a triumph of German nationalism and that the Nazis revered it indicates how often people have looked at epic works and seen in them only what they expected: reflections of national glory and calls to heroic action. But if traditional literary heroism is passé, is epic still possible? It is, because the epic and the heroic are not the same things and the epic does not have to be heroic. If every age develops its own epic, then an age that does not believe in the value of the heroic will not produce heroic epics, and an age in which the heroic code is not an issue will not even produce epics that critique that code. Thus the works that will be studied in subsequent chapters address many important issues, and one of those issues may focus on what constitutes the heroic in the twentieth century—but none of the works display vestiges of the heroic code.

This shift in the epic's attitude toward the heroic, of course, has had a profound influence on the role of the hero. In the *Iliad*, Homer provides many characters with an *aristeia*, a moment of shining glory on the battlefield, but almost all those characters end up as failures. Hektor dies, and we know that the other Trojan warriors are doomed as well; but the Achaians and their allies fare little better. Achilleus, we also know, is doomed; and, except for Odysseus and Menelaos, most of the others will die either before they reach home or, in the case of Agamemnon, at homecoming. And even Odysseus and Menelaos will have their difficulties. Virgil's Aeneas is often regarded as a glorious hero; but his whole story consists of a series of tragedies, and his final triumph over Turnus covers the whole of his story with ambiguity. Lucan's *Pharsalia*, an anti-*Aeneid*, is critical of heroism from the beginning; and Statius' *Thebaid* has barely a single admirable character. Beowulf does well against monsters, but he is incapable of saving his people and the poem ends with an elegy not only for the hero but for the community that verges on destruction. The climactic battle of the *Mahabharata* gives the heroes a chance to display their martial prowess, but the battle is defined before it begins as evidence of failure. In short, the alleged heroism of these heroes is suspect.[44]

Actually, the careers of each of these epic heroes must be seen in the context of his community and its fate, which the heroes can do little to change. It is no accident that Achilleus tells Odysseus in the Underworld that he would rather be a living peasant than a dead hero, which is as devastating a comment on the heroic code as anyone ever made. What each of those epic heroes finally confronts is not his own glory, his success as a warrior or as the savior of his people, but his mortality, the limits of his heroic possibilities. Through much of the *Iliad*, Achilleus seems like a spoiled baby, pouting in his tent, which to some extent he is. But then we hear about the choice that he faces—the choice that all the warriors face, though they do not address it so clearly: he can stay, fight, win glory, and die young, or he can go home and live in obscurity to an old age. From the traditional heroic viewpoint, the choice is between glory and obscurity, but from the poet's viewpoint—from Achilleus' viewpoint in the Underworld when he tells Odysseus, "I would rather follow the plow as thrall to another / man, one with no land allotted him and not much to live on, / than be a king over all the perished dead" (11.489-491)—the choice is more properly between life and death, and Achilleus' withdrawal to his tent represents a more serious crisis than we earlier realized. Some will argue that this way of framing the issue is peculiar to the twentieth century, that more "heroic" ages were not so inclined to such views. I would respond that the distance between us and them is not so great, that they were not so barbaric and we are not so civilized that the paradigm has shifted drastically. The evidence is in the epics, in their treatment of the heroic code and of the heroes. When Aristotle treated the epic alongside the tragedy, he knew what he was doing.

Further support for this view of the epic can be found in the roles of women in epic literature. Epic has almost always been viewed as a male genre. Keith tells us that "Roman definitions of epic from Ennius to Statius adapt ancient Greek genre theory to characterize the subject of the genre as the 'greatest accomplishments of the fathers . . . primarily, though not exclusively, in warfare.'"[45] There have been very few female epicists, and none until relatively recent times. In H. D.'s magnificent *Helen in Egypt*, war is not precisely incidental, but it is presented as a fairly silly thing that men do, an attitude that differs significantly from what are considered traditional views. And while the term "epic hero" sounds quite natural, "epic heroine" has a faintly oxymoronic ring to it.

As I have been arguing, epic poetry is a symbol of civilization; war symbolizes a lack of civilization. If we regard epics as glorifications of traditionally masculine values, we are much mistaken, for almost all epics (as opposed to heroic poems) call into question at least some of those values. One way in which they do so is by giving us glimpses into the ways various female characters understand their worlds.

A significant reason that this aspect of the epics has been so frequently overlooked is that the women play such small—not minor, but small—roles in the poems. Despite the infrequency and brevity of their appearances, however, the female characters add an essential dimension to the epic vision, a dimension that helps to transform the entire vision.

As we have seen, on one level the *Iliad* is a great poem about a war, which makes it also a poem about the mortality of warriors, that is, of men. While the poem focuses on Achilles, all of the men share his predicament: they can either risk dying gloriously now or they can die later, less gloriously; but die they must. Consequently they have choices about their own destiny, about when and how they will die. Given the inevitability of death, they still have options. But what about the women? Not only can they not choose to go out to the battlefield, that is, not exercise that particular kind of choice over their destinies, but their destinies are entirely determined by the fates of the men, who generally make their choices without considering the women.

We can see this point in the encounter between Andromache and Hektor that we looked at earlier. When Andromache pleads with Hektor to bring his troops into the city, she is not asking him to abandon the battle but only to fight in a safer way. Hektor responds that he cannot appear to be a coward, even though he knows that the city will be destroyed. What really bothers him, though, is the thought of Andromache's fate, and he closes his speech with the hope that he will be dead and buried before she becomes another man's captive.

Hektor, relying on his male notion of glory, makes the decision for himself and for her, knowing full well what the consequences are likely to be. He allows himself to be trapped by an idea of glory in fighting a war that he knows is basically dishonorable and that he himself could end relatively quickly by returning Helen to Menelaos. And while the decision to continue fighting is certainly not an easy one for him, the consequences that he foresees for Andromache are surely worse than those he will face: he will die, which may not be a good thing but which happens quickly, while Andromache, who does not share his idea of glory and who has no role in making the decision, will continue to suffer for years. Thus does Homer once again undercut the heroic ethos. We cannot say that Andromache is, after all, only a woman, that her fate is not terribly important. Homer makes it important, and he tries to force his audience to focus on it, though admittedly generations of androcentric readers have tended to overlook it.

Nor is this an isolated episode, short though it may be. We may remember that the whole crisis of the *Iliad* occurs over the status of the captive Briseis, who, despite the centrality of her position for the story, does not actually appear until book 19, when she laments the death of Patroklos:

> "... [Y]ou would not let me, when swift Achilleus had cut down
> my husband, and sacked the city of godlike Mynes, you would not
> let me sorrow, but said you would make me godlike Achilleus'
> wedded lawful wife ...
> Therefore I weep your death without ceasing. You were always kind."
>   So she spoke, lamenting, and the women sorrowed around her
> grieving openly for Patroklos, but for her own sorrows each.
>   (19.291–303)

This is a strong condemnation of the male ethos of battle glory, and it is no accident that Homer puts it in the mouth of the woman Briseis. Like Andromache, who lost her father and brothers in battle, Briseis lost her husband and brothers; but neither Andromache nor Briseis mentions the cause or the outcome of these fatal battles, because ultimately the battles were not themselves important, nor do the causes concern the women. The battles simply resulted in the loss of men's lives and the transformations of women's lives. Andromache, fortunately for her, has been happy with Hektor, while Briseis has been turned into a war prize.

Furthermore, Homer's narrator makes a significant comment here: as Briseis laments, so do the women who are with her, "openly for Patroklos, but for her own sorrows each." Briseis' lament is ostensibly for her rescuer Patroklos, but on a deeper level it is a lament for herself, for the sorrows that she, as a woman, has suffered because of the men's wars. Her father and brothers are dead—that is, their suffering is over. Hers, and those of her female companions, continues. From the men's point of view, the result of war is either victory and the glory of triumph or defeat and the glory of heroic death. For the women there is no glory, but there is always the possibility of inglorious suffering and servitude.

It is true, of course, that these episodes concerning Andromache and Briseis, even if we add to them those concerning Helen, comprise only a few lines out the thousands that make up the *Iliad*. Nevertheless, these few lines are essential for fully understanding the work. Yes, the *Iliad* is largely concerned with examining how human beings confront their mortality, but if we focus only on the male heroes, we get only a partial view. These few lines about women not only provide another view of human mortality, but they transform the glorification of the male ethos. No one who is aware of these few lines can claim that the *Iliad* glorifies war or the hero. They are a reminder to anyone who thinks that Homer's gorier descriptions somehow recommend the joys of carnage, and they underscore the poem's antiwar sentiments. Without them, the *Iliad* would be a far different poem.

We can see the same phenomenon in *Beowulf*. Like the *Iliad*'s earliest audience, *Beowulf*'s audience was probably largely, if not entirely, male; and yet this much briefer poem contains even more references to women, references that again undercut the stereotypical male glorification of honor and battle. We can see the *Beowulf*-poet's critique of male evil just about every time that a female character is mentioned. One of the best examples occurs in the Finnsburg digression, in which we hear of the deaths of Hnaef, the brother of Hildeburh; Finn, the husband of Hildeburh; and Hildeburh's unnamed son. It is significant that throughout this digression, the poet's focus is on Hildeburh: "And no need had Hildeburh to praise the good faith of the Jutes: blameless she was deprived of her dear ones at the shield-play, of son and brother." (2.1071–74).[46] We hear of her preparation of the funeral pyre for her kin and then of the death of her husband, because Hengest is more concerned with revenge than with anything else. Hengest may preserve his honor, he may save face, but he does so at the expense of peace; and the character who suffers most, of course, is the woman Hildeburh.

Similarly Wealþeow, the Danish queen, becomes the focus of a brief episode that occurs immediately after the Finnsburg story. At the feast celebrating Grendel's death, Wealþeow approaches Hroþgar and Hroþulf; and when she addresses her husband, she says, "'I know my gracious Hroþulf, that he will hold the young warriors in honor if you, friend of the Scyldings, leave the world before him'" (2.1180–83). The audience, of course, knows that Hroþulf is treacherous, that when Hroþgar dies, Hroþulf will kill his nephews and seize the throne and ultimately lead to the destruction of Heorot. It is significant, therefore, that Wealþeow is so central to this scene, for like Hildeburh she will be a primary victim, losing both her husband and her sons. Not only do we see the villainy of Hroþulf, but we have the effects of that villainy underscored by the poet's focus on the main sufferer, a woman who cannot take part in the kind of male activity that constitutes the treachery.

Finally, it is important that near the end of the poem we hear of the Geat-woman who lamented the death of Beowulf and its effect on the Geats. The point is not simply that women traditionally sang dirges (the *Iliad* concludes with the laments of Helen, Andromache, and Hekabe) but that the collapse of the Geat men, evidence of which we have seen in Hygelac's foolish and unnecessary wars and in the behavior of Beowulf's retainers in his various battles, will lead to awful consequences, primarily for the women, who are trapped in the male world of violence and treachery, with no opportunity to make decisions or to act independently.[47]

In more recent times, as women have achieved more public roles in society, their role in epic has also changed. In the epics that form the main body of this study, women play prominent roles and are among the most memorable characters. And one of the epics, Olivia Manning's *Fortunes of War*, is the work of a woman. All of these works demonstrate, along with other examples of epic evolution, an evolution in the way epic regards women and their concerns; but women have always been important in the epic tradition.

One of the implications of my argument thus far has been that epics are anything but simple, straightforward works describing heroic behavior in the service of nationalism. The great epics of world literature, like all great literature, pose more questions than they answer. This view stands in sharp contrast to Bakhtin's notion that the epic is monologic while the novel is dialogic. Much more to the point is Susanne Wofford's study, which explores the ways in which poetic language undercuts the apparent surface meaning in classical and Renaissance epics. That language enables epic to "express and define an entire cultural system while also revealing its contradictions and the costs of its ethical paradigms and political solutions."[48] Epic is subversive.

An important area in which to apply this concept involves the relationship between the epic and nationalism, or between the epic and the sources of power. It has long been felt that epic catered to the power elite and promoted a rather simple-minded form of nationalism. Evidence of this feeling can be found in works like Ronsard's *Franciad*, but the feeling became especially strong in the very nationalistic nineteenth century, so much so that it became almost imperative that nations discover or create national epics, as the *Kalevala* was assembled to be the national epic of Finland.[49] A number of recent critics have seized on such nationalistic feelings to attack the epic as an imperialist tool, most significantly critics like Elizabeth Bellamy and David Quint, whose studies are fascinating but ultimately—dare I say it?—monologic. Bellamy, for example, argues that epic has "a heavy investment in the Symbolic of imperial ideology. Epic—and its ethical superstructure of *pietas*—is an explicitly ideological genre, and its epic narrative is the aesthetic tool of imperialist ideology."[50] Unfortunately Bellamy neither proves nor supports this damning judgment, nor does she define what she means by epic. Quint concentrates more precisely on Virgil, whom he views as the archetype of the epic poet working in tandem with the imperialist state. The focus of his study is the way in which Virgil appropriated the Homeric epic "for the ends of empire: as a source of inspiration or authorizing model for political domination on a mass scale."[51]

It is undeniable that Virgil loved Rome and that his poem glorifies the new-born empire, but it is an error to view the *Aeneid* as Roman propaganda or as a justification for everything Augustus did. Certainly Virgil praises Rome and Augustus, but he also offers criticism and warnings.[52] The character of Aeneas himself raises vital questions. Aeneas is often criticized as being less than an ideal character.[53] He often seems like a stick figure, a hero who makes few choices and does what he must, illustrating the ways in which every Roman man must do his duty regardless of the personal sacrifices that such duty requires. From some perspectives, such behavior may seem like an ideal, but not from Virgil's perspective. When Aeneas tries to act—when he wants to run back into burning Troy to find his wife and in his whole affair with Dido—he is prevented from doing what he wants; and while there may be something heroic about his devotion to duty, there is also something profoundly sad about his progressive dehumanization. When he does act on the basis of his feelings, as he does at the very end of the poem, it is not entirely clear that his actions are admirable. If Aeneas represents the empire whose founder he is, then Virgil is not simply celebrating the glory of that empire. He may celebrate the potential glory of the empire, but he surrounds that celebration with warnings about dehumanization of self and others in the cause of empire. He loves his country, but he sees in its character the seeds of its own destruction, and he includes those in his poem.[54]

The same can be said about most of the epics that continue to be read. As Winnifrith says, "Writers of bad epics in the seventeenth century and bad epic theorists in the nineteenth century liked to think that an epic ought to celebrate a nation's glory."[55] The corollary is that good epics may celebrate a nation's glory, but they do far more. *The Faerie Queene*, for instance, is a good example, even if it is not purely epic. Spenser is sometimes regarded as a sycophantic poet who wrote in praise of queen and country for both mercenary and patriotic reasons, but *The Faerie Queene* criticizes English policy nearly as much as it praises it. Certainly the first three books are more optimistic than the last three, but even the first book contains the episode with Lucifera, who is clearly an infernal parody of Elizabeth. At the very least, Lucifera is a warning about what Elizabeth could become, but even at that level, her inclusion in the poem is striking. *The Faerie Queene* is full of such critiques. Spenser may well have written them as part of his patriotic stance, but his poem is hardly an uncritical portrait of either England or Elizabeth.

An even clearer example is Alonso de Ercilla's *La Araucana*, a truly astounding sixteenth-century epic about the Spanish conquest of Chile, focusing on the Spanish triumph over the Araucanian Indians. Ercilla, who took part in the campaign, without doubt favors the Spanish, but he is not averse to praising the Araucanians and disparaging his own people:

>La sincera bondad y la caricia
>de la sencilla gente de estas tierras,
>daban bien a entender que la codicia
>aún no había penetrado aquellas sierras;
>ni la maldad, el robo y la injusticia,
>alimento ordinario de las guerras
>entrada en esta parte habían hallado.
>
>Pero luego nosotros destruyendo
>todo lo que tocamos de pasada,
>con la usada insolencia el paso abriendo
>les dimos lugar ancho y ancha entrada;

> y la Antigua costumbre corrompiendo
> de los nuevos insultos estragada,
> plantó allí la codicia su estandarte
> con más seguridad que en otra parte.
>
> (36. st. 13–14)

(The sincere goodness and the cares of the simple people of this land help to show that greed still had not penetrated into these mountains; not evil nor theft nor injustice, the usual food of wars, could be found to have entered there.

But then we, destroying all that we touched in passing, with our usual insolence clearing our way, we gave them a wide space and a broad entrance, and corrupting ancient custom with new insults, greed planted there its banner with more sureness than anywhere else.)[56]

This startling passage shows that the *Araucana* may be more forthright in its critique than some other epics, but Ercilla is hardly unique in using the epic as an instrument of self-analysis for the community that produced it. Of course there are aspects of the epic that support dominant ideologies, which invariably require the subjection of both people and other ideologies. Poets are human beings and are subject to the same forces as other people. Nevertheless, the major epics do not accept those dominant ideologies uncritically, a tradition that subsequent chapters will show continuing into the twentieth century. From Homer on, in the Western tradition, through such medieval epics as *Beowulf* and *The Song of Roland*, through Renaissance epics like *La Araucana* and Camoes' *Lusiads*, and on to the present, epicists have demanded that readers look critically at a community's deepest beliefs. That readers have so often chosen not to do so, have chosen to see epics more as glorification than critique, is not necessarily the fault of the writers or of the genre.

From this discussion, it should be obvious that epic literature has a unique relationship with history. Ezra Pound's dictum that an "epic is a poem including history"[57] may be a bit oversimplified, but it is basically accurate, as is Spenser's reference to "Poetes historicall" in the letter he addressed to Ralegh arguing that his poem was epic. Because the epic deals with the lives of individuals and communities at pivotal periods in the histories of those communities, its tie to history is very close. At the same time, it may be too simple to say, as Bellamy does, that Renaissance epic, or any sort of epic, is "a kind of repository for national history."[58] Epic writers do indeed focus on the past, whether on the distant past, as in Homer or Virgil, or the more recent past, as in Lucan and Ercilla. Even so, their works are not just historical curiosities. Writers write for the present, and epicists use the past to illuminate the present. That past may be largely legendary; it may convey the collective mythology of the community. Even so, it opens that mythology to examination.

Epicists are not historians. They use history. They may believe that the history is true, as does Djeli Mamoudou Kougalé, the griot who recited the epic of *Sundiata*. He says that griots "are the memory of mankind" and their function is to "teach kings the history of their ancestors so that the lives of the ancients might serve them as an example, for the world is old, but the future springs from the past."[59] Djeli Mamoudou Kougalé did not need to read Philip Sidney to find this emphasis on the epic as a handbook of virtue, but Sidney allows the poet to adjust history in order to create even better examples, while the griot claims only to report history. He may well believe that Sundiata could tear up a baobab tree by the roots and bring it to his mother, but we do not need to believe in the historical veracity of that episode, or of any episode in epic, to understand that the epicist uses the past to comment on and to affect the present.[60] As Philip Hardie notes, Lucan alluded to the *Aeneid* in describing the deserted city of Troy in order to create an allegory commenting on what Caesar was doing to Rome.[61] Lucan's epic on a subject from relatively recent history, then, refers to very ancient history in order to illuminate the present. H. V. Routh, in contrast to Bakhtin's position that the epic is totally Other, totally alien to the present, says, "it is the essence of an epic to blend the past with the present."[62] The epic relies on history, but it also creates and adapts history to make its point about the present and the relationship between the past and the present. Homer is not writing for its own sake about a battle that took place in the past. He uses that battle and the legends that had grown out of it to explore the perennial problems of human mortality and the human propensity to hasten mortality.

There are, of course, other kinds of works that also rely in various ways on the use of history, and it is worth considering how they differ from epic. A number of writers in the nineteenth and twentieth centuries have written long, multivolume accounts of historical periods. Among the best-known such accounts are Balzac's *Comédie Humaine*, Zola's Rougon-Macquart novels, and Anthony Powell's *Dance to the Music of Time*. These are all wonderful works, but they are not, I argue, epics. They are descriptions of an era rather than of a moment. They are, to put them in another genre, chronicles, records of the passage of years, retelling many of the events of those years without focusing on a single pivotal moment that somehow, like the founding or the destruction of a community, changed history. As

Powell's title indicates, they move with time rather than centering on a moment.⁶³

An interesting question, though it involves a slight digression, is whether the Bible is an epic. It is sometimes claimed to be one, but the Hebrew Testament seems more like a chronicle, covering the history of Israel from its beginning to the destruction of the First Temple and, overtly in Ezra and Nehemiah, even beyond that. The whole of the Christian Bible, covering the period from creation to apocalypse, all of history, is too broad; and the Greek Testament is more of an anthology than a unified narrative. Perhaps the Five Books of Moses, which have historically been counted as a separate unit within the Bible, can be seen as epic, describing the origins of the world and of the Children of Israel but focusing on the pivotal moment of the Exodus, which is foretold to Abraham and is the subject of Exodus, Numbers, and Deuteronomy. Hegel, reflecting nineteenth-century nationalism, says that "the epic work is the Saga, the Book, the Bible of a people, and every great and important people has such absolutely earliest books which express for it its own original spirit."⁶⁴ On the other hand, he adds that not all bibles, and specifically not the Hebrew and Greek Testaments, are epics.

Another genre that we must briefly consider is the historical novel. Walter Scott's historical novels, the earliest to be written, obviously have a historical setting, but they are romances rather than epics. That statement takes us back to the Renaissance controversies over the status of poems like *Orlando Furioso*. We may marvel at the amount of attention that was devoted to this controversy, though, as I mentioned earlier, the conflict involved more than mere generic classifications. Nevertheless, the distinction between epic and romance is a vital one, and understanding the differences helps to clarify both genres.

The distinction, however, remains controversial. For example, it is usually understood that Homer (or whatever we believe "Homer" to have been) wrote two epics, the *Iliad* and the *Odyssey*, but the astute reader will have noticed that the *Odyssey* has not heretofore been discussed in this study. In Voltaire's essay on epic, he, too, moves from the *Iliad* to the *Aeneid*. The reason for these apparent lapses is that the *Odyssey* is a romance rather than an epic.⁶⁵ It does not focus on a pivotal moment in history. It is true, of course, that Odysseus must return home to preserve the kingdom of Ithaka for his family, but the fate of Ithaka never really surfaces as an issue in the poem. What is at issue is Odysseus' personal and family life. We never hear the history of Ithaka or whether Odysseus was a good ruler or a bad ruler or the effect his return has on the people of Ithaka. Those subjects are irrelevant to the poem. We hear, rather, about his relationship with his wife and son, about how that wife and son have coped with his absence, and about his own development as a human being, fascinating matters all, but without historical significance. Their significance remains personal and domestic. Furthermore, the *Odyssey* lacks the serious, often tragic, grandeur that characterizes epic, even though it describes numerous deaths and foretells the fate of Odysseus.[66]

The romance, then, since it does not focus on the pivotal historical moment, treats history differently. As Bellamy puts it, epic is "the historicization of fiction" while romance is "the fictionalization of history."[67] This is an important distinction. We might say that epic pretends to convey history while the romance pretends to use history. For epic, the historical moment is a vital focus; for romance, the history provides background, while the focus is elsewhere, on the leading characters, their feelings, and their adventures. In Renaissance French "epic," for example, the poems focus on the noble victims of killing or on dignified single combat as opposed to the bloody free-for-all of the *Iliad*. These works, which are really romances, focus on the single characters while the epic focuses on the community.[68]

The Middle Ages saw a major shift from epic to romance. We need only compare *Beowulf* to the romances of Chrétien de Troyes to see the differences. As Morton Bloomfield indicates, the former is heroic, the latter chivalric. In the epic, love is subordinate (if it is there at all), while in the romance, which cares so much for its characters and their feelings, love is a driving force.[69] Beowulf fights to protect communities, Danes and Geats; Yvain and Lancelot fight to establish their own glory and only in a very secondary way for Arthur's court (which, to the extent that it was thought of as real, did not even exist in Chrétien's country).[70] Romance, as Patricia Parker says, has come to be associated with "the escapism of 'pure fiction,'"[71] which may be unfortunate but which reflects the ahistorical nature of its origins.

Another factor in considering the relationship between epic and romance is that because there can be no such thing as a pure example of a genre, they have on occasion been successfully combined. *The Faerie Queene*, like some of its Italian predecessors, combines elements of romance and epic, and the *Nibelungenlied* is an epic that was at least strongly influenced by romance.[72] Still, the fundamental differences between the two genres remain. Epic is tied to history while romance plays with history (if we can think of "play" in a nontrivializing way). In epic, however important individuals may be, the overall focus is on a community; in romance, however important the community might be, the overall focus is on individuals.

The joining of epic and romance brings us to yet another problem, the relationship between the epic and the novel. All of the Western epics that have been discussed so far have been epic poems. Gradually, however, epic poems were largely replaced by verse romances and verse romances by prose romances. And then came the novel. Critics often discuss "the novel" as if it were a single genre, but it is no more a single genre than is "the poem." Just as there are epic poems, lyric poems, elegies, ballads, and others, so there are historical novels, romance novels, and probably to no one's surprise, epic novels. What, then, is an epic novel?

In the early history of the novel, in the eighteenth century, Henry Fielding wrote one species of epic novel by grafting his Augustan understanding of the epic onto the form of the novel. His notion that "a comic Romance is a comic Epic-Poem in Prose" may not be very helpful for our purposes, but Fielding does make a statement that justifies the existence of the epic novel against all those who argue that the last real epic was written by Milton:[73]

> When any kind of writing contains all other Parts, such as Fable, Action, Character, Sentiments, and Diction, and is deficient in Metre only; it seems, I think, reasonable to refer it to the Epic; at least, as no Critic hath thought proper to range it under any other Head, nor to assign it a particular Name to itself.[74]

Just as Milton justified not only the ways of God to man but the writing of an epic without the usual heroic framework, so Fielding justifies writing an epic in prose rather than in verse. In both cases, the authors implicitly recognize the differences between the conventions, those elements that ornament the epic, and the essence of the genre. Fielding's actual practice, however, is less satisfactory. *Joseph Andrews* does not appear to be in any sense an epic, while both *Tom Jones* and *Amelia* rely more on an eighteenth-century conception of epic conventions than they do on the central characteristics of epic. We might argue that allegorically *Tom Jones* has an epic, Miltonic scope and structure. *Amelia*, on the other hand, is an eighteenth-century adaptation of the *Aeneid*, relying on the formal conventions of the genre but not depicting a pivotal moment.

Fielding, then, continued to rely on many of the accepted epic conventions. Could the novel achieve epic status if it did not, like *Amelia*, rely heavily on the pattern set by classical epic? Bakhtin, who regarded the epic as a strict, solitary genre rather than as a type of narrative, said that it could not, that treating novels as though they were epics in prose flattened out the differences between them.[75] Lukács was more ambivalent. On the one hand he said that "epic had to disappear and yield its place to an entirely new form: the novel"; but forty pages later he wrote, "The novel is the epic of a world that has been abandoned by God."[76] What Lukács appears to be saying through this ambivalence is that the epic as it used to exist can no longer be written but that the essence of epic can be transferred to the form of the novel, that epic can be adapted to a new age. I would only add that epic has been adapted throughout history to the needs of many new ages.

Lukács recognizes in these statements that from Homer through the Christian epics, the gods or the divinities played a major role. Perhaps the best example of a work by a poet who thought that he had to include epic conventions of the gods in his poem is Camoes' *Lusiads*, in which the Olympian deities discuss and control the voyages of Vasco da Gama in what almost seems like a parody of the genre. Epic writers are well-advised not to take that path, but in the modern world they cannot take Milton's path either. Of course, in Milton's time, pivotal historical events were still given divine explanations. In the modern world, in the modern novel, we often look elsewhere for explanations. Again, the central subject of epic is consistent, though the conventions surrounding it have changed.

The epic novel, then, is not a contradiction in terms, though it may still be difficult to attain. The number of true epics is relatively small, and there is no reason to expect that there will be a greater number of epic novels. Even so, such novels do exist, and the greatest of them is Tolstoy's *War and Peace*, the first novel (that I know of) that combines the epic and the novel without an overt reliance on classical models. It is a work that casts an enormous shadow over the epic novels that will be considered in this study.

Woody Allen once said that he had taken a speed-reading course and then zipped through *War and Peace* in twenty minutes. "It's about Russia," he said. In a special way, he is correct. Many of the novel's characters—Natasha, Andrei, Pierre, Maria, Nicholas, Kutuzov—are indeed memorable, but ultimately the novel is about Russia as it weathered (in more ways than one) the Napoleonic invasions. *War and Peace* focuses not only on those memorable characters but on the Russian people. They are the heroes, and to some extent they are represented by those memorable characters, perhaps especially by Platon Karateyev.

In writing his epic novel, Tolstoy could not use the figure of a typical martial epic hero. Achilleus, Hektor, Aeneas—none of them could represent a nineteenth-century hero. Milton needed a different kind of hero for his Christian epic, and Tolstoy needed a new kind of hero for his nineteenth-century epic. Of course Tolstoy's theory of history, propounded at great length in the pages of the novel, by itself precludes the use of a traditional epic hero, as Tolstoy casts doubt on the efficacy of so-called "great men." It was not Napoleon who caused millions of Frenchmen to take up arms, he says. It was something in the French. Napoleon himself is depicted as much less than a great man in the novel. On the Russian side, Kutuzov, although he is the victor, is hardly a traditional epic hero either. His greatness lies not in his martial prowess or his scientific strategy. It lies in his knowing that all he has to do is allow Russia to be Russa and Russians to be Russians. For Tolstoy, a Platon Karateev will triumph over a Napoleon any time.[77]

Prokofiev certainly recognized this aspect of the novel when he transformed it into an opera. The early scenes deal with the characters, but the later scenes, bombastic and jingoistic though they may be (a Stalinist and Second World War legacy), are, like the novel, about Russia, about the threat to its existence and its eventual victory. The memorable characters who people Tolstoy's pages are all trying to understand themselves as human beings, specifically as Russian human beings, in a time of crisis. Prince Andrei dies in the search, but the other characters survive. One of the most amusing scenes in the Homeric romance the *Odyssey* occurs when Telemachos visits Menelaos and Helen and finds them to be a very ordinary middle-aged couple. Of course they have become the stuff of legend, but their reality, after the war and its aftermath, is quotidian. Tolstoy uses the same effect. After well over a thousand pages of crisis, battle, and privation, he provides a romance ending for his novel by presenting the home life of two happy couples, Nicholas and Maria, Pierre and Natasha, and their children. They are so ordinary that it seems hard to believe that they played their roles in the crisis, and therein lies Tolstoy's point. They have survived the crisis, the pivotal moment. They are surely not the same as they were earlier, but they have attempted to return to everyday life; and to a large extent, they have succeeded. Lukács says, "Tolstoy's great and truly epic mentality, which has little to do with the novel form, aspires to a life based on a community of feeling among single human beings closely bound to nature, a life which is intimately adapted to the great rhythm of nature."[78] Lukács still seems afraid to admit that a novel can be epic, so he downplays that aspect of *War and Peace*. He recognizes the importance of community in making *War and Peace* an epic, even if he does not recognize the critique of culture that Tolstoy's work shares with earlier epic.

Tolstoy's epic novel influenced all of the writers whose works will be examined in the following chapters. It should not be surprising that his monumental novel had so profound an impact on writers whose century produced so many pivotal moments. The works that I shall examine are all among Tolstoy's heirs, though several of them have been largely ignored by the academic-critical establishment. There are several possible reasons for this situation. One is that these works are all quite long, and such long works—"large loose baggy monsters," in the words of Henry James—are not fashionable.[79] Another possible reason is that readers who expect a novel are puzzled when what confronts them is an epic, just as a person expecting a brownie will be unpleasantly surprised by the taste of a stuffed mushroom.

And there are other reasons as well. The first work to be considered is Sholem Asch's *Three Cities*, a Yiddish epic novel. Few people read Asch any more. Relatively few people read Yiddish literature at all, and Asch, though he was once quite popular, is largely ignored even by those who do. The next two works are Olivia Manning's *Fortunes of War* and Paul Scott's *Raj Quartet*, both of which have been made into television series and shown on Masterpiece Theater. Edward Whittemore's *Jerusalem Quartet* has simply been ignored by the critical establishment. The only one of these epics that has received extensive critical attention has been Lawrence Durrell's *Alexandria Quartet*, to which I take what is, I hope, a new approach.

It may at first appear to be a coincidence that all of these works have such similar titles: *Three Cities* (with individual volumes entitled *Petersburg, Warsaw,* and *Moscow), The Fortunes of War* (comprised of *The Balkan Trilogy* and *The Levant Trilogy), The Raj Quartet, The Jerusalem Quartet,* and *The Alexandria Quartet*.[80] Each of them describes the number of volumes, three or four, marking them as long works. And each of them incorporates the place names—Russian (and Polish) cities, geographical areas, British India, Jerusalem, and Alexandria, which are pivotal loci. These titles are vital parts of the works to which they are attached, proclaiming both the extended scope of the work and its relation to a geographical and historical locus.[81]

These works, as I hope the following chapters will illustrate, continue the epic tradition through the twentieth century. As we have seen, some readers claim that epic died with Milton or that the works of Homer are the only true epics. Such positions are far too narrow. The epic impulse is far more durable and inclusive than these judgments allow, nor is the impulse confined to the Western tradition. The *Mahabharata*, the *Ramayana*, and *Sundiata* are clearly epics. The epic vision takes the reader outside of himself or herself, outside of a single society, and reveals something about the individual, the individual's relation to history, and the meaning of that history. It questions, it probes, and it inspires. All of the works that are about to be examined partake of that vision. They may differ in important ways from their forebears—the *Iliad*, the *Aeneid, Beowulf, Paradise Lost*—but they are related to those earlier works, just as individual people differ from their great-grandparents and yet remain part of the same family. Or, to return to Genette's metaphor, they are palimpsests, written over the older texts. In either case, perhaps recognizing that these works are indeed twentieth-century epics will increase interest in them and in the whole tradition of epic.

2
Sholem Asch's *Three Cities*

THE TWENTIETH CENTURY WAS CERTAINLY FULL OF PIVOTAL MOMENTS, FROM the First World War to the Second, from Korea to Vietnam, from the end of the British Empire to the rise of the American Empire, with many less global events thrown in. Some of these events, like the Korean War and Vietnam, have not yet produced literary epics, and they may never do so. Others, like the end of the British Empire, have produced several, two of which will be considered in later chapters of this book. Those epics, the works of Olivia Manning and Paul Scott, will use the Second World War as part of the background of the empire's disappearance, but they do not focus on the war itself. The war, while obviously important, served as a catalyst, speeding up processes that were already underway before 1 September 1939. In India, for instance, Gandhi was already a formidable figure before the war, but Britain's treatment of him and other Indians as a result of the war made the British withdrawal from India happen more quickly, and more inevitably, than might otherwise have been the case.

The same point can be made about the First World War and the Russian Revolution. Russia under the czars had long been a land full of dissatisfaction and protest. The Russian-Japanese War of 1905, militarily disastrous for Russia, had nearly brought the country to revolution, but it was the First World War, with its military mismanagement, the governmental corruption that it made even more visible than usual, and the intensified suffering of the Russian people, that made the Revolution a reality. Again, the war was already a central event, but the pivotal moment for the Russian people was the Revolution, and that revolution is the subject of several significant epic novels, among them Mikhail Sholokhov's *Quiet Flows the Don*, Aleksandr Solzhenitsyn's *The Red Wheel* (of which two volumes, *August 1914* and *November 1916*, have been published), and Sholem Asch's *Three Cities* (the name given to the English translation of the Yiddish *Farn Mabul, Before the*

Flood).¹ These three long works, covering the same period of history, ostensibly depicting many of the same events, differ considerably from each other and illustrate a number of facets of the twentieth-century epic novel.

One of those facets is the dependence of the form on the work of Tolstoy. In fact, near the beginning of *August 1914*, Solzhenitsyn mentions Tolstoy many times and even includes him as a character whom Sanya meets. This character, however, is not the Tolstoy of *War and Peace* so much as he is the later, more peasant-like and mystical Tolstoy, the Tolstoy of *Resurrection,* perhaps:

> On the wooden staircase at the back of the house an idyllic view of Tsarskoye Selo looked down on the top step, and Tolstoy, plowing, on the bottom one, both painted by an Italian artist brought in from Rostov (21). . . . [There was] yet another Lev Tolstoy on the way, this time in the act of mowing."²

Solzhenitsyn, it seems, plans to outdo Tolstoy, and so he shows Tolstoy taking the role of a peasant rather than that of a writer. We will see how well he succeeded shortly, but both Solzhenitsyn and Sholokhov, like most writers of twentieth-century epic novels, are clearly indebted to Tolstoy. Herman Ermolaev describes *Quiet Flows the Don* as "a blend of historical drama and a tragedy of individual love," an apt description for *War and Peace* and for most of these works that combine the qualities of epic and the qualities of the novel.³ Perhaps what has made *War and Peace* seem like the perfect novel to so many readers is its balance between the historical and the private (even if many readers feel that Tolstoy's philosophical reflections about history are occasionally overwhelming). Neither Sholokhov nor Solzhenitsyn achieves that balance. Even if Sholokhov comes close to it. His novel still lacks, as Ermolaev says, "the philosophical complexity of *War and Peace*."⁴

The reputation of *Quiet Flows the Don*, which Sholokhov began in 1925 and completed in 1940, has had a checkered history.⁵ In the USSR, "critical reaction to the completion of the novel was enthusiastic. *The Quiet Don* was acclaimed as a real epic, a great ideological and artistic accomplishment by a writer of the new socialist type."⁶

At the same time, Sholokhov, who was patronized and protected by Stalin, was not personally popular, and the taint of Stalin affected the status of the novel. Many Russian readers, including Solzhenitsyn, have accused Sholokhov of having plagiarized the novel, either by having appropriated documents related to the time he describes or by having appropriated the entire manuscript of the novel from an unknown soldier who died in his presence. Such claims sound ludicrous. Novelists who write about history must use historical documents—Tolstoy and Solzhenitsyn certainly do—and the argument about the unknown soldier sounds like the kind of argument made by people who cannot believe that Shakespeare wrote those plays and so find someone else who must have been that genius, as though such genius would be more comprehensible in someone besides Shakespeare. The real problem with Sholokhov, however, seems to have been Stalin, though a careful reading of the novel makes one wonder why Stalin would have protected the novelist. Many important passages in the novel offer overt criticism of the Reds and support the Cossacks in their resistance to the Communist government. Sholokhov did not sell out the Cossacks, whom he so greatly admired. Instead, he depicted their lives before the upheaval, during the war, during the Revolution, and into the Civil War. These pivotal events are depicted in great detail, but always from the point of view of the Cossacks, so that the epic focuses ultimately on the Revolution, its causes, and its consequences, but from a particular perspective.

The reader who approaches *Quiet Flows the Don* expecting it to be a simple novel is likely to be disappointed, while the reader who approaches it as an epic is more likely to be satisfied. Sholokhov does occasionally provide a bit more historical background than the reader needs, so that the narrative bogs down; but in a novel of over thirteen hundred pages, there are bound to be a few slow spots. Nevertheless, *Quiet Flows the Don* is a fascinating and moving portrayal of a society at a pivotal moment. Ermolaev describes the novel's epic qualities in terms similar to those that I have used in the first chapter: "The epic character of *The Quiet Don* stems from a predominantly dispassionate and broad portrayal of a nation at a crucial period of wars, revolutions, and drastic social and political changes that were to have far-reaching consequences for the entire world. If an epic is expected to convey a belief in the basic dignity of man and to be marked by a certain grandeur, heroism, patriotism, and violence, Sholokhov's novel has all of this in abundance."[7] Grigory Melekhov, the "hero" of the book, is a particularly interesting character. He does indeed display the grandeur that we would expect from an epic hero, though, like most epic heroes, he is hardly a saint. He can be brutal, unfaithful, and callous; and yet he, like Achilleus, manages to rise above those flaws as his story approaches its end. And like Achilleus, despite those shared flaws, he also shows himself to be a sensitive person whose interests transcend the immediate and tend toward the larger issues that always bedevil human existence.

Reading *Quiet Flows the Don* requires a good deal of patience, but the effort is clearly repaid by the rewards the book offers. Solzhenitsyn's work is quite different. The first two volumes (or "knots," as the author calls them) comprise almost two thousand pages and do not even get to the Revolution. Large portions of the first volume and even larger portions of the second are devoted to what Solzhenitsyn calls "historical matter," and he explains its inclusion as the result of distortions in the teaching of Russian history.[8] If his point is that he is being more objective, he must be quite mistaken, since his account is as ideologically driven as any other account. Furthermore, that "historical matter" simply overwhelms the rest of the novel. Individual characters or even whole families are introduced only to be dropped—some never reappear while others may appear over a thousand pages later. And even the narrative bits generally serve as introductions to long political conversations that may have been fascinating for Solzhenitsyn but that tend to obscure the novelistic aspects of his work. Clearly he has a Tolstoyan model in mind—Vorotyntsev is a latter-day Prince Andrei—but *The Red Wheel* lacks the balance and the artistic focus of *War and Peace*. A good editor might have done for Solzhenitsyn what Maxwell Perkins did for Thomas Wolfe, but the absence of such an editor prevents this sprawling work from even achieving the status of a "loose baggy monster."

On the other hand, Sholem Asch's *Three Cities*, while it never achieves the status of *War and Peace* (and what work could?), is much more like *Quiet Flows the Don* both in its artistic success, that is, as a unified and coherent whole, and in its depiction of that pivotal historical moment. And, like Sholokhov's epic novel, it depicts that pivotal moment not from the perspective of all Russia but from the perspective of one of the Russian minorities. Sholokhov chose the Cossacks, the people among whom he had lived, though he himself was not a Cossack. The Cossacks tend not to have a good reputation: In some circles their name became synonymous with brutality and an indifference to human life. Sholokhov acknowledges those traits, but he also shows why those traits arose and he depicts other traits as well, while Asch explores that pivotal moment in Russian and world history from the perspective of the Jews, another despised minority. Sholokhov's epic novel, then, is not simply about the First World War and the Revolution. It is about those events in relation to the Cossacks. Similarly, Asch's epic novel is about those events in relation to the Jews.

It may, at first, seem odd to focus a chapter of this study on a Yiddish writer, especially on a Yiddish writer who was quite popular in the early twentieth century but whose works, long out of print, are seldom read now. It is unfortunate that so much Yiddish literature, like so many of the characters it describes, has been ghettoized. Not only is much Yiddish literature of the highest quality, and not only do individual works have great historical interest, but the course of Yiddish literature, until the Holocaust and the

Stalinist purges destroyed so many of its writers and readers, was a microcosm of the development of Western literature, especially of the novel, as a brief survey will illustrate.

Yiddish is a Germanic language that is printed in Hebrew characters. It stems, ultimately, from that period during the Middle Ages when Jews lived in German-speaking countries and spoke the vernacular with their neighbors and among themselves. As the Jews were expelled from these territories and moved to the east, into Poland and into territories that were later incorporated into Russia, they took that language with them, incorporating words from Hebrew, Slavic, and other languages. In the nineteenth century, as European Jews began to be emancipated, many of them, especially in Germany, also became assimilated. To their refined German ears, Yiddish sounded like the language of the ignorant. It was regarded by non-Jews and by educated Jews as a bastard language, a kind of jargon, and speakers of Yiddish were regarded with scorn. A number of writers arose who began to write in Hebrew, a language that had been used only for religious compositions for hundreds of years. That revival of Hebrew was a remarkable phenomenon, but we must realize that only a very small audience could read such Hebrew writing or even cared to read it. After all, those who were proficient in Hebrew tended to be part of the religious establishment and had no interest in reading novels in any language.

At the same time, a number of works had appeared in Yiddish. These works were important because they could be read by the large body of Yiddish speakers, the everyday masses of the Jewish people. These works, however, tended to be much like the earlier European romances, and not even like the best of those. They could be melodramatic and contrived. But then, at the end of the nineteenth century, appeared the author who transformed Yiddish into a literary language. His name was Shalom Ya'akov Abramovitsch, but his works appeared under the name Mendele Mocher Seforim, Mendele the Book Peddler. Abramovitsch was a well-educated, well-read *maskil,* that is, a member of the Jewish Enlightenment. His early goal was to write Hebrew literature (which he did); but he soon realized that if he had something to say to the people, he had to say it in the language that the people understood, Yiddish. Consequently, he wrote a series of novels in Yiddish that show great originality but that also show his familiarity with the wider world of European literature. He was influenced not only by such Russian writers as Tolstoy and Turgenev but by other writers, like Balzac and Dickens. His novels range from the picaresque to the allegorical to the ultra-realistic. He touched the masses, and his alter ego, Mendele, became a kind of folk hero.

Abramovitsch was followed by someone who is better known in the English-speaking world, Sholom Aleichem (whose real name was Shalom Rabinovitz). Rabinovitz used a pseudonym because he did not want to embarrass his father by using his real family name. Just as Samuel Clemens used the river cry "mark twain" as his pseudonym, so Rabinovitz used the popular greeting "peace be upon you" as his. Americans know Sholom Aleichem as the author of the Tevye stories, the source of *Fiddler on the Roof,* but the stories themselves are in many ways quite different from the musical adaptation. Sholom Aleichem also wrote many other works—epistolary novels, realistic novels, novels of social protest. So famous did he become that a well-known story has him saying to Samuel Clemens, "I'm told that I'm the Yiddish Mark Twain," to which Clemens responded, "I'm told I'm the American Sholom Aleichem."

After Abramovitsch and Rabinovitz had shown that Yiddish was not jargon, was in fact a legitimate language, numerous Yiddish writers appeared. The third of the "founding fathers" of Yiddish literature was Yitzchak Leib Peretz, another fine writer who wrote short stories and plays. All three of these Yiddish pioneers helped to transform Yiddish into a powerful literary language, a language that could be used to describe both the beauties and miseries of Jewish life in Eastern Europe. All of them, like the rest of the Jewish masses, were subject to Russian anti-Semitism, to pogroms, to oppressive laws, and to the poverty that beset so many Russians, Jews and non-Jews.

By the time Peretz appeared, Yiddish literature was no longer a novelty, and the Yiddish language had been used in a wide variety of genres. It remained for one of Peretz's disciples, Sholem Asch, to write a Yiddish epic. Asch is in many ways a strange figure. He grew up in an extremely religious household, but as a teenager he, like the earlier writers, came into contact with Enlightenment ideas and quickly abandoned the world of orthodoxy. Nevertheless, throughout his life he identified with Jews and Judaism, and he became enormously popular as a writer of plays, stories, and novels. That popularity, as we will see, came to an abrupt end, and though he died in 1957 as an acclaimed figure in Israel, he has never regained his early level of popularity.

It is true that Asch has a number of flaws as a writer. But while he was never a great prose stylist, many of the translations of his books, like *Three Cities,* suffer from having been made from German translations of the Yiddish. They are, that is, translations of translations. Furthermore, in a number of cases, references in the Yiddish to biblical or Jewish subjects are often homogenized for American audiences. There is also a broad streak of melodrama in Asch's work, and his attempts at presenting psychological analyses are often less than successful. At the same time, some of his alleged flaws, like the weakness of his main characters, are not flaws at all, as I hope to demonstrate. Like almost any writer, Asch produced lesser and greater works, but he is a writer worth reading. He wrestles in his work with large moral and historical problems, and he often adopts an idealistic stance that can seem hopelessly outdated to contemporary readers, though whether that perception is his problem or ours remains an open question. It certainly created problems for him.

Asch's first novel, *Mottke the Thief* (*Mottke Ganif*, 1916), contains many of the strengths and weaknesses of his later work.[9] The novel offers a picture of the Jewish poor and of the criminal class that flourished in their midst. The descriptions of Mottke's childhood and of his environment are Dickensian, as are the descriptions of criminal life, except that they are more explicitly sexual than anything in Dickens. Asch, however, is not issuing a call for reform. He is, rather, exploring, and the focus throughout is on Mottke himself, a young man who suffers from his evil surroundings but who never considers trying to rise above them, not, that is, until the end of the novel when he falls in love with an angelic young woman and tries to reform himself. By then it is too late, and the novel concludes as he is arrested for murder in her presence.

While *Mottke the Thief* presents an interesting picture of the life of its characters, it has its share of flaws. The two halves of the book, Mottke's youth and his adulthood, have very different tones. The first half shows Mottke as a troublesome scamp in terrible surroundings, while the second half focuses much more seriously on his criminal career. Mottke himself is a problematic character. He is, first, fixated on his mother, a common characteristic for Asch's protagonists. Whether or not Asch had Oedipal problems, many of his characters do, and their attachments to their mothers often contribute to the melodrama of the novels. The second major problem with Mottke, a problem that also afflicts many of Asch's characters, is his sudden conversion. Because of his love for the angelic young woman, he suddenly drops his criminal activity—he is, at the time, a pimp for several prostitutes, control over whom he transfers to his competitors—and he tries to make himself worthy of her love. The situation is ludicrous, melodramatic, and contrived and makes the end of the novel unworthy of the beginning.

Many of Asch's novels show these flaws, in varying degrees, but his next important novel manages to overcome them. This is a brief work whose English title, *Sanctification of the Name*, requires a word of explanation. *Sanctification of the Name* is a direct translation of the Yiddish title, *Kiddush*

Ha-Shem. (These words are actually Hebrew, but the expression is also used in Yiddish.) Kiddush Ha-Shem means martyrdom; someone who dies for "sanctification of the name" is a religious martyr. Not only does this title indicate what the novel will be about, but its subtitle is even more explicit: *An Epic of 1648*. Jewish history contains a number of large-scale slaughters, the most famous being the Holocaust. Less well known is the havoc caused by the Crusaders in the early twelfth century, and even less well known are the Chmielnicki massacres of 1648, when the Jews of Eastern Europe were caught between the forces of an oppressive anti-Semitic government and anti-Semitic rebels against that government. The result was the most massive killing of Jews before the Holocaust and a transformation of subsequent Jewish history. Asch presents one small but poignant episode from that awful time, which he bases on seventeenth-century chronicles aided by his own imagination.

The novel is relatively brief—about one hundred fifty pages—but length is not necessarily a defining factor for epic. Is *Sanctification of the Name*, then, an epic? Not really. It does indeed deal with a pivotal moment in Jewish history, but it deals with that moment in a very focused and specific manner. The action takes place in the remote village of Zlochov. Asch provides no background for the events that took place there, no analysis of those events, and no consideration of the consequences of those events. The novel lacks the grandeur, the panoramic view, and the worldly sweep that epic requires. It is a fine novel, better handled than *Mottke*, but it is not an epic. Even the melodramatic ending, when the beautiful Jewish maiden tricks her captor into killing her so that she can avoid marrying him, fits into the context of the book, as the ending of *Mottke* does not.

Sanctification of the Name was written in 1919, while Jewish life in Eastern Europe was again being transformed, thanks to the war and the Russian Revolution; and Asch's attitude toward these events is revealed by the epigraph to the novel: "We are ashamed to write down all that the Cossacks and Tatars did unto the Jews, lest we disgrace the species man, which is created in the image of God." He is aware of the horrors that afflicted people, but he never loses his idealism. Yes, people did terrible things; they behaved worse than wild beasts. But we cannot forget that human beings were created in the image of God. Even in the wake of those horrors, there is still a faith, in both God and in human beings. Asch may not have been observant in the traditional Jewish sense, but he was deeply religious in the sense that he believed that human beings have specific responsibilities to each other and that by meeting those responsibilities they can create a better world.

Interestingly, Asch did not see the United States as a solution to the problems faced by Jews. In his two most famous novels set in America, *Uncle Moses* (1917) and *East River* (1946), he is quite critical of the materialism and greed that he sees in the United States and that afflict not just immigrants but, even more powerfully, their children. These novels attack the sweatshops of the garment industry with Dickensian ferocity, and *East River* especially offers an idealistic picture of a way in which life could be improved for everyone.

Of course, many people in the late 1920s and 1930s believed that the Communist regime in Russia presented a blueprint of how society could be more equitably organized. At the beginning of our new century, we may laugh (or cry) at their naiveté, but such people saw the inequities that beset society and sought a way to abolish them. Their solution may have been mistaken, but their recognition of the problem and their idealism certainly were not. Asch, as we have seen, was acutely aware of the problems, but he was not taken in by the rhetoric of Lenin and Stalin. His masterpiece on this subject, *Three Cities*, is indeed an epic treatment of the Russian Revolution, as we will see. First, however, we need to see the rest of Asch's career, because it illustrates much that he wrote about in *Three Cities*.

After *Three Cities*, Asch wrote the work that is often considered his masterpiece, *Salvation* (whose Yiddish title is *Der T'hillim Yid, The Psalm Jew*, 1934), a beautiful and moving novel that has its share of melodrama but that overcomes that melodrama to present an idealized religious vision. Its hero, Yechiel, is perhaps a little more attached to his mother and to various mother figures than he should be; but eventually he overcomes his Oedipal tendencies and, even more profoundly than *Three Cities*' Zachary Mirkin, he arrives at a vision not only of how the world should be but of how it actually might be.

All of the novels that have been mentioned so far are clearly about Jewish life, though they also have universal implications. They were, of course, written in Yiddish, but they were translated into many other languages. They were no more intended for strictly Jewish audiences than Sholokhov's epic novel was intended solely for Cossacks. In fact, *Three Cities* was very popular with Jewish and non-Jewish audiences, but Asch's next major works brought about a drastic change in his reputation. These works—*The Nazarene, The Apostle*, and *Mary*—are about Jesus, Paul, and Mary. Christian readers found these books valuable, and at the moment that I am writing, *The Nazarene* is the only one of Asch's novels that is still in print. Jewish audiences, however, were largely outraged. We must remember that when these books were published, ecumenicism had not become popular. People generally focused not on what religions had in common but on what separated them. For Jews, the approach of the Holocaust, added to almost two thousand years of persecution, had made them at best suspicious of Christians. Not only had there been few attempts at religious reconciliation, but even the thought that reconciliation might be possible would have been regarded with scorn and alarm, which is precisely the way that the Jewish world responded to *The Nazarene*. Asch's writing was banned from Yiddish periodicals and his earlier accomplishments were quickly forgotten. He had few defenders in the Jewish world.

In light of this controversy, it is indeed an interesting experience to read these books now. If one were not already aware of this history, reading these books would not lead one to imagine the controversy they caused. In fact, what these novels do is to point to what scholars have been discussing at great length in recent years, the Jewish origins of Christianity. Asch's Jesus is, in modern terms, a nice Jewish boy who has no intention of starting a new religion. He and his followers (whether they believe in his messiahship or not) regard him as an idealist, someone who sees the social implications of Judaism that have been obscured by the self-seeking priestly families in the Temple. Asch, true to history, demonstrates the similarities between many of Jesus' statements and those of such Talmudic sages as Hillel and Yochanan ben Zakkai. And in *The Apostle*, Paul, too, is an idealist, though he does become interested in starting a new religion for mistaken reasons.

I have gone on at some length about these novels because they help us to understand *Three Cities* and to see what makes that work an epic, which they, despite being a trilogy, are not. Those three works on the beginnings of Christianity stand as independent novels, with separate leading characters, telling related but not unified stories and not focusing on a single pivotal moment. *Three Cities*, on the other hand, is a continuous narrative, tracing its action through St. Petersburg, Warsaw, and Moscow, maintaining a consistent cast of central characters (with, naturally, a changing cast of lesser characters), offering scope, presenting an epic hero whose behavior raises questions about being a hero, and focusing on events leading up to and then away from a pivotal moment, the Russian Revolution.

As is the case with many of these epic novels, *Three Cities* begins innocently, with only hints of what is to come. The reader of the *Iliad* or the *Aeneid* in any age would have recognized from the verse form and the opening words—"Sing, Muse . . ." or "Arms and the man I sing"—that these are epics and would have been prepared for the epic conventions (and the variations played on them) that followed. The reader of the epic novel has no such expectations. *War and Peace* opens with rather confusing conversations at the home of Anna Scherer, conversations that only begin to make sense as the novel progresses. Tolstoy worked hard to achieve that effect, having tried a large number of possible openings for his novel. The epic novels of Olivia Manning and Paul Scott open with domestic scenes that seem innocent enough but that contain the seeds of the crises that will follow. So, too, does *Three Cities*. It begins in a Petersburg winter with a description of the sledges making their slow way through the snow. The drivers try to stay warm, while they and their horses "breathed heavily as they struggled through the dirty gray gutters." Occasionally, however, these sledges are passed by speeding troikas. "These little one-horse sledges were conveying the riches of the south into the capital of the Czar," such riches as French champagne, fresh flowers from the south of France, fruits, perfumes, and cosmetics.[10]

In the contrast between the mass of struggling sledges and the speedy troikas with their luxurious cargo we can see the entire struggle that will occupy the rest of the epic novel. In fact, the whole work is structured on the basis of this contrast. The first volume, *Petersburg*, shows us life among the relatively wealthy Jews of the capital, while the second volume, *Warsaw*, takes us to the poverty-stricken ghetto of the Polish city. With that contrast clearly drawn, the third volume, *Moscow*, takes us to that city after the October Revolution and allows us to see the struggle of the nation and of its individual citizens, particularly Zachary Mirkin, as they try to right the wrongs that the trilogy's opening paragraphs have delineated.

The contrasts between the rich and the poor are further emphasized as the scene shifts to the offices of the lawyer Solomon Ossipovitch Halperin. Halperin is a complicated figure, in large part because a person in his position would have led a complicated life. Halperin is quite wealthy, as the accoutrements of his home indicate. He is wealthy because "though a Jew, Halperin was celebrated far and wide in Russia for his acuteness, his eloquence . . . and his influential connections" (5). That sentence indicates at least part of his problem. He is an excellent lawyer, greatly in demand by rich and poor clients alike, but he still suffers from the restrictions placed on Jews. He knows that he, like many other Jews, is in Petersburg only because he has received special permission, in effect a license, to be there, and that that permission could be withdrawn at any time. He does a good deal of what we might call *pro bono* work, helping oppressed minorities, Jews and others; but of course his prestige comes from his wealthy and well-known clients, who naturally are ushered into private waiting rooms rather than having to wait with the rabble. In short, Halperin is on a sort of tightrope. He has extremely high standards—so high that he turns down the case of an openly anti-Semitic government official who has been caught stealing government funds, even though turning down the case could lead to trouble—but at the same time he is proud of his wealth and his status. He walks the tightrope well, but he seems to know that he cannot stay on it forever.

Halperin's tenuous status can be seen in other ways. He is, for example, a Russian patriot: "To my way of thinking Russia is not an empire, not a state or a nation; Russia is something more, something greater. Russia is a philosophical conception, a form of life." In the same speech, however, he acknowledges that Russians live "under an unjust, dreadful system of oppression [that] has itself created in us a common ideal of freedom and an intense longing, a thirst for justice."(29). In fact, after the dinner at which he makes this speech, he mounts yet a different tightrope, as he introduces his rich friends to a young revolutionary and urges them to contribute to his cause, which involves smuggling out of the country documents containing information about the influential anti-Semitic organization called the Black Hand. When one of the wealthy magnates demures, Halperin exclaims, "No decent man in Russia is against the revolution, and least of all a Jew" (35). He and the revolutionary know that they are using each other, he to eliminate the anti-Semitism that restricts him and all Jews, the revolutionary to obtain money from the capitalists that will be used to overthrow the capitalists. Both are playing a dangerous game and both will ultimately lose, but the fact that they both knowingly play that game indicates the precariousness of their respective positions. They live in troubling times, and they know, or hope, that change is imminent. They both work to implement and control that change, but as the rest of the trilogy demonstrates, such expectations are fruitless.

Adding to Halperin's problems is yet another tightrope (if the presence of three tightropes does not overwork the metaphor). Halperin grew up in a traditional Jewish home, but he has moved far from that environment. He seems to be almost perfectly assimilated, a good Russian in nearly every way—"A stranger who knew nothing of the circumstances might have concluded from hearing the conversation that he was not among persecuted Jews, but in a company of Russian patriots" (27–28)—yet his Jewish background frequently manifests itself. For example, as he considers a problem, "he accompanied his thoughts with words uttered in the sing-song rhythm of the Talmud school from which, all his life, he had been unable to wean himself" (8).[11] Similarly, "when he had guests for dinner he always felt an irresistible compulsion to harangue them, just as his forbears had been wont to elucidate the Torah at table to their Chassidic followers" (31). Despite his attempts to escape his Jewish background, he cannot. He is like a yeshiva student, like a Chassidic rebbe, and the qualities of that traditional life, based on close reading of texts and detailed argumentation, have undoubtedly contributed to his success as a lawyer. Do what he can, he cannot escape that background; and the same can be said for his wealthy Jewish colleagues, including, as we will see, Zachary Mirkin's father.

This desire to escape from traditional Jewish life, even if it is not totally successful, is another common motif in Asch's work. As Charles Madison says in describing two of Asch's early plays, *The Messiah Period* and *The Inheritors*, "Asch is at pains to demonstrate the spiritual bankruptcy of the middle generation and to point out how the youth are desperately seeking to forge a new religion."[12] Halperin and his colleagues are part of that middle generation, occupying the time between ghetto life in the Pale of Settlement and the hope for complete emancipation and assimilation. Unfortunately for such people in Asch's world, they seem to have given up what was best in the previous generation in favor of an emptiness in the present. Madison's judgment is also accurate regarding many, though not all, of the children. Halperin's own children are a good example. His vivacious daughter Nina differs from her literary ancestress, Tolstoy's Natasha, only by being on her way to total spiritual bankruptcy. She has no serious interests aside from being pampered, and when she becomes engaged to Zachary Mirkin, she seems to think that the pampering will only increase. In one of the novel's memorable scenes, she goes to a restaurant with her fiancé and her prospective father-in-law and orders, in the middle of the Russian winter, cherries. Remarkably, the restaurant has some cherries, which had been ordered "for the Grand Duke Boris" (132). If the waiter serves the cherries to Nina, he is likely to be whipped by the Grand Duke, but Mirkin's father insists that she be served. Still, when the cherries arrive, she eats one and sends the rest back, because she does not want the waiter to be beaten, and she explains to old Mirkin, "I wanted the cherries because I thought they couldn't be got. Now that I see they can be got I've no further desire for them" (133). Like an idealist, like her fiancé Zachary, she wants what is beyond her reach, what might not be possible; but unlike the idealist's, her desires are material, cherries in winter, a symbol of conspicuous consumption. If Halperin still feels the pull of his traditional religious upbringing, if he bases his legal practice on the highest standards of integrity, he has managed to raise his daughter with none of the virtues that her tradition should have taught her.

And his son Misha is even worse. The good-looking Misha is loved by one of the Halperins' servants, Anushka, and he takes advantage of her by borrowing money from her. Eventually, in his quest for funds to pay for his pleasures, he steals a piece of jewelry and allows Anushka to take the blame, which means that she is severely beaten by the police. Halperin is appropriately outraged when he learns what his son had done. He proclaims to his wife, in one of his typical orations, "In my house . . . justice will always be upheld. Here has always been an asylum for the oppressed and persecuted, here protection from violence and injustice could always be found. And now the meanest, the most contemptible form of crime has crept into my household. I shall root it out with my own hand and deliver it over to justice!" (271). Of course, as his wife points out, he will do no such thing, and he is struck dumb as she comments on his empty oratory. And the first volume of the trilogy ends as Olga Michailovna Halperin delivers some of the truest words in the novel: "We're to blame for everything!" (273).[13]

Halperin may well believe that he has stood for justice and that he has defended the oppressed and the persecuted. We have, in fact, seen evidence that he has done so. Still, he has done so in a very pragmatic way, in a way that would not inconvenience him. He supports the revolution not because he sees the entire panorama of injustice that is czarist Russia but because he wants equal rights for the Jews. This goal is not evil, certainly, but it is, for Asch, only a partial goal. Halperin wants the revolution to succeed to the extent that it will provide him and other Jews with full emancipation, but he does not want it to succeed to the extent that he would have to share his considerable wealth with the poor. Halperin is not a villain, but he lacks the idealistic outlook that an Aschian hero requires.

Furthermore, Halperin's insistence on playing by the rules is problematic. As we saw, he has denied his aid to a corrupt government minister, as though there were another kind of government minister. Later, he tries to help a poor Jewish woman gain freedom for her son, who has been imprisoned for striking an officer who tried to force-feed him nonkosher food. Halperin is unsuccessful in his legal maneuvering, but Zachary's father Gabriel succeeds. He simply gives the minister money to replace the funds he has embezzled, tells him the boy's story, and encourages him to tell the Czar, who is so moved by the melodrama that he has the boy released. Which methods are more admirable, those of Halperin, who tries to make the law work while the young man sits in prison, or those of Mirkin, who indulges official corruption but who succeeds in gaining the young man's release? The contrast here is not between the pragmatist and the idealist. It is, rather, between two kinds of pragmatists. They both aim at the same laudable goal, for which they are hardly to be condemned; but neither of them is willing to challenge the underlying corruption of the system.

The second volume of the trilogy offers the strongest possible contrast to the first, both in the situation it presents and in its characters. Zachary, having broken his engagement to Nina, goes to Warsaw, to the home of Frau

Hurvitz, another woman who had come to Petersburg in an attempt to rescue an imprisoned son. Zachary, with all his ties to Petersburg cut, has nowhere else to go, though he is hardly impoverished, unlike everyone whom he meets in Warsaw. Poland was under Russian control at that time; and Russian restrictions on the Poles, Jews and non-Jews, were terribly oppressive. Asch focuses on Jewish life, but clearly everyone was suffering. As a result, life in the Hurvitz household is quite different from life at the Halperins'. At the Halperins' we saw wealth and plenty. We saw a dinner to which numerous people were invited without any thought about how many people had to be fed. The Hurvitzes, too, have a full house, but to the Hurvitzes, who rely on Solomon Hurvitz's meager salary, supplemented by his daughter's smaller earnings, every additional guest means less for everyone else. Still, there is never any hesitation about inviting in the hungry. When Zachary appears, he is welcomed; and when a young man from the provinces appears because his father has thrown him out of his house for undertaking secular learning, he, too, is not only welcomed, but Frau Hurvitz finds lodging for him. Her attempt to find a bed for the young man provides Asch with an opportunity to illustrate the poverty of the community, as she goes from family to family. They are poor; they are ill. They live in misery:

> It was a typical tenement barracks with a labyrinth of courtyards where workshop leaned against workshop.... And the barracks [an unfortunate translation] surrounding the uncannily dark workshops were packed full of human bodies that worked at machines of some kind from morning lamp-light until evening lamp-light; weaving-machinists, knitting-machinists, bag-makers and strap-makers. From the open windows in summer issued the sad songs of apprentice work-girls who bartered their young eye-sight for half-pence during the long summer days and the longer winter evenings. (293)

Such descriptions—and there are many of them in *Warsaw*—go on for pages, driving home the point that these people live inhuman lives. (Similar descriptions, incidentally, can be found in *East River*, in which Asch decries abuses in the American garment industry.) The contrast between Warsaw and Petersburg, between the Hurvitzes and the Halperins, is striking. Nina, as we saw, wants cherries in the winter, despite the other luxuries in her life. Frau Hurvitz, on the other hand, "did not lament her destiny; on the contrary she was content. Could she have lived her life over again she would have taken the same path" (321). Her life, for all its difficulties, has meaning and purpose, whereas Nina's life is empty. Asch has done a masterful job of setting up what appears to be a clear dichotomy between these two families and the social circles that they represent.

Another area of contrast involves their attitudes toward their religious backgrounds. Solomon Ossipovitch Halperin (who is always addressed in the Russian style, with his first name and patronymic) feels strongly that Jews should have equal rights, and he harbors memories and even habits that stem from his religious upbringing; but he feels no attachment to Judaism itself, and his wife and children are almost completely detached from the religion. Even more detached are the Mirkins. Zachary has been raised with no indication that he is Jewish, and his father "had seriously considered going over to the religion whose usages he had always kept" (54), that is, Christianity. Zachary learns about his religious background only because his father's housekeeper reveals it to him.

The Hurvitzes have also left behind formal religious observances—almost. The hesitation of that "almost" is central to the Hurvitz's lives. They are not ritually observant. Hurvitz loves secular literature and philosophy, especially the philosophy of Spinoza, who was regarded as a heretic by religious Jews. Nevertheless, on Friday evening, Frau Hurvitz lights the Sabbath candles, and the Friday night meal is the best of the week:

> For although Frau Hurvitz regarded herself as a progressive woman, and although her husband was notorious in Warsaw as a "renegade" who seduced pious Jewish youths from the straight path, Rachel-Leah could not bring herself to deny her upbringing and to ignore the Jewish feast-days that involved her often enough in conflict with her "progressive" views, and yet—on Friday evening the Sabbath began for Rachel-Leah. To deny that would have meant for her renouncing something that betokened a higher life. (343)

Nor is this only Frau Hurvitz's practice. For her husband, too, freethinker though he may be, Friday evening is a special time, a time when "the blood of his forebears cried aloud in him" (347). Unlike Halperin, Hurvitz does not suppress that cry. On the Sabbath and the festivals, the candles are lit and dinner becomes a celebration. It is true that most of the holiday rituals are ignored, but the holidays themselves are not. Asch's point seems to be that in many ways, the Hurvitz's customs are adaptations of the religious rituals. Thus the tenth chapter of *Warsaw* is entitled, in the English, "Sabbath Music," but the Yiddish title of the chapter is "Z'mirot." That Yiddish word is much richer than the English translation, even though the translation is literally accurate. Z'mirot are the songs people sing around the Sabbath table. They are, to be sure, religious in nature, but to say that people are singing z'mirot is to say that there is a fellowship, a community, and a sense of celebration. Naturally the Hurvitzes do not sing such songs. Their z'mirot consist of Hurvitz's reading of patriotic Polish poetry, works forbidden by the occupying Russians, works by Mickievicz and Wyspianski; and later, the Hurvitz's guests do sing songs, dangerous revolutionary songs, songs about liberty and an end to tyranny.

These activities may not be the activities of religious Jews, but they are the activities of people who believe in prophetic Judaism, of people whose answer to the question "Am I my brother's keeper?" is an emphatic "yes." Halperin sincerely believes in justice, but he does not embody justice the way the Hurvitzes do. The Halperins' lives have a certain emptiness, despite their wealth, while the Hurvitzes give meaning to life, despite their poverty. After dinner

> As Mirkin descended the staircase he saw the Sabbath lights gleaming from every window in the large courtyard. The building in which Frau Hurvitz lived had always seemed to him unspeakably wretched and gloomy, but today there was a remarkable change; the Sabbath shone out of every Jewish dwelling. Zachary felt its radiance in himself as well. (366)

Certainly this is a romanticized picture, but it is a picture that was very common in Yiddish literature and that held a great deal of truth for the Jewish people. There was a saying that the Jews in Eastern Europe lived buried in mud up to their necks, and their foreheads touched heaven. Abramovitsch, in his novel *Dos vintchfingerl* (*The Magic Wishing Ring*), presents a family who live in absolute poverty, but on the Sabbath they and their hovel of a home are transformed. Asch uses that same image here to indicate the spiritual vitality of the Hurvitz family and of all who lived the way they did. They themselves may have abandoned the rituals of their religion, but they have not abandoned its essence. The Halperins and other Petersburg Jews have abandoned both.

This point is emphasized later when Mirkin, in the service of the revolutionaries, visits Lodz and sees the appalling conditions in which the workers exist.[14] While there, he visits a decrepit little synagogue, the kind of place for which his Petersburg circle would have had contempt, and he makes an important discovery: "Unutterable pity seized him not only for the human beings but also for the God that lived here. The Jewish God seemed just like the men who came here, a poor Jew just like them. He had left His glory behind Him in Heaven, and had come down among these people to dwell with them in their stinking court" (488). Like Stephen Daedalus's remark that God is a "shout in the street," Zachary's realization here concretizes the immanence of God.[15] Furthermore, it acknowledges the divine mandate for and the divine association with social justice (which, incidentally, helps to explain one factor that lay behind Asch's writing of *The Nazarene*, Jesus's passionate devotion to social justice). Halperin, too, seeks social justice, but he does so at a remove from his wealthy surroundings, where there is nothing of the divine; but in Lodz, amid the squalor and the poverty, Zachary takes a vital step on his way to becoming a fully developed human being, as we will see.

Asch explores this connection between the revolutionary life and Jewish life, two systems theoretically dedicated to achieving social justice, and he does not come up with easy answers. In this connection we need to recall that young man who appeared at the Hurvitz's door. He wants to be a writer, though he has had minimal contact with the secular world. Later we learn that he has had some pieces published and that a "famous Yiddish writer living then in Warsaw and regarded by the younger generation almost as their mentor, considered that the young man had a brilliant future before him" (565). The likelihood is that the older writer is Peretz and the young man is Asch, who is including autobiographical details in his novel. Thus, when the young man achieves success as a Yiddish writer, the Hurvitzes, who had considered Yiddish to be merely "jargon," are persuaded that it is indeed a literary language. But this young man represents Asch in yet another way. For instance, at that "Sabbath" dinner that we have seen, he asks, with great trepidation, a question that has bothered him:

> "I only want to ask one thing. . . . In your opinion, now, what do you think . . . is there any reward for us in a future world or not? Is there guilt and expiation in a future world or not? I've heard everything discussed in this circle except the main thing, the great fundamental question, what happens *after* our life; about that I've heard nothing at all." (359)

What he is asking, using the traditional religious language of reward and punishment, is whether the world has a transcendent meaning, whether there is any extraworldly basis for determining human morality, whether, in effect, there is a God. Hurvitz's reaction is that he "sat petrified; this was a question for which he was not prepared," but Hurvitz is seldom at a loss for words, so he takes the young man aside and talks to him: "In stating his views he fell involuntarily into the Talmud sing-song which he had caught from the young Chassid." Again, then, he is like Halperin, unable to escape his religious roots, lapsing into a Talmudic mode; but his answer differs from what Halperin might have said. He avoids religious clichés while still giving a religious answer, which is that we cannot know about a transcendent world but that with "enough knowledge and culture . . . you can be assured that we won't need to look for Paradise in another world! Then all men will be brothers . . . Paradise will be in *this* world" (359). If these words are not religious clichés, they certainly sound like revolutionary clichés, except for their close resemblance to the prophecy of Isaiah

> And He shall judge between the nations
> And shall decide for many peoples;
> And they shall beat their swords into plowshares,
> And their spears into pruning-hooks;
> Nation shall not lift up sword against nation,
> Neither shall they learn war any more.
>
> (Isaiah 2:4)

What Isaiah said some twenty-seven hundred years ago combined the revolutionary and the religious, but too often people who consider themselves either revolutionary or religious divide those two realms, as does the young man when he responds to Hurvitz, "But if there's nothing to expect from a future world, what's the good of everything? Is *this* world . . . the kind of world in which it's worth a man's while to live?" (359). The point that Asch makes here and elsewhere in his works—and it is important to remember here that the young man represents himself as a young man—is that neither of these positions is incorrect, but that without each other they are incomplete.

Thus, Asch spends considerable time in this epic-novel that focuses on the Russian Revolution portraying various kinds of poverty. Most immediately obvious are his descriptions of the physical poverty in which so many people live. Lodz is so awful that it appears almost surrealistic, and when Zachary is shown through the city's power plant, the Dickensian influence is obvious, as Asch pictures the plant as a great automaton that oppresses and devours the people who work in it. These visions of poverty and oppression are certainly disturbing, and they help the reader to grasp the forces that lay behind the revolutionary zeal of so many Russians; but Asch also reveals a spiritual poverty in the country. Much of the first volume, *Petersburg,* focuses on such spiritual poverty among the materially wealthy, but we also see it in *Warsaw* and especially in *Moscow* among the lower classes. It is that spiritual poverty that allows the Revolution to become a mockery of the ideals that lay behind it for so many people, people like the Hurvitzes, who are betrayed by the Revolution, people like Zachary, whose life, as we shall see, becomes a struggle to overcome both sorts of poverty.

Asch himself, with this book and others—particularly *Salvation* and *The Nazarene*—tried to reconcile the two views, the immanent and the transcendent, the material and the spiritual. That he was unsuccessful is not surprising. How could he have succeeded? The vision of Isaiah is properly regarded as messianic, because, as we know from world events, we are not yet ready to realize it in actuality.

As Asch wrote *Three Cities* in the early 1930s, he presented not only a metaphysical view of the world but a picture of a specific situation, the Russia that resulted from the Revolution. The Revolution was, from its earliest days, a brutal instrument based on a desire for power, as Sholokhov, too, showed. Even so, social activists around the world, led on by their idealism, were willing to ignore the brutality or even to make excuses for it. By the early 1930s, however, there was ample evidence that the Revolution had betrayed its ideals, that Lenin and then Stalin were not proletarian heroes. Far more accurate is Marfa Kryukova's description of Lenin and Stalin in the form of the traditional Russian *byliny*:

> On a morning it was, on an early morning,
> At the rise of the fair red sun,
> That Ilich stepped out of his little tent,
> He washed his fair face
> With spring water cold,
> His face he wiped with a little towel.
> As he played on his birchbark horn,
> The whole people heard him,
> The whole people gathered and thronged.[16]

Amusing though it may be to imagine Lenin summoning the people by playing on his birchbark horn, Kryukova's image of him as Russian warlord, which she obviously intended as flattery, reveals an important aspect of his approach to leadership.

Furthermore, by the time Asch was writing *Three Cities*, Stalin's tragic policies in the Ukraine had produced millions of victims, so that Sholokhov even protested to Stalin. The Soviets may have been adept at manipulating the truth of what was happening in the Ukraine, but they were not so adept that their apologists were not required to engage in their own self-deception. Asch uses no such self-deception. Instead he faces the contradictions inherent in the Revolution.

The third volume of *Three Cities*, then, focuses on the failure of the Revolution. *Petersburg* focused on the wealthy, with occasional views of the poor; *Warsaw* focused on the poor, with occasional views of the wealthy. That dichotomy between rich and poor is central, but it is not simple. The complicating factor in Asch's scheme is the role of the Jews. There are, of course, rich Jews and poor Jews, but there is also a division between Jews and non-Jews, regardless of economic status, which makes it very difficult to determine social status; and the status of individuals was a vital factor in the Revolution, since it helped to determine who constituted the enemy. The rich and the poor obviously were at odds, but so were Jews and non-Jews, so that non-Jews, divided though they may have been by economics, were united in their dislike of Jews. Economic status and inequities, therefore, were not the only causes of the Revolution and of its failure.

This point is easily illustrated. One of the first episodes in *Petersburg* involves Halperin's interview with the minister Akimov, who admits to having embezzled funds; but when Halperin refuses to defend him, Akimov accuses the lawyer of having obtained his confession "simply out of pleasure in your cunning, your Jewish cunning" (16), and he threatens to denounce him to the Czar. Much later, during the First World War and just before the deposition of the Czar, Zachary is in a little railway station, where he sees a startling scene. As a group of Austrian prisoners pass through the station, a peasant woman offers them food, on the theory that "then their mothers will give our sons something to eat if they're taken prisoners" (652). Zachary is so moved by the generosity of the peasants, at the signs of humanity that it shows, that he follows the woman, grabs her hand, and kisses it as a tribute to her. "The peasant woman gazed after the stranger in alarm, then she spat and crossed herself" (653). So much for humanity. She would share her bread with enemy prisoners, as indeed she should, but she would also recoil from the touch of a Jew. She and Akimov, though worlds apart, have that in common. Asch's description of the Revolution, then, does not convey a simple perspective. It is not just a matter of rich and poor but of Jew and non-Jew, insider and outsider, as well. Thus, one soldier shouts, in his frustration, "They should all be strung up together on the same trees, Kerensky, Lenin, and the other Jews" (614), as though "Jew" were just another word for "enemy."

Asch, of course, is aware of other factors in history, for the Revolution was a complex historical event and Asch, like Sholokhov, is particularly good at portraying the confusion that reigned through its early years. A key question closes the first chapter of *Moscow*. As Vassily Andreyevitch tries to make his way through the chaos of Petersburg, he asks his cab driver, "What the heck are Bolsheviks?" to which the driver responds, "I can't begin to know" (*Moskva* 18).[17] Nor are bystanders like Vassily Andreyevitch the only ones who do not understand the Revolution. In the governor's palace, now occupied by revolutionary troops, those troops try to find out exactly what they stand for. When one asks, "Tell us, won't you, what Bolsheviks really are?" the unsatisfactory answer is that "these men are Bolsheviks," to which the reply is, "I know that—I'm a Bolshevik myself. But nobody has told us yet what the Bolsheviks are. . . .What *is* a Bolshevik" (614–15). The soldiers reveal the confusion—yes, they are Bolsheviks, but no, they have no idea what a Bolshevik is. And a series of speakers manage to cast no light on the question, because no one in the assembly actually does know what they stand for until Comrade Sofia, the sister of Zachary's second fiancée, addresses the crowd. Her words, while they energize her audience, actually provide very little in the way of an answer. She does, however, reveal what a Bolshevik is in her discussion with Zachary, whose comment on her performance is, "I liked your speech, because it stirred the crowd to action. But surely it isn't necessary to tell lies?" But, as Sofia shows, she does not understand his point: "Oh, you bourgeois! You've come with us to the very gate of the Governor's palace—but you've kept your sentimentality" (624). Zachary's conviction is that the Bolshevik cause is so just that it does not have to rely on lies, whereas Sofia believes that the end justifies any means. She demonstrates this belief yet again when she tells Zachary that the Red Army will "turn Russia into a sea of blood" if the need arises (831), while Zachary finds himself less able to justify inhumane behavior in the cause of saving humanity. Sofia's determination may be understandable in light of what happened to her family—the oppression they suffered, the execution of her brother—but as Asch, and history, make clear, her reaction was not the one that would save Russia: "If it was necessary for the revolution . . . I would kill off a certain species—with pleasure" (804)

Neither Asch nor Zachary, it should be emphasized, is unsympathetic to the need for a revolution. Zachary himself participated in the October Revolution and even took part in the actual fighting, thereby transgressing his own pacifist tendencies. Asch provides ample proof in his writing that the Revolution was necessary, from his descriptions of conditions in Warsaw and Lodz to the disaster that was World War I. Perhaps his best comments on the need for revolution occur in the episode involving the massacre in Warsaw and the events at the Hotel Metropole. The Warsaw massacre (which foreshadows a similar episode in Scott's *Raj Quartet*) occurred when Russian troops fired on a peaceful demonstration of the poor, who found themselves trapped in a blocked-off square with no way to escape. Such murderous actions called out for redress.

The Hotel Metropole sequence is more amusing but equally revealing. As the hotel is being besieged by Bolshevik troops, including Zachary, the hotel's guests, including Halperin and Zachary's father, are taken to a safe area in the basement. Without realizing the seriousness of the problems they face, they continue to lead their privileged lives, dining on caviar and champagne and being waited on by their servants and by the hotel's employees. As the siege continues, however, those servants begin to rebel, rejecting not only the demands of their "social betters" but even the notion that such people may be their "social betters."

Asch is obviously unsympathetic to those upper-class parasites, but he is equally unsympathetic to those who would solve the problem by killing them. Particularly interesting in this regard is his treatment of Lenin, who appears several times in *Three Cities*, much as Napoleon appears in *War and Peace*, but who is almost never mentioned by name. Just as Tolstoy focuses so often on Napoleon's hands, Asch focuses on Lenin's eyes, referring to him as the man with "the Kalmuck eyes" (659). On his first appearance, Lenin is presented as an ambivalent figure: some people regard him as a traitor while others "saw in him the Messiah who alone could bring salvation, a new Moses who had miraculously appeared to lead a helpless people out of the abyss into which their countless enemies had pushed them" (659–60). It is this latter Lenin who speaks against the war, who urges his listeners, "Sacrifice yourselves for peace instead of for war as these people over there bid you do" (662). Somewhat later, however, in a chapter called "The Great Illusion," in a long interior monologue, he finally concludes, "Undeterred by the shrieks of farewell, regardless of the sufferings of those who fall by the way, we shall blaze a path for ourselves and for those who will follow us. And if it is necessary to help on man's forward march with a whip, we shall use it" (771). Asch implies that Lenin, like the Revolution, could have gone in either direction. The course followed by both the individual and the movement resulted from a lust for power among those who were (or seemed to be) in charge in addition to the greed of those less significant characters who stood to make material gains, characters like Ryshkov, who uses his new position to get himself a mistress, or Ossip Markovitch, who moves his family into Halperin's home. Lenin, Asch implies, was indeed responsible for much of what happens, but Lenin was not alone. In the absence of law, both the legislative and moral varieties, the will of one man in conjunction with the baser instincts of many others is allowed to triumph. As Charles Madison says, "Asch is here as much the social historian as the imaginative novelist."[18]

Here, then, lies the historical core of this epic novel, though it differs in significant ways from the historical core of other epics. In most other epics, the historical core has a singular focus. In the *Iliad* that focus is on the fate of Troy; in the *Aeneid* it is on Rome, in its ancient and Augustan manifestations; in *Beowulf* the focus is on the decline of the Geats, and in *War and Peace* it is on the Napoleonic invasion of Russia. In *Three Cities* there are two historical foci, the Russian Revolution (with its prologue in the First World

War) and the fate of the Jews. With this double focus, *Three Cities* again resembles *Quiet Flows the Don*, which treats the Revolution and the parallel history of the Don Cossacks. *Three Cities* opens with Halperin's interview with Akimov and Akimov's anti-Semitic outburst, and one of the book's last episodes describes Halperin's death at the hands of a violent, anti-Semitic mob. This continuing anti-Semitism indicates that the revolution has done little, if anything, to improve the society that it claimed to have reformed. Ben Siegel argues that *Three Cities* focuses on the Romanovs and on the revolution and uses the Jews as "sensitive barometers of social change."[19] Siegel is correct, up to a point, for the Jews function not only as a barometer but as a counterpoint to the Revolution. The ongoing anti-Semitism is indeed one indication of the Revolution's failures, but the Jewish life that Zachary discovers functions as a major theme on its own terms as well.

Zachary Mirkin, the novel's major figure, is problematic in several ways. As Madison says, "in a novel of profound social crisis the main character must possess the dynamic inner drive which enables him either to ride the crest of the forces unharnessed by the cataclysm or to stand up against his explosive environment and be destroyed by it. Zachary, however, is a weak and worried man, neither accepting nor fighting the life about him."[20] Madison's evaluation of Zachary has merit, but Madison falls into the trap of creating an either/or situation in which the proper answer is neither. It is true that many epic heroes fit into Madison's scheme. Achilleus, we know, like Hektor, stands up against his environment and is destroyed by it. Pierre, on the other hand, as unlikely as it seems at the beginning of *War and Peace*, does develop the drive to ride the crest of the forces unharnessed by Napoleon's invasions. But Pierre is only able to do so, finally, with the aid of Platon Karateyev, who appears only briefly in the novel and whose lesson for Pierre seems almost commonplace; yet that lesson makes all the difference. Zachary, despite the differences between himself and Tolstoy's hero, is very much like Pierre.

Zachary is certainly an extraordinarily weak character in the early sections of *Three Cities*. Born to a wealthy Jewish magnate, he is raised almost entirely by his father's housekeeper after his mother leaves Russia. Like so many of Asch's heroes, Zachary develops a mother-fixation that nearly cripples him. The only affection he receives is from that housekeeper, who eventually reveals his Jewish origins to him. Zachary is repelled by that revelation—a normal reaction, undoubtedly, to learning that he belongs to an outcast group—but he is also fascinated by it. Somehow, and we are not told how, this weak and whining boy becomes a lawyer, works in Halperin's office, and eventually becomes engaged to Halperin's daughter, though their unsuitability for each other should be obvious to everyone. One major difficulty is that, true to his Aschian heritage, he is more attracted to Nina's mother than he is to Nina.

That attraction, it probably goes without saying, is a problem, but there is another problem as well. As part of his lawyerly duties, he comes in close contact with poor Jews from outside Petersburg who have come to seek legal aid from Halperin. Again he is repelled and fascinated by these people who are his people, and soon he finds that he is more comfortable with them than he is with his usual social circle. As Nina gets closer to Zachary's father and reveals more of her frivolous nature, Zachary draws away from her. When he makes love to her mother, we can be pretty certain their engagement is over, and he does break it off and leave Petersburg, making his way to the Hurvitz home in Warsaw.

Told this way, with the absurdities highlighted, the story seems at best melodramatic and seamy. But this is not the sense one gets while reading it. Certainly the affair with Nina's mother is embarrassing and the reader is likely to think that Zachary's issues with his mother would have been of interest to Freud (who was practicing in Vienna at the time), but Zachary is redeemed by his growing attachment to Judaism, about which, however, he still knows very little. Nevertheless, he is attracted to the inner beauty of the people with whom he comes in contact. On one level, he is sensitive to their plights, to the injustices from which they suffer; but he is also attracted to their patience, to their hope that justice will be served, and to their faith in a divine force that will support them. Asch makes this point in what can charitably be described as a very awkward way. Zachary has gone to the lodging of these poor Jews and listened to the problems of Halperin's most recent client, an old Jewish woman who speaks only Yiddish: "Mirkin had not expected that his encounter with the old Jewish woman would make such a deep impression upon him. Most remarkable of all, he had understood all that she said. How could that be explained? A hidden nerve seemed to have set to work, taking up her incomprehensible words and conducting them to his brain. Soon he had quite mastered the idiom" (112). If we can overlook the unlikelihood that Zachary understands a long, complicated story in a language he does not speak and that he then quickly learns the language, we can see that Asch is here making a serious point.

Zachary has been lost in his Petersburg environment: He is out of place in Halperin's office, he is engaged to the wrong woman, he still yearns for a mother who will take care of him. He is largely estranged from his father. He is adrift, but his experience with these poor Jews, whose different language represents their apparent distance from him, touches something deep inside of him. He feels attracted to them, to their values, and to their way of life. His exposure to them is the beginning of a transformation in his life, a transformation that will take years to be accomplished and that will require him to go through many stages of development. In effect, Zachary is being reborn here and he consequently acts like a child on a number of occasions, which may be the reason that for so long he hardly seems like the hero of an epic. Of course, no epic hero behaves in a more childish fashion than Achilleus seems to through much of the *Iliad*, so childishness does not disqualify one from being an epic hero. And equally important, *Three Cities* differs from the *Iliad* and therefore requires a different kind of hero. The hero of a twentieth-century epic does not have to be a warrior, but he does have to face his situation, especially his mortality, heroically. So *Three Cities* requires not an Achilleus but a Zachary Mirkin.

Sol Liptzin has made a significant point about one of Asch's early plays, *The Messianic Age (Moshiachs Tseiten)*. Liptzin sees in the play a tension among the three generations pictured there: there are the pious grandparents, the bourgeois and assimilating middle generation, and the children, each of whom tries to find a personal kind of messianism. One turns to Polish patriotism, one to socialism, and one to Zionism; and one, with no such faith, has no purpose in life. He stands at the crossroads and does not know which way to go. "This despairing conclusion voiced the dilemma of the uncommitted Jewish intellectual during the revolutionary year 1905."[21] Liptzin's astute analysis can be applied to a number of Asch's works even after 1905, as Asch shows his concern with the confrontation between Judaism and modernity. He frequently refers to an older generation that was pious and traditional in its observances. Sometimes that generation is described at length, as it is in *Salvation*, and sometimes it is only mentioned. The next, or middle generation, has moved away from the piety and traditions of the parents. They have taken advantage of the emancipation, however limited that may be, and largely accepted the secular traditions of the society that surrounds them. Members of the third generation, however, discover the hollowness at the core of the second generation, a hollowness that consists of weakened or nonexistent values and a heightened materialism. They often rebel by turning to some movement that requires their faith: they may return to religion (though in a form different from that of their ancestors' religion) or they may turn to social movements such as Zionism or, in *Three Cities*, the revolution.

This pattern applies not only to those of Asch's novels set in Europe, in "the old country." It applies as well to a work like *East River*. And naturally the pattern does not apply to everyone. In *Three Cities* there are also members of the middle generation like the Hurvitzes who do have strong commitments to movements and to values that transcend their own immediate interests; and there are also members of the third generation, like Nina, who are perfectly happy with the materialism of their parents. Nevertheless, the pattern does help us to make sense of the trilogy. Halperin, as we saw, is a thoroughly modern man, but he still reflects his shtetl past by thinking talmudically (probably a good thing for a lawyer to do) and by reverting to a talmudic melodiousness when he argues with himself. Zachary's father, Gabriel Haimovitch Mirkin, is perhaps even further from his Jewish roots than is Halperin—he has a non-Jewish mistress and has considered converting to Christianity. Even so, as Zachary got older, his father "spoke more and more frequently to him of his forbears and his race. He often expressed regret that he had neglected his traditional religion so much and passed his whole life in a foreign environment" (80). Mirkin's nostalgia for the old ways is not prompted by any religious feeling, however. He is not motivated by a distrust of materialism or a yearning for spirituality. He reacts, rather, to the "universal reactionary atmosphere in the country, and more specifically the Antisemitism and the oppression of the Jews" (80). Consequently, despite his nostalgia, Mirkin never actually undertakes Jewish activities. He simply yearns for a past to which he could not and would not return, thereby leaving his son even more confused. After all, if his father expresses regret for the world he has left behind and yet does nothing to return to that world, Zachary has no basis for making a decision about his own relationship to that world. In Liptzin's words, "He stands at the crossroads and does not know which way to go."

It is understandable, then, that Zachary, in the early sections of *Petersburg*, shows no passion for anything. Until his encounter with the old Jewish woman, "he had brought to the daily examples of injustice which came the lawyer's way a purely professional interest of a somewhat lukewarm kind" (12). Halperin, with his shtetl roots, still has a passion about what he does, even if his passion is, paradoxically, dispassionate. Zachary, until this point, shows none of that passion at all. Now, however,

> it was a far greater thing that moved him; he stood trembling and amazed before a thousand-year-old mystery, before an inaccessible and secret mystery which nevertheless still had a strong and deep life in all the members of his race: shaken, he stood before a faith which he himself had never possessed. (113)

Only now does Zachary begin to feel passionate about things, even though he still operates in ignorance. His feelings are engaged, not his mind. His attraction is emotional rather than rational, but it also comes from the depth of his soul. Whenever he has free time, he visits the dwelling of these poor Jews, because then "he felt *heimish* and good—as if he had become a whole other person, as though he belonged to a whole other world" (*Petersburg*, 313).[22] The word *heimish* literally means "familiar" or "intimate," but it is a word with strong connotations that give the sense of being at home, precisely what Zachary feels in this company. He is at home with them; he is where he belongs, even if his social status, his dress, his language, in fact almost everything about him separates him from them. All of those formal elements he can and will change, though with some difficulty; but he has discovered his identity.

Of course, Zachary has help in his rebirth. The old woman and Frau Hurvitz befriend him, but the key is provided by Baruch Chomsky, another poor Jew from the provinces who has come to Petersburg seeking justice.[23] Chomsky understands the vagaries of human law, so he reinforces his quest with a belief in divine justice, which, he explains, "always conquers" (231). When Zachary expresses his doubts on this issue, Chomsky interrupts him and explains, "I've come to the certainty that there is finally a world order that binds everything together. I've come to that conclusion quite simply . . . one only needs to feel it as I feel it" (231). Chomsky here may be talking about faith, though he does not use that word, but what he says about feeling is not so different from Zachary's feeling that he belongs with these people. Chomsky goes on to describe the world as a giant organism, a living thing in which every other thing plays a part, and he tells Zachary, "Rise out of yourself, young man! Tear yourself free from the darkness of your own petty life; then you will see the great light, will feel the mighty pulse, the great heartbeat of the world!" (233).

Zachary is astounded at these words, feeling that Chomsky has somehow read his mind, but he is still not fully convinced, as he tells the old man, "Everything's indifferent to me," prompting Chomsky to explain, "[T]here's nothing that's 'indifferent'; there's only the way of those who help or fail the world." (234). Asch wisely does not allow Zachary to undergo a complete metamorphosis as a result of this epiphany. Zachary's education remains a gradual process. He does indeed break off his engagement soon after this episode and then he makes his way to Warsaw for the second volume.

Like all recent converts, Zachary is full of enthusiasm for his new way of life. To his new acquaintances at the Hurvitz home

> he poured out . . . in fiery words all that he had experienced and all the new convictions he had acquired, believing in good faith that every person who

belonged to the mass of Jews or had any connection with them must be filled with the same national sentiments that had fired him so instantaneously; he could not even imagine that any genuine Jew might have a different viewpoint. (325–26)

He recounts for them his experiences in Vilna, where he attended synagogue services for the High Holy Days (and where Asch confuses the Torah reading for Rosh Hashanah and Yom Kippur). He also announces that he has begun to learn Hebrew and that he has become interested in Zionism and is planning to move to Eretz Yisrael, the land of Israel.[24] For the first time in the trilogy, Zachary seems truly alive, though, as Hurvitz and the others point out, he is guilty of idealizing what he has seen. Zachary has gone from one extreme to the other. By the end of *Petersburg*, he has rejected the worldly, totally secular society of the capital. Now in *Warsaw* he must begin to see the everyday life of ordinary people. He tries, but for a long while he also relies on his family's wealth for support. Eventually, though, he rejects that crutch as well and accepts a life of poverty, trying to live with the people as one of the people. He is not fully successful in this endeavor because his background always marks him as an outsider, but eventually he is accepted for his good intentions.

One particularly striking scene involves his visit to the soup kitchen. Having rejected his family's money in his attempt to be one of the people, he decides to eat in the communal soup kitchen. Asch's description of this establishment conveys the horror of the place, but Zachary forces himself to eat the nauseating food. Unfortunately—or perhaps fortunately—he cannot keep that food down, and he becomes upset at his own softness, vowing that "I'll conquer the fine gentleman in me, even if I've got to thrash him with a cudgel" (397). This episode offers a good contrast to the episode of Nina and the cherries. Whereas Nina tries to rise above her rank, ordering the cherries that had been obtained for the Grand Duke, Zachary abases himself, trying to make himself one with the lowest class of society. Just as he idealized the religious life that he saw in Vilna, he tries to romanticize the life of poverty. What he learns is that poverty can be borne, but it cannot be romanticized. Poverty is the result of injustice, not the cause, but it is certainly not a virtue.

Zachary has another obstacle to overcome as well. We have already commented on his attraction to older women who take the place of his mother, resulting in his semi-incestuous relationship with Nina's mother. In Warsaw, too, he is attracted to Frau Hurvitz, but she, unlike Nina's mother, encourages him to grow up, to act like a man instead of a little boy. In the process of doing so, he is again helped by Chomsky, whom he meets during one of his visits to a synagogue. Once more the older man takes on the role of a father toward the floundering young man. For a second time Chomsky acts as something of an oracle, a biblical prophet who appears at a crisis in Zachary's life and tells him how to behave. Novelistically the technique is weak, and in an ordinary novel it would surely appear as a defect; but in the kind of epic novel we are considering, the technique is no more out of place than are the speeches of Nestor in the *Iliad*—except that Chomsky is not nearly as long-winded and his advice is better.

Chomsky's words, though not very different from what he told Zachary earlier, are not what we might expect from such a traditionally religious Jew, but they do incorporate some of the main themes of the trilogy:

> "The main thing . . . is to believe in everything one does. God does not care in what fashion you believe in Him, so long as you believe there is a power for good directing the world, and resign yourself to it so as to serve its purpose, and do what you can to increase it. . . . [I]t does not matter whether the things you have to do are small or great; they all come from *one* source, they all have *one* purpose: to accomplish God's work on earth." (515)

It should be clear now that Asch is not simply offering a dichotomy between Jewish and non-Jewish life, urging the superiority of the former. More precisely, he offers a dichotomy between the religious and the nonreligious life, he defines what he means by the religious life, and he does indeed urge its superiority. He reconciles the doubts of the young man from the provinces and the answer of Hurvitz, and he provides a pattern by which to judge what happens in the third volume, in which we see the Revolution in action. It is easy to see, incidentally, from passages like this what led Asch to write *The Nazarene*, in which he sought to describe the common elements shared by Judaism and Christianity. The kernel of that novel can be found in Chomsky's prophetic words to Zachary.

Once again, however, Asch wisely does not allow Zachary to undergo a sudden metamorphosis. Chomsky teaches him well, but Zachary must discover how to apply that teaching to his life. Chomsky's major effect on him at this point is to help him preserve his idealism. At times that idealism has gotten him into trouble, particularly when he assumed that his ideals were consonant with those of his audiences; but when the First World War breaks out and one of the Hurvitz lodgers, known as the Shachliner, expresses his delight in the coming catastrophe, Zachary makes an impassioned speech in which he expresses his belief that human beings will someday overcome their murderous and oppressive tendencies: "A dark night is falling upon us, but I have no fear, because I trust humanity. It will emerge again from the dark night, the dark wood, and find its own path." No one responds, because everyone feels that "the sacred faith of a human soul had been laid bare to them" (571), and the second volume ends.

Such idealism must surely strike most readers as jejeune. It seems bad enough that Zachary says such things, but it is obvious that Asch feels them as well, and our tendency in the early twenty-first century is to reject them and to reject the works in which they appear as well. We would be mistaken to do so in the case of *Three Cities*. Asch is examining in this work a pivotal historical moment, culminating in the Russian Revolution, a moment that was theoretically founded in idealism. The third volume of the trilogy focuses particularly on that moment and examines the various ideologies that operated then, testing their legitimacy against a standard that he has established in the first two volumes. If most of those ideologies are found wanting, Asch's analysis has been confirmed by historical events; and if he proposes yet another approach, it seems illegitimate to disqualify it because it does not suit modern tastes.

Zachary himself, in living through the events of the Revolution, tries out various ideologies, even when the actions that they require lead him to do things he abhors. During the war he is a noncombatant who tries to help refugees, especially Jews, who, as Russians, were considered to be the enemy by Germans and, as Jews, were considered to be the enemy by Russians. Asch's descriptions of the devastation they suffered—written in 1933!—foreshadows accounts of the Holocaust and of other refugee crises, but in the middle of that devastation is Zachary, risking his life in the attempt to bring aid to others.

Nevertheless, when the Revolution begins, Zachary is so caught up in it that he is made the commander of a machine gun emplacement in Moscow: "He, who all through the war had striven against the horrors and bloodshed of armed warfare, was lying now beside a machine gun.... It seemed to him that he had been caught in a vicious circle which he had been perpetually trying to avoid." (668). Zachary is no longer a bystander. He is an active participant who constantly tries to understand his participation. In the excitement of the moment, and again with the enthusiasm of a recent convert, he even takes part in events of which he disapproves, though he quickly gets past that stage. While he tries to understand the rationale behind the Revolution's methods, he gradually realizes "that he had not been a witness merely, but an accomplice in a revolting crime" (754).

Zachary's final revelation comes from Comrade Anatol, the man who had been the most radical of the revolutionaries in Warsaw and who, now that the Revolution has arrived, is dismayed by what it has become. When Zachary, despite his true feelings, tries to defend the Revolution—after all, he has committed himself to it—Anatol tells him

> "Keep only one thing in mind . . . the original feeling for justice and truth that exists in all of us! It is the deepest meaning of socialism. Everything rests on it; it is the foundation of our humanity, it is the divine in us. . . . The world has seen already to what lengths men can go when they exchange their natural feelings of justice for inquisitorial dogmas." (757–58)

Strangely enough, this advice from the still devoted socialist resembles the advice from Chomsky, the devoted Jew. Both of them preach fidelity to an ideal rooted in the divine. Although ideals may be perverted, as the Revolution perverted the ideal of socialism or as fanaticism perverts religion, the ideals themselves remain pure.

Zachary is thus torn between the ideal of the Revolution, which is also the ideal of his religion, social justice, and the misery that the Revolution has actually brought. The words of Chomsky and of Anatol have had their effect on him, but it is not clear that he has internalized them until he has a long conversation with Sofia. Zachary persists in calling her by her Yiddish name, Sosha, though she now goes by the more Russified Sofia, from the Greek for "wisdom." Her wisdom is the wisdom of the Revolution, which justifies any means for its end. Her sister, Helene, has been at home in Warsaw caring for the family and operating her father's school, while Sofia has been in the forefront of the Revolution. When Sofia expresses no reservations about the Revolution's excesses, when, in fact, she defends them, Zachary, in a passage that makes him sound like the Nazarene, says, "I believe there is only one morality for all humanity and all ages—to speak the truth and love your fellow-men!" (807). Again, these words do not constitute a startling new creed. They are simply basic to human existence. From this point on, Zachary is like someone who has been reborn, as Asch emphasizes by having him catch pneumonia and nearly die. After his illness, he reestablishes relations with his father, not, by any means, accepting his father's values but respecting him as a human being.

Finally, when Halperin has been killed while trying to escape from Russia and Zachary's father has been shot in a Russian jail, Zachary returns to Warsaw, where he finds Helene still teaching in her school, and he thinks, "While I've been jumping over the tops of houses *she* has been spending herself here day after day, drop by drop." (899). In comparing his service to the Revolution with her steadiness at her job, he sees the value of her perseverance. It may not have been exciting and it may not have proclaimed its own virtue, imagined or not, but it was honest and important. It involved no betrayal of her self or of her ideals. We know from history—and in 1933, Asch, too might have guessed—that Zachary and Helene were probably not destined to live happily ever after. Nevertheless, Zachary has returned to a place and to a state of mind where, despite what others do, he can maintain his integrity. Like the main characters of *War and Peace*, Zachary has lived through tumultuous events and has discovered that he must put his ideals into practice in his private life before they can be expected to appear on the world stage.

This discussion of Zachary has been prolonged because he is such an important character, such an important epic hero. An epic hero is not, of course, the same as the hero of a heroic poem. *Three Cities* is not a heroic work. It is an epic novel that focuses on a pivotal historical moment and considers that moment in conjunction with the development of a central character. Ben Siegel says that some early reviewers thought that Zachary was too pallid to be a hero, and he quite rightly comments, "These readers missed not only Asch's basic conception of his hero but his central theme: to die is relatively easy, whereas to keep living—to keep hoping and trying—requires courage and endurance. Because Zachary does endure, and without compromising his principles, he embodies hope for himself and for all men."[25] Zachary may not be a great warrior—actually he is a terrible warrior—but he is like Achilleus or Aeneas in some significant ways. Although, like them, he is flawed, he transcends those flaws. Furthermore, he explores and comes to terms with the conflict between his own mortality and the significant events in which he takes part. Our focus is on those events as much as it is on him, just as Achilleus' story is part of the story of Troy and Aeneas' story is part of the story of Rome.

In addition, it is important to remember, as I mentioned earlier, that Asch has written an epic novel that actually has two points of focus, the Russian Revolution and the situation of the Jews. The Holocaust may have added another layer of poignancy to the latter aspect, but even in 1933 it would have been significant for Asch's Yiddish-speaking audience. *Three Cities* is the story of an individual, Zachary, and a people, the Jews, living through the social turmoil of a pivotal historical moment. That moment is central to the work, but so, too, are the stories of Zachary and his people. This multiple focus is not the same as the multiple plot structure that we so often see in romances. In a work like *Orlando Furioso* or the romance sections of *The Faerie Queene*, we follow multiple strands of plot as they intertwine. They may be thematically related, but they form individual stories. In a work like *Three Cities*, all the strands of the plot form a single story. What happens to Russia, under the czars or under the Revolution, directly affects the Jews, and what happens to Russia and to the Jews directly affects Zachary. The options that Asch presents for Jewish survival—assimilation, Zionism, traditional religious life, or life transformed by ethical monotheism—are the options that really existed as the Jews faced the anti-Semitism of both pre- and postrevolution Russia. Zachary tries all of these options, as he copes with injustice and conflict. For Tolstoy's characters at the end of *War and Peace*, the crisis has passed and they can look forward to a return to normalcy. For Asch's characters at the end of *Three Cities*, both crises, that of Russia and that of the Jews, continue.

After the passage of almost seventy years, we know what his characters had to look forward to, but even in 1933 their outlook was bleak. In this sense, *Three Cities* shares the scope and the tragic grandeur (though certainly to a lesser extent) of the *Iliad* or the *Aeneid*. It is not an epic in exactly the same way that those works are epics (and even they differ from each other), but it is not a novel in quite the same way that *Great Expectations* is a novel. It is, rather, a fusion of the two, an adaptation of epic themes to the form of the novel. Like the rest of the works to be examined in this study, it is a twentieth-century epic novel.

3
Olivia Manning's *Fortunes of War*

OLIVIA MANNING WAS A RELATIVELY PROLIFIC NOVELIST, THOUGH MOST OF her novels are seldom read. She has received virtually no critical attention, probably as a result of a combination of factors: She does not seem to have been terribly popular with her contemporaries, and she tells her stories using unremarkable prose and a straightforward narrative technique, without any of the modernist techniques favored by many of her contemporaries.[1] Her novels are certainly worthy of being read, however. They seldom contain particularly memorable scenes or picturesque language, but they do provide an interesting perspective on British life in the middle of the twentieth century. Her protagonists may not always look back in anger, but they do share a similar sort of malaise. Invariably they feel alone, cut off from their families and their society. In *The Play Room* (1969; called *The Camperlea Girls* in its American edition), Laura Fletcher's father is a failure and her mother has lived her whole married life using that failure as a lever to gain power over her husband and children. Similarly, *The Doves of Venus* (1955) tells the story of Ellie Parsons, who tries to escape the stultifying world of her mother. Ellie has terrible problems making human connections, and her situation is not helped by the fact that her father abandoned her by dying.

That locution may seem odd, but there is a sense in Manning's novels that parents consistently abandon their children, whether by ignoring them, dying, or committing suicide. It is interesting, furthermore, to note that many of Manning's novels focus on the crises in men's rather than women's lives. In *A Different Face* (1953), for example, Hugo Fletcher returns to his childhood home of Coldmouth (a descriptive and uninviting name), but he has no friends or relatives left there and he has no idea of how to behave with people. The bombed out ruins of Coldmouth, the result of the Blitz, are an apt symbol of the society he finds and of his own psychological state. In *Artist among the Missing* (1949), Geoffrey Lynd is aware of "his old inability to cope with human beings" (15), while his wife Vi shows no fear or hesitation about dealing with the unpleasant circumstances in which she finds herself. As is often the case in Manning's novels, traditional gender roles are reversed, with results that are none too satisfying. Geoffrey notices things that "a more masculine man" (17) would not see, which lead him to a psychological crisis, while Vi treats him with often brutal disregard for his problems. Of course, if the roles were more traditional—if Geoffrey were stronger, more brutal, and Vi more sensitive—their relationship would not be any better. They, like so many of Manning's characters, are unable to touch each other. Their alienation from each other and from the world is frightening.

It should not be thought, however, that Manning's novels are simply copies of each other. There is a great deal of variety in them, but taken together they create a picture of an arid and alienated society. Even the possibility of art, for those of her characters who think about art, cannot transcend the bleakness she portrays. Her novels are reminiscent of Joyce's *Dubliners* in their portrayal of national paralysis, a paralysis that extends, in her case, beyond the British Isles and into the rest of the British Empire. *Artist among the Missing* takes place in the Middle East during the Second World War, and *The Rain Forest* (1974) is set in Al-Bustan in the twilight of the Empire.

Manning's novels, then, are serious works that deserve more consideration than they have received, but her masterpieces are the two trilogies that are the subject of this chapter, *The Balkan Trilogy* (*BT*) and *The Levant Trilogy* (*LT*), the former written between 1960 and 1965, the latter between 1977 and 1980.[2] The trilogies (or the hexology, as Bernard Dold calls them) have been combined under the title *The Fortunes of War*. Like Manning's other works, these six novels are seldom read, but, like another of the twentieth-century epics that I am considering, Paul Scott's *Raj Quartet*, they have been dramatized for public television's Masterpiece Theatre, the former as *The Fortunes of War* and the latter as *The Jewel in the Crown*. It is neither accident nor coincidence that these works have received such treatment. As twentieth-century epics, they have the breadth that a Masterpiece Theatre serial requires. They both intertwine the stories of interesting characters and pivotal global events, and, notably in the case of these two works, they do so in fascinating and exotic locales. Such works lend themselves wonderfully (unfortunately, in my opinion) to literate dramatizations. These are not empty tales of passion and intrigue but powerful studies of global events and their effects on the lives of people who live through them. And to repeat a point I made earlier, just as the *Iliad* is not the *Achillead*—just as that poem is named for the city rather than for a leading character—so Manning's works are *The Balkan* and *Levant Trilogies*, not the Guy and Harriet Pringle stories. The characters are vital, certainly, but the story of Guy and Harriet, had it taken place in London in the 1920s, would not have been epic. It is epic because its subject is not the travails of Guy and Harriet but Guy and Harriet in the context of the Second World War and the beginning of the dissolution of the British Empire.[3] As we see in the work of both Manning and Scott, those two events are inseparable, a mid-twentieth-century crisis for the British, a pivotal time that is appropriate for epic treatment.

While Manning's trilogies differ in numerous ways from her earlier works, they are not her first foray into political literature. Her very first novel, *The Wind Changes* (1937), effectively combines the personal and the political in the context of Dublin in the early 1920s, with a focus on Elizabeth Dearborn, whose reactions to events, as a woman, differ markedly from those of the men who are most involved in the political activities of the time. This focus foreshadows the trilogies, in which the reader sees events largely through the eyes of Harriet Pringle, who frequently contrasts her perceptions with those of the men who surround her. As we saw in the introductory chapter, epic has often been viewed as a male genre, that is, a genre reflecting, monologically, the concerns of men, primarily in terms of military activity and conventional definitions of the heroic. While such treatment has oversimplified the epic, it has prevailed in discussions of the genre. Manning's approach overtly challenges that treatment. Perhaps the dialogism of the *Iliad* or of *Beowulf* has been obscured by centuries of monologic reading, but Manning's skillful use of Harriet and her exchanges with Guy and with so many other characters develops the new epic perspective that Tolstoy used in *War and Peace*. The novel form helps to emphasize the dialogic, but it does not create it; and Manning's use of Harriet further emphasizes what has always been part of the epic.

Did Manning set out to write an epic? Are the trilogies the result of a conscious generic decision? Such questions cannot be answered, but we can say that there are epic references woven throughout the novels, most notably the references to Troy that run throughout *The Balkan Trilogy* and the recollections of *War and Peace* in *The Levant Trilogy*. Such references indicate an awareness that these works are part of a tradition.

The references to Troy are particularly noticeable. Guy, ever the English teacher, decides to mount a Shakespeare play in Bucharest, as the Rumanians justifiably worry about the intentions of Russia and Germany after Germany's invasion of Poland. Guy, who tries to avoid political actions, cannot be bothered with such considerations. He wants to help his students learn contemporary English, which makes Shakespeare something less than a natural choice; and having to choose among *Macbeth, Othello,* and *Troilus and Cressida*—the three plays of which he has copies—he chooses *Troilus and Cressida*, not one of the more famous, or more accessible, plays. It is a very odd choice for Guy, who assures Harriet, "It will be tremendous fun" (*BT* 222), words that may never before have been spoken about this thorny play, a play that presents a particularly cynical view of one of the great subjects of epic. There is no heroism in this play. There are "Words, words, mere words, no matter from the heart" (5.3), which is a fair description of what we see in Bucharest, as refugees from overrun countries, Rumanians, and the British colony try to grasp and deal with their precarious and constantly changing situation. Few characters act out of conviction. Self-interest rules. Even Guy, who seems so magnanimous, tends only to make the opening gestures of magnanimity, to say the words, allowing the burden to fall on others, usually Harriet. So *Troilus and Cressida* is an appropriate choice both for Guy and for Manning; and the pun at the end of the first novel, *The Great Fortune*, is too delicious to be accidental, for when the production is over, having been quite a success, we read, in a chapter called "The Fall of Troy," that Paris has fallen. Paris and Troy, two doomed cities, are joined together as part of a tradition, but no one learns from that tradition. When word comes during rehearsals that Calais has fallen, "Yet what could be done about it? Nothing. It was a relief for them all to turn their attention to the fall of Troy" (*BT* 253). The play is, for the British in Bucharest, mere words. It has nothing to do with their world. Only Harriet and the reporter Gilpin seem to take the larger events around them seriously, and Harriet has been excluded from the play by Guy's fear of having her there. Guy and his actors are rather like his friend David, who complains that he read the first volume of *Anna Karenina* to brush up on his Russian and now is having trouble finding the second volume because he would like to know how it ends:

> "Haven't you read it in English?" Harriet asked.
> "I scarcely need to brush up my English."
> If this were a joke, David gave no indication of the fact. (*BT* 173)

Although he cares about how *Anna Karenina* ends, his main concern is with the language, the words, not the human characters. This novel about a young woman in an oppressive marriage giving in to an adulterous temptation—very nearly Harriet's situation in the third novel—is for David a Russian language textbook. Like so many of the characters in the trilogies, he cannot get past the words to consider the substance.

This affliction particularly affects the numerous bureaucrats who populate the novels, from the various directors of the organization that employs Guy up to Neville Chamberlain, who is mentioned occasionally along with his promise of peace. It is, to return to Troy, very much like the situation in that beleaguered city. Thus, when Dobson says that the play's cast "stuck to your posts like Trojans" (*BT* 401) or when Mrs. Brett reports that her husband "worked like a Trojan" (*BT* 619), words that on the surface are intended to be complimentary actually indicate that people have been devoting themselves to a lost cause. Elizabeth Bellamy's description of Troy "as the paradigmatic memory-trace for all epic history," is certainly appropriate here, for the story of Troy informs the whole of *The Balkan Trilogy*.[4] Robert K. Morris comments that "Bucharest becomes the battleground for a kind of primal survival . . . and a Troy fallen anew."[5] Guy and Harriet may not be the precise counterparts of Hektor and Andromache, but, as we shall see, Guy does put everything else ahead of his wife's well-being.

Guy, like many leftists in the 1930s and afterward, romanticizes the Spanish Civil War. Clarence has already told Harriet, "In Spain there was colour and heat and danger. Things were significant there. Life should be like that" (*BT* 190), and Guy often regrets that he could not fight in Spain. Thus, toward the end of *The Levant Trilogy*, he reacts badly when Aidan Pratt tries to teach him some political truths:

> "The Germans haven't found Franco as docile as they'd hoped, and we should be grateful for it. If the government had won, Spain would have been occupied when war broke out. It would have been an important stronghold for the enemy. We would certainly have lost Gibraltar."
> Guy, frowning, said: "That's merely supposition." (*LT* 515)

Aidan changes the topic, but Guy is so irritated with him that he decides to break off their friendship, leading to Aidan's suicide on the train. Guy is not someone whose idealism can be trifled with, and he certainly does not allow practical matters to divert him from what he sees as his duty, much like Hektor in the sixth book of the *Iliad*.

This kind of romanticization can also be seen in an episode that has comic overtones but a potentially tragic outcome. As the Germans close in around Rumania, Guy and his friends are summoned to a secret meeting where Sheppy invites them to be part of "Striking Force . . . Big plans are afoot. We'll be blowing things up. One of them's the Iron Gates. Remember, this isn't a lark: it's an adventure" (*BT* 183). What, one must ask, is the precise difference between a lark and an adventure? There is none, except in the way the words sound. This collection of minor functionaries and an English teacher would certainly make up an unintimidating Strike Force, but Sheppy promises them, "There'll be lots of fun, and we're letting you in on it" (*BT* 183).

Even before Sheppy is forced out of the country, Harriet, who cannot tell how serious either the plan or Guy is, forbids her husband to take part. Of course, there is no real plan, but Guy keeps the "Top Secret" document he has been given, because, like Hektor, he has a notion of heroism that he thinks he must live up to. When Yakimov steals the plan and reveals it to others, including Germans, Guy is put into real danger. Nothing actually happens, but that is only a matter of Guy's luck.

The point in all of this discussion is that Manning is making the same kinds of points as Homer. There are real dangers in the world, and they must be considered and confronted. Automatic responses, attempts to win glory, whether through Sheppy's absurd plans or Guy's equally absurd dedication to students who never show up for his classes, are worse than self-defeating. If people wish to bring defeat upon themselves with empty gestures, that is their business; but their defeat usually means the misery of others as well. Harriet may not be as totally dependent on Guy as Andromache is on Hektor; but she is attached to him, and if anything happens to him, she will suffer, a fact that he never takes into account.

As we saw, the women's role in the *Iliad* and other epics, while small, is absolutely vital. In the trilogies, women play a larger and equally vital part. Of course, we see the world in these works largely through Harriet's eyes, so we know her attitude toward things, but we also hear other women and plenty of men. What is surprising (though perhaps it should not be) is how similar the attitudes of Manning's men are to those of Homer's men, created nearly three thousand years earlier. Almost the first thing Harriet is told when she arrives in Bucharest is that there is an order that "the ladies must return to England," and when she questions the order, Woolley, who had told her about it, was "surprised, it seemed, not only by the edge on her voice but by the fact she had a voice at all" (*BT* 28). While the men might not be warriors or "heroes" (Woolley is described as "hairless, with toad-mottled skin"), women are still expected to be silent, invisible, and compliant; and Harriet, who is a strong woman, who would never emulate the self-condemnation of a Helen or the meekness of a Lavinia, antagonizes a number of the men.

In fact, throughout the trilogies, Harriet is engaged in a quest to define herself. People, especially men but also some of the women, define her entirely as Guy's wife. While she often likes, or at least does not object to, that designation, she gradually realizes that that is not what she is, that while being a wife is part of her, she is something quite different, something more than Mrs. Guy Pringle. At one point she has a conversation about this matter with her friend Clarence, although she only recognizes much later the deeper implications of what is said. Harriet begins

> "I want . . . I want to be . . . "
> Clarence concluded smugly: "What you are not?"
> "No. What I am. The 'I' that is obscured by my own feminine silliness. In some ways, I suppose I am just as absurd as Sophie or Bella."
> Clarence laughed. "I suppose you are. Women are like that, and one likes them like that."
> "No doubt you do. But I don't imagine I exist to enhance your sense of superiority. I exist to satisfy my own demands on myself, and they are higher than yours are likely to be. If you don't like me as I am, I don't care."
> Clarence was unruffled. "You mean you do care," he said, "that's the trouble. Women want to be liked. They can never be themselves."
> "And you, my poor Clarence, can never be anything but yourself." (*BT* 209)

This conversation is rather like the one between Jesus and the Samaritan woman in the Gospel according to John, in which the interlocutors are speaking on such different planes that their words simply go past each other. Clarence speaks on the basis of feeble stereotypes. When he says, "Women are like that, and one likes them like that," it is clear that "one" is supposed to be normative, and therefore male, superior, and entitled to pass judgments on women as a whole, as though women were an alien species—which, to men like Clarence, they are. "Women want to be liked," he says, feeling fully justified in characterizing all women, while Harriet responds, "And you, my poor Clarence . . . ," addressing only him and in fact characterizing him quite accurately.

Harriet's mistake is in thinking herself "just as absurd as Sophie or Bella." Sophie and Bella lack conviction. They are typical on two levels: they are the kind of women who exist to please men, who see it as their role to please men—their "feminine silliness"—and they are typical of the moral ambivalence that underlies the crises, the "pivotal moments" that are at the center of the trilogies. Harriet must discover what it means to be herself, to be both Harriet Pringle and Guy's wife. Through most of the trilogies, she tries to be Guy's wife. After all, they are newly married when the work begins, she is following the expected pattern for a new wife, and she is arriving in a foreign country where Guy is well-known and she knows no one. Then, in the last novel, she goes off on her own, but she has no more success in that role. To be herself, she must play both parts. On a purely personal level, she makes a vital discovery, and she understands that both roles will require constant reexamination, redefinition, and reinforcement, which is why, when Guy asks her, "You'll never leave me again, will you?" she can truthfully answer, " 'Don't know. Can't promise.' Harriet laughed and squeezed his arm: 'Probably not'" (*LT* 568). That laugh and squeeze are not "feminine silliness," not her attempt to set him at ease. After what she has learned, she probably will not leave him, but she cannot promise more than that. Guy does not change—he may be incapable of changing—but she does. On the one hand she says, "I'm not much good at being alone. My home is where Guy is" (*LT* 540), and on the other she can tell Guy, "Angela helped me when I needed help; now if I can, I'll help her. So don't try and influence me against her. You have your friends; let me have mine" (*LT* 561). Guy's reaction to this outburst is revealing:

> Guy was startled by her tone and she remembered how Angela had advised her to box his ears. And that, in a sense, was what she had done. After his first surprise, he was clearly uncertain how to deal with the situation. Harriet was moving out from under his influence. She had gone away once and had, apparently, managed very well on her own. He was unnerved by the possibility she might go away again. (*LT* 561)

In fact, she had not done very well on her own, but her lack of success is irrelevant if Guy thinks she was successful and that she can manage on her own. Her discovery that she could be Guy's wife and still be herself, and his perception that she had done very well on her own, combine to allow her to move out from under his influence and allow him to accept that new situation.

Of course, if this were just a story about the marital problems of Guy and Harriet, it would be a fine novel or perhaps a romance. It would not be an epic. Their marital problems, however, are fitted into much larger contexts. One is the Second World War and another is what I will call personal and national imperialism. The war dominates the first trilogy, and national imperialism dominates the second, but personal imperialism, the attempt to impose one's power on others, runs through both. It is what is at stake in the Pringles' marriage and in every gender relationship in the novels. Sophie's obvious and feeble attempts to lure Guy away from Harriet arise partially from her need to protect herself as the Nazis approach Rumania and partially from her need to assert her sexual power over the plainer Harriet, who has inexplicably managed to wed Guy. At the same time, the only power an ordinary woman like Sophie can have in the context of the novel is sexual, and we must be careful before we condemn her for using it. Still, when Clarence reveals in *The Levant Trilogy* that Sophie married him in order to escape Rumania and has now left him, we remember how adept she is at using people. She is not much different from Angela when she hires a prostitute and a potential customer to put on a sex show for her friends, a performance that revolts Harriet and Simon not because it is sexual but because it is a naked display of power, of the ability to transform people into things.

It could be argued that the women, to the extent that they attempt to seize power, are often forced to do so. When Woolley ordered Harriet back to England and she challenged him, he was surprised "by the fact that she had a voice at all," so that anything she might say, aside from total acquiescence, would appear as a challenge to his power. For the men, the story is rather different. They almost automatically engage in the politics of power in their most ordinary relationships. Even Yakimov, who shows no evidence of pride when it comes to sponging off of everyone he knows, plays the power game on the one occasion when he has more money than someone else: "'Dear boy'—Yakimov suddenly remembered his position of power—'it is I who should offer [hospitality]'" (*BT* 52). And despite his constant begging and stealing, he never wearies of telling people that his fur coat, which becomes increasingly threadbare as time passes, was a gift to his father from the Czar. This boast is an assertion of his power, and it becomes more and more grotesque as the coat proceeds to disintegrate.

Similarly, Inchcape, who is totally ineffective in his executive position, is nevertheless zealous in guarding his power:

> "So you've got yourself married!" he said and turned with a mocking half-smile towards Harriet. She saw that beneath the smile his glance was critical and vulnerable. One of his men had brought back a wife—an unknown quantity, perhaps a threat to his authority. When Guy made the introductions, she greeted Inchcape gravely, making no attempt to charm. (*BT* 34)

Inchcape worries about his authority, possibly because he actually has so little and must therefore guard every shred of it; and Harriet refuses to play the game, refuses to smile, to play the compliant woman and assuage Inchcape's fears.

Such encounters occur frequently in the trilogies. Characters are constantly trying to outflank each other either in order to maintain their power or to gain it. Toby and Dubedat are particularly notable examples. Guy, because he is naive and generous (especially when his generosity makes no specific demands on him), hires the two incompetents, who flee from Rumania the instant that they feel threatened. Later, when the Pringles arrive in Egypt, they discover that Toby and Dubedat have arrived first, have taken over the position that should belong to Guy, and now exercise their power by refusing to give him a job. Because they are such incompetents, their attempt to seize and exercise power is both obvious and unsuccessful, but other characters are far better at it. Gracey and Pinkrose are both petty bureaucrats, but they know how to get and use power in their own behalf. Their methods are obvious, occasionally even brutal, but effective.

There are, however, other methods, more subtle, perhaps, but equally coercive; and Guy is a master of such methods. People like Sophie, Toby, and Dubedat are looking out for themselves; their manipulations and self-interest are obvious to everyone, including themselves. They know what they are doing, and they have no concern about how they are perceived. (In fairness, Toby does seem a trifle embarrassed, but his embarrassment does not stop him.) Guy, in contrast, adopts a wholly different technique. He assumes, first, that he knows what is best for everyone. Often what he thinks is best for someone else works to his advantage, but he never seems to think of his advantage. His concerns appear to be altruistic. And he is, after all, such a nice Guy that neither he nor his friends seem to think that he is being coercive. He is just being Guy Pringle, everyone's friend. Consequently, scores of people volunteer to be in his production of *Troilus and Cressida* and the shows he organizes to entertain soldiers in Egypt. Virtually no one objects to his invariably being late for appointments or leaving meetings early. Guy expects people to do things; and because they like him, they do. The only opposition he receives is from those like Pinkrose, who see him as a threat, and, not surprisingly, from Harriet, who does not always think that Guy knows what is best and who does tire of Guy's lateness and his general lack of consideration.

For example, when the Pringles visit the Druckers, Guy is offered a ride back to the university, and Harriet rises to leave with him; but the Drucker women clamor for her to stay for tea. "'Of course she will stay,' said Guy. Harriet gave him an anguished look but he did not see it. 'She has nothing else to do. She would enjoy it'"(*BT* 105). It is not clear whether Guy is looking at Harriet when she gives him her anguished look, and the implication is that he would not have noticed it even had he looked directly at her. He is unaware of his assumptions—that he can decide for her, that she has nothing important to do, that she can function and probably wants to function as his surrogate while he goes off to something more important. At this stage, Harriet does not know how to respond, because she is not yet at the point of rebellion. Only much later, after enduring many more indignities, does she begin to think that she has had enough. It is true that she is attracted to Charles in Greece; but Charles, though more suave than Guy (almost everyone is more suave than Guy!), is really no less demanding of her. Although she is tempted to have an affair with Charles, she is not ready at that point to betray Guy or herself by doing so.

Only when Guy takes the brooch that Angela gave her does she move to rebellion. At the moment she is sick in the hospital, so she cannot react properly, but the scene is fairly shocking. As Guy is visiting her in the hospital, he sees the brooch and takes it as a gift for Edwina. When Harriet objects, he replies

> "Surely you don't want it. You couldn't be seen wearing a thing like that. It's a theatrical prop . . ."
> "It's a valuable piece of jewellery. They're real diamonds and cost a lot of money."
> "Even so, it's tawdry. It looks cheap."
> Smiling his contempt, he held the brooch away from him and she saw it degraded from a treasure and a talisman into a worthless gewgaw. (*LT* 344)

Guy has been quietly coercive throughout the trilogies, but his behavior here is overt and intolerable. Harriet is in no position to defend herself, and Guy takes the brooch from her in two ways: he physically steals it from her, and, perhaps more important, he takes away its value. As a result of her outrage, Harriet decides to return to England, leading almost to her death (had she boarded the ship) and certainly to the extended separation that precedes their reconciliation on new terms. Earlier we had been told that Guy "was conscious of a natural authority, the authority of the upright man" (*BT* 613); but quite clearly, when Guy finds that authority challenged, especially by someone as helpless as Harriet in the hospital, he has no qualms about behaving in a less upright manner. This is an important point, to which we will return.

First, however, there is one more example of personal imperialism to consider, the case of Guy's friend Ben Phipps. Phipps appears only in the third volume of *The Balkan Trilogy*, but he is a particularly nefarious presence there. Harriet, who begins the trilogy as a perceptive observer and becomes even more perceptive as time passes, recognizes that Phipps "had to have controlling power somewhere. Ousted from the Phaleron circle, he had taken over Guy and he wanted no distracting gestures from Harriet" (*BT* 786). Manning's wording here is significant: Phipps needs "controlling power" and he has "taken over Guy." Guy's personal imperialism is generally more subtle, but Phipps is an imperialist with a vengeance. Not only has he "taken over Guy," but he has done so by dealing in lies and slanders. Phipps captivates Guy by telling him about "the Zoippus Bank, the Bund, and certain Wall Street Jews who had financed Hitler in the hope of forcing the whole Jewish race to move to Palestine," and he adds that Hitler came to power through the machinations of the wealthy and the Vatican (*BT* 786–87). He is, in short, not just a left-winger—there are several of those in the trilogies, including Guy—but a fanatic who seeks to enhance his power through deception and outright fictions.

Guy is, apparently, taken in by Phipps's ravings, but Harriet is not; and she finally confronts him with his lies, to which he responds, somewhat less than intellectually, "You know fuck all" (*BT* 791), which may be a strong response today, but in the 1940s would have been considered incredibly rude. Nevertheless, after Harriet insults Phipps in return, Guy prevails on her not to leave the restaurant. Though Phipps does not play a major role in the novel after this point, it is no wonder that Harriet regards Guy as "a gaoler who hemmed her in with people who did not interest her and talk that bored her. She had found no release in marriage. It had forced her back into the prison of herself" (*BT* 791).

But once again, if these novels were only about the problems between Guy and Harriet, they would not constitute an epic. What makes them epic is the realization that the conflicts and the personal imperialism I have been describing are the microcosmic version of what is happening in the macrocosm of Europe—and beyond. The Pringles' crises, like those of numerous other characters, mirror the national crises that surround and subsume them, focusing on the war, on imperialism (particularly British imperialism), and the dissolution of the British Empire. Manning quite skillfully manages, through her use of British communities in Bucharest, Athens, and Cairo, to devote attention to the general European crises while focusing on the particularly British aspects of those crises. The years covered by the trilogies, 1930–1943, were indeed a pivotal time for Britain, involving the failure of British diplomacy, the Blitz, the initial battle losses and subsequent victories (El Alamein plays a large part in *The Levant Trilogy*), and the turning of the war to eventual triumph. Furthermore, these war developments led directly to the formation or the development of independence movements in many parts of the Empire, from Palestine and Egypt to India (as we will see in *The Raj Quartet*) and elsewhere. These trilogies are certainly not the same as the *Iliad* or *Beowulf* in foreshadowing the complete destruction of a civilization. They are more like the *Aeneid* and *War and Peace*, illustrating a pivotal time in a civilization, examining the assumptions of that civilization, assumptions that contain the seeds of their own destruction, and then going on to reflect on the aftermath of that pivotal moment. Thus, Manning's "Coda" to *The Levant Trilogy* is truly a coda in the musical sense, a brief return to the main ideas leading directly to the end of the work:

> Two more years were to pass before the war ended. Then, at last, peace, precarious peace, came down upon the world and the survivors could go home. Like the stray figures left on the stage at the end of a great tragedy, they had now to tidy up the ruins of war and in their hearts bury the noble dead. (*LT* 571)

The simile in the third sentence is particularly notable, as it perches on the edge of literalism. The survivors are not only "like the stray figures . . . at the end of a great tragedy." They *are* those stray figures, and they have indeed passed through a great tragedy; and the "noble dead" whom they have to bury include not only the literal dead but the selves that they were before the tragedy. Kent, at the end of *King Lear*, is not the same as Kent at the beginning, and the same is true for these characters—and for England.

Manning has no trouble keeping our attention on the war, even though the closest the Pringles get to actual fighting is the bombing of Piraeus while they are in Athens. We read about the arrival in Bucharest of refugees from Poland, about the evacuation of Dunkerque, about the fall of Paris, and about the Blitz. Each of these elements requires only a brief mention, enough to allow it to reverberate, to remind readers of what was happening in the world outside of Bucharest, Athens, and Cairo. We also watch as the Pringles flee from Bucharest to Athens to Cairo, with the threat that they might have to go even further. We hardly need to be reminded that this war, like all wars, is a matter of power, the same contested power in the macrocosm that we saw in the microcosm. Manning makes the connection directly as she describes the rise of the Rumanian Iron Guard, who make a martyr out of Codreanu, who was assassinated near the trilogies' beginning. Guy argues that "Codreanu was a murderer, a Jew-baiter and a thug. He had a following of nonentities who wanted only one thing—power at any price" (*BT* 390), and he denies, probably correctly, the possibility that if they actually got power, they could remake their country.

The Iron Guard, as we know from the novel and from history, truly were thugs, but it is interesting to compare Guy's reaction here to the response of Sir Brian Love when he is asked how conditions are in England. Sir Brian—he is always called Sir Brian—says that England is "changed for the better," by which he means that there was "a new sense of comradeship . . . which was breaking down class-consciousness in England." Sir Brian continues:

"Your secretary calls you 'Brian.' . . . I like it. I like it very much. . . . After the war we shall see a new world. . . . A classless world, I should like to think." (*BT* 564)

There are surely different kinds of thuggery, but one's perception of thuggery depends a great deal on which side of the power divide one occupies; and Sir Brian and his associates, though they are more refined, are no more inclined to rebuild a better society than are Codreanu's thugs.

This is not to say, of course, that the Allies were as evil as the Nazis and their sympathizers, but it does mean that power tends to operate on the same principles everywhere. Hitler wants power for evil purposes, and his opponents obviously want to prevent him from getting it; but, like Guy in his relationships with people, especially with Harriet, that desire is not necessarily altruistic. Both sides want to retain power, even to extend it if they can.

This point brings us to the subject of imperialism. *The Balkan Trilogy* deals primarily with the war. We hear about events in Europe, we see the Polish refugees, and we follow the progress of the German armies. In *The Levant Trilogy* we see our only real battle, as Simon wanders the battlefield; but later in the trilogy, the war turns. The British in Cairo are justifiably nervous, but throughout the trilogy the Germans move further and further away until they are no threat at all. This scheme may oversimplify the actual progress of the war, but it does allow the second trilogy to take up the vital and related issue of the British Empire.

In the first trilogy, we see the Pringles and other British subjects carrying out their duties in Bucharest. Why, one wonders, are they in Bucharest at all? Is their presence there an imperialist beachhead? The answer is no, at least not in the sense that the British built an empire in non-European locales. Guy teaches in the English Department of the University of Bucharest, but he seems to think that his duties include the importation of British culture into Rumania. The decade of the 1940s, of course, was not a time when multiculturalism was valued, and most of the British in Bucharest display an attitude toward the Rumanians that can most nicely be described as condescending. This attitude is reinforced by the Rumanians, who, as long as they believe the British will protect them, behave ingratiatingly. The true ambivalence of the Rumanians, which might be interpreted as lack of conviction or, more positively, as a technique of self-preservation, can be seen in a single incident:

> The waiter brought tea and toast for Harriet, then, unasked put on the table a plate of ball-shaped chocolate cakes pimpled over like naval mines. "Siegfrieds," he announced.

"Not our line," said Dobson, imperturbably, in English.
At once the waiter whipped away the plate, retreated a few steps, returned and put it down again. "Maginots," he said, and went off well satisfied by Dobson's amusement. (*BT* 118)

This is, on the surface, a comical scene. The waiter is apolitical: If he thinks his customers are Germans, he is pro-German, and if he learns that they are British, then he is just as happily pro-Allies. In fact, however, his attitude portends great danger for the British, because the waiter, like so many of his compatriots, has no special love for the British, who behave as though the Rumanians should admire them, simply because of British superiority. As soon as the Germans start to win, however, and with the rapid rise to respectability of the Iron Guard, hostility toward the British increases. One reason for such hostility must be self-preservation: if the Germans are indeed about to arrive, as looks probable, it would not be healthy for a Rumanian to have been allied with the British. On a deeper, if not more practical level, the British have never taken a real interest in Rumania. The British colony has remained separated and superCilious. Men like Inchcape and Woolley and most of the others are not the sort to inspire loyalty in a beleaguered nation.

The most interesting example of Rumanian ambivalence is Harriet's friend Bella, who is both British and Rumanian and who follows nothing but her own self-interest. What she says, though, probably expresses the feelings of many Rumanians. Moreover, what she says, repugnant though it may be, also contains some truth. One afternoon, as the situation is becoming desperate in Rumania, Bella and Harriet meet near the Athenée Palace, "under the Nazi flag." Bella is exultant because, as the Germans approach, the economy is seeming to improve:

Harriet glanced up at the swastika. "Doesn't that disturb you?"
Bella looked up again and gave an uncertain laugh. "Does it?" she asked. "I don't know. In a way, it makes me feel safe. It's nice to be protected, even by Germans. And, you know," she gazed seriously at Harriet, a rather petulant gleam in her eye, "Rumania has been very unfairly treated. . . . No wonder we've been in an awkward position. You can't blame the Rumanians for wanting the foreigners to go." (*BT* 550)

When Harriet points out that Germans are also foreigners, Bella reveals that she has been passing as German, to her great advantage. Harriet realizes that Bella "had found a means of managing her situation: she was shuffling off her own identity and taking on an aspect of the enemy" (*BT* 550). Bella's behavior is certainly reprehensible, but she is correct in her assessment of how Rumania had been used. As the trilogy presents the situation, the British have exploited the oil fields at Ploesti, supported an unpopular king, and reneged on their military assurances to the nation. (This last point can be explained by the military situation in which the British found themselves, but with the German army about to swoop down on Rumania, and with a history of British exploitation, such details are easy to overlook.)

As Harriet had recognized much earlier, they were living in a "disintegrating society" (*BT* 292). What she, and we, come to recognize is that they live in a disintegrating world. As the German war machine rolls across Europe, old verities no longer hold. At the very beginning of the trilogy, as Yakimov wanders through Bucharest, "he saw windows masked with the harem grilles of the receded Ottoman Empire" (*BT* 18). That reference to the Ottoman Empire is an early reminder of the transient nature of empire. Similarly, late in *The Balkan Trilogy*, when the Germans invade Greece and overcome the defenders in the Rupel Pass forts, a journalist says, "It was a Thermopylae. Another Thermopylae" (*BT* 861). The journalist's reference is more accurate than he can know, for just as the Greek defeat at Thermopylae preceded their ultimate triumph, so the tragedy at the Rupel Pass marks the loss of a battle, not of the war. The Reich, another attempt at creating an empire, will also pass away.

These references to past empires, brief though they are, help to provide a context for the war that is so much the focus of *The Balkan Trilogy*. They also help to prepare for *The Levant Trilogy*, in which the British Empire becomes a focus very like the personal imperialism we saw earlier. In the first trilogy, the British virtually all assume the legitimacy of British sovereignty. In the second trilogy, that assumption has begun to crumble; and once the crumbling begins, the whole assumption gives way. As usual, the most perceptive person is Harriet, who, once the Pringles had arrived in Egypt, managed to secure a position at the American Embassy, where she finds her assumptions questioned:

> Having grown up in the belief that Britain was supreme in the world and the British the most fortunate of people, she had been shocked to find that to the Americans she was an alien who rated less than a quarter of the salary paid to an American-born typist. She protested to her superior, a Mr. Buschman, saying, "I'm not an alien—I'm British." Mr. Buschman liked this so much that he managed to get her a rise in salary. (*LT* 71–72)

Harriet may be the most perceptive character, but ingrained assumptions die hard. Her line, "I'm not an alien—I'm British," is wonderful in its assertive obtuseness. There she is in Egypt telling an American that she is not an alien. What she means, of course, is that she is not only British but light-skinned. As a white British woman, she belongs everywhere, an assumption that sounds very much like an argument for imperialism. She is not a "native," with all the negative connotations of that word.

Harriet is shocked to realize it, but to the American Mr. Buschman she is just as alien as Iqal, an Egyptian employee of the embassy. Harriet is, however, set apart from most of the other British because she does very quickly come to understand the situation, and the situation is not very pleasant, as Iqal demonstrates: "What do you British do with my country, Mrs. Pringle? You come here to rule yet when the enemy is at the gate, you run away" (*LT* 73). Obviously issues are being raised that Harriet has not considered previously; and although Harriet argues with Iqal, she knows his assessment is accurate.

The Germans take advantage of anti-British sentiment among the Egyptians, leading to this long exchange between Harriet and Iqal:

> "See here, Mrs. Pringle, they exhort us, 'Rise against your oppressors,' they say, 'kill them and be free.'"
>
> "You don't think the English are oppressors, do you?"
>
> Iqal raised his great shoulders. "Sometimes, yes. Sometimes, no. When they break through the palace gates and tell my king what to do, what would you call them? Are they not oppressors?"
>
> "We're fighting a war, Iqal. If the Egyptians really felt oppressed, they would turn on us, wouldn't they?"
>
> "Ah, Mrs. Pringle, we are not fools. My friends say, 'Time enough when the Germans are at the gate—*then* we cut the English throats."
>
> "O, come now, Iqal, you wouldn't cut my throat?"
>
> Iqal giggled. "Believe me, Mrs. Pringle, if I would cut your throat, I do it in a kind and considerate manner."
>
> "You wouldn't hurt me?"
>
> "No, no, Mrs. Pringle, indeed I would not." (*LT* 131–32)

This conversation presents a number of interesting points. First, Harriet still cannot think of herself and her compatriots as oppressors. She still thinks that she and her fellow Englishmen are the ones who bear the burden, while Iqal, showing the deference of a colonial subject, cannot answer her as directly as he would like so he admits only that the British are occasional oppressors, though he goes on to imply that he would not be sorry to see all of their throats cut. And when Harriet tries to have herself exempted from that threat, he only says that he would cut her throat "in a kind and considerate manner." When he says that he would not hurt her, he does not say that he would not cut her throat, just that he would do it painlessly, giving us some indication of the anger that lurks below the surface.

At one point, Harriet explains Guy's predicament by saying, "He knows he's been defeated by people for whom the whole of life is a dishonest game" (*LT* 113). People like Gracey and Pinkrose do indeed treat life, consciously, as if it were a dishonest game. Guy and Harriet, whatever their other failings, do not do so consciously, but Harriet's conversations with Iqal illustrate what a dishonest game colonialism is. Harriet cannot conceive of herself as an oppressor and can barely think of Iqal as oppressed, while he, recognizing his oppression, cannot bring himself to say what he really thinks. They are both trapped by their roles on either side of the imperialist divide. Perhaps the best symbol of that division is the Anglo-Egyptian Union, a club which "existed to promote friendship between the Egyptians and their British rulers" (*LT* 68) but to which Egyptians seldom went. Whether the Egyptians avoided the Union because they felt rejected by the British members or because they chose not to create sham relationships with their "British rulers" is unimportant. Just as Harriet and Iqal cannot have an open conversation, so the British and the Egyptians cannot share a club or establish friendships. As long as they are rulers and ruled, there is an unbridgeable gap between them.

Harriet, of course, quickly understands the situation, not only because she is perceptive but because, as we saw, it is also her situation. She is, in national terms, the British colonizer; but in personal terms, she is the victim of Guy's imperialism. Thus, when she is discussing Egypt with the newly arrived Simon, who believes British verities about its colonies, he says, "You don't really think they'd turn on us after all we've done for them? . . . We've brought them justice and prosperity, haven't we? We've shown them how people ought to live" (*LT* 24). Harriet, who is only a few years older than Simon, finds herself thinking how young he is. His naiveté is striking today, but he is merely voicing the ideology of imperialism; and when Harriet responds

> "What have we done here, except make money? I suppose a few rich Egyptians have got richer by supporting us, but the real people of the country, the peasants and the backstreet poor, are just as diseased, underfed and wretched as they ever were." (*LT* 24)

he recognizes his ignorance and changes the subject.

In Simon, then, we can see most plainly the way the war functions as a catalyst in the collapse of British imperialism, for Simon's experience is repeated thousands of times as soldiers actually come into contact with the countries and people they have supposedly been civilizing and are exposed to their hostility. Simon, however, is young and inexperienced. What is even more surprising is that Guy, hardly the most perceptive character, finally recognizes the same thing: he could

> see the futility of his reserved occupation. Lecturing on English literature, teaching the English language, he had been peddling the idea of empire to a country that only wanted one thing; to be rid of the British for good and all. (*LT* 514)

This is an important realization for Guy, though it in no way marks a transformation in his character. In fact, it comes only pages before his rejection of Aidan Pratt because of his practical view of the Spanish Civil War; and Guy has yet to learn what he needs to about the role of personal imperialism in his relationship with Harriet (who, to be fair, he thinks has died). Nevertheless, it is vital to see what a change this realization is for Guy. He may have felt earlier that life was a "dishonest game," but now he begins to see his role in that dishonest game. His own righteousness (even were it not flawed) cannot keep him from being a player in the dishonest game that is represented by the British Empire.

The Pringles' marital problems, then, while certainly interesting, are not the sole focus of these trilogies. Those marital problems are examined in the context of world imperialism. The war itself, of course, represents a pivotal moment for many people; but for the British it is tied into the end of the empire, another pivotal moment, as we shall see again in considering *The Raj Quartet*. The Pringles are important because individual human beings are important—but the trilogies offer a far wider scope than a more usual study of marital problems could have. They examine cultural ideologies on a broad scale at a crucial time in history, and they show how individual human beings are used by and can react against those ideologies.

It is interesting that in her introduction to a reprint of Manning's first novel, *The Wind Changes*, Manning's friend Isobel English writes that the author had "a marked admiration for imperialism, and a belief that in an imperfect world Britain's rule in her colonies had been for the most part a beneficent one. But this, in her view, did not apply to Ireland" (xv).[6] I would not want to dispute what Manning may have told English in private conversations, but English's assertion is certainly undercut by what we see in these trilogies, where there is no evidence of a beneficent British presence and ample evidence of a presence that is, if not overtly malevolent, at best debilitating to both sides, both in Rumania and in Egypt. And, incidentally, we can find the same assessment in Manning's novel *The Rain Forest* (1974), which was written between the two trilogies. In all of these works, British imperialism is shown to be a corrupt and self-serving system, which not only deserves to be dismantled but which is actually on the verge of being dismantled.

Thus, like Hektor and Andromache or Pierre and Natasha, Guy and Harriet live in a time that is more than merely interesting. Their times are flash points and turning points for their societies. The historical events and the historical context are not simply used to supply local color or to add an air of authenticity. They are, in a real sense, the center of the works, the elements that help to provide meaning for what the characters go through; and they also help to provide that epic scope which is such an important part of the genre. Manning provides further scope by referring several times to much earlier history. In the last volume of *The Balkan Trilogy*, set in Athens, the characters make several trips to the Acropolis, while in Egypt there are visits to the pyramids and various other tombs, at one of which Harriet, explaining why a bit of painting from ancient Egypt went unfinished, says

> "The usual reasons. Demand falling off. New religions taking over. New ideas. Or price going up and the tomb-makers going out of business. It's interesting to see that in ancient Egypt things ended just as they have always done." (*LT* 26)

Coming at the beginning of a work that deals with things ending, this is an appropriate comment. Harriet sees the continuity of history, the recurrent feeling of beginnings and endings that so often runs through epic, with its larger view of the world. The Athenian Empire, which expressed its glory in the Parthenon, and the Egyptian Empire are gone. So, as we see when Harriet is in Damascus, is the greatest caravanserai in the world, once known as the "Hub of the World" (*LT* 438). Now there are the Reich and the British Empire, but those, too, will pass away. As is so often the case in epic, even in those that celebrate the glorious birth of a nation or civilization, there is a pervasive sense of melancholy here because epic is so aware of the inevitability of rises and falls. It may be celebratory, but it knows that even in the celebration lie the seeds of mourning. Guy's words at *The Levant Trilogy*'s end, therefore, apply not only to the Pringles but to humankind. When Harriet asks if he really thought they would survive their frightening, sudden departure from Athens, he says, "Yes. I knew we'd make it somehow or other. We always do" (567). They, human beings, must persevere, no matter what happens around them.

One of the things that the Pringles must persevere against, strangely enough, is anti-Semitism. This anti-Semitism is not, of course, directed against them, but they encounter it frequently in *The Balkan Trilogy*, and it reveals a great deal about them and about the people whom they encounter. Guy and Harriet are remarkably free of this prejudice. Guy, in fact, puts himself in some jeopardy by taking on Jewish students and even keeping the school open when only Jewish students are left. Many characters take the opposite approach. Yakimov's landlady, Doamna Prolopopescu, is especially outspoken, as she blames the Jews for the war; and when Yakimov jokingly refers to Count Horvath, who "had the finest Jew-shoot in Hungary," she approves, lamenting that Rumanians are too easy-going. Even Yakimov, who virtually never shows anything related to a principle, is disconcerted (*BT* 205). On the other hand, there is Bella, who also lacks all principles. At one point she refers to the Jews disparagingly when she mentions that Drucker has been paying to have his son exempted from the service: "Trust *them*" she says (*BT* 336). What is significant is that she has been doing the same for her husband, though clearly she considers heself one of *us* rather than one of *them*. Her fear of being taken for one of *them* appears somewhat later, when she shows some concern about the Jews after the Iron Guard has threatened them, an attitude that surprises Harriet until Bella explains "that she was worried on her own behalf. In this country of dark-haired Latins, the Jews, contrary as ever, were notably blond or red-haired. As a result, Bella had always been suspect" (*BT* 462). Her concern for the Jews, then, is nothing more than self-interest (rather like Angela's sorrow in the second trilogy when she hears that the Axis troops are retreating, because Allied successes jeopardize her future with her lover). Such self-interest is an issue throughout the trilogies. Early in *The Balkan Trilogy*, when the Pringles visit the Druckers, one of the Drucker sisters asks a legitimate question: "Why do they hate us? Even the *trăsura* driver when angry with his horse will shout: 'Go on, you Jew.' Why is it?" (*BT* 102). But then the Druckers—whether understandably or not makes no difference—begin a lengthy attack on the Rumanians that mirrors the Rumanian attitude toward them. This conflict has centuries of history behind it, but in the end it comes down to what we have been examining all along, questions of power, domination, and personal imperialism. Groups of powerless people, Rumanians and Jews, argue about who has power, or more accurately, who appears to have power.

But Manning takes the role of Jews much further than this, as the Pringles become involved with Sasha, the son and heir of the Drucker family. When Harriet first meets him, she thinks that were one to meet him in any capital in the world, one would think not "Here is a foreigner" but "here is a Jew." Though he would be recognisable anywhere, he would be at home nowhere except here, in the midst of his family. Despite the fact that he did undoubtedly belong . . . there was something about him, something so vulnerable and unprotected that Harriet's sympathy went out to him. (*BT* 97)

Harriet indicates somewhat later that she seems to believe that Jews purposefully exclude themselves from society—"Your first loyalty is to your own race" (*BT* 102)—but at the same time, when meeting Sasha, she recognizes that his status as an outsider is largely thrust upon him. Her distinction between "foreigner" and "Jew" is significant. A foreigner is, to use a word that came up earlier, an alien, someone who belongs somewhere else. A Jew, as Harriet uses the word, belongs nowhere. Such, of course, was the traditional view: Nations that for centuries had excluded Jews from everyday life blamed the Jews for separating themselves and when Jews did try to assimilate, those nations blamed them for that as well. Consequently, in most places and in most times, the Jew was indeed a perpetual outsider. Throughout the trilogies, the Pringles are foreigners, but there is always an England to which they can, at least in theory, return. But they also, wherever they are, become part of the British colony. Their first loyalty, too, is to their own nation, for which no one blames them; but they are British, not Jews. And the Pringles are clearly interlopers, British citizens in Rumania, Greece, Egypt. The Druckers were German Jews living in Rumania because they had been forced to flee from Germany. There is nowhere they can go where they will belong. Their existence, as Jews in Europe, is precarious.

In fact, shortly after Harriet meets the family, the elder Drucker is arrested and has his fortune taken from him, while the rest of the family is scattered. The Pringles manage to rescue Sasha, who, as long as they are in Rumania, remains hidden in their apartment, at great risk to them. Unfortunately, Sasha has not responded well to his and his family's difficulties. While he is in hiding, he takes no advantage of Guy's teaching, and he seems to have withdrawn utterly from any meaningful activity. Still, we must remember that Sasha not only has nowhere to go, but if he goes anywhere at all, he is in danger of being recognized and imprisoned. He is not, while he stays with the Pringles, especially appealing. There is no reason he should be.

And yet he is much less appealing toward the end of the trilogy when Harriet meets him by chance in Athens. Sasha, having inferred from Iron Guardists that the Pringles had betrayed him, remains very distant from Harriet, almost hostile. "Yet one lie—less than a lie, a hint that he had been betrayed by friends—had precipitated the settled doubts of his race. . . . He now accepted the perfidy of the world and acceptance was born in him, an inheritance not to be changed" (*BT* 858). Sasha's judgment is surely defective, but he was young, spoiled, and probably unaware of the risk the Pringles took in sheltering him. Nevertheless, his recent experience and his experiences as a Jew combine to make him more insular and isolated than he needs to be. He does not know whom he can trust, and so he trusts no one. Harriet's reaction to this encounter sounds uncharitable, perhaps even anti-Semitic, but it is not: Sasha and his uncle

> belonged not to a country but to an international sodality, the members of which had more in common with each other than they had with the inhabitants of any country in which they chanced to be born.
>
> "Jews are always strangers," Harriet thought, yet when Sasha followed his uncle upstairs, she felt a sense of loss.

Epics almost always deal in some fashion with peoplehood or nationhood, and Manning's trilogies adapt that tradition. Harriet's reflections on the Jews fit into that concern. We see her reactions to the Rumanians, the Greeks, and the Egyptians, as well as the British. Her reflections on the Jews help to give depth to received ideas about nationhood that have been valuable but that have also caused so much trouble in the areas that are of primary concern to these works, war and imperialism. (I should note, incidentally, that Manning herself spent the war being evacuated from Bucharest and Athens to Egypt and then to Jerusalem, so she knew about these places from personal experience.) As is so often the case in literature, people's reactions to the Jews reflect more about the people who are reacting than they do about the Jews, who thus serve as a kind of barometer.

Sasha, then, never does fit in, but at the same time that he is in hiding with the Pringles, they have another guest (though against Harriet's wishes), Prince Yakimov, one of the most interesting characters in the trilogies. Unlike Sasha, Yakimov never allows himself to be an outsider, at least not for long. Like so many of the "princes" in Russian novels, Yakimov has nothing noble about him, and he is virtually always without funds and in debt. He takes advantage of everyone, generally has no principles aside from those that assist his self-interest, and even turns on the Pringles when it suits his purposes; and yet almost everyone puts up with him. Many characters find him amusing, and despite his poverty and his inability to earn money, he seldom goes without food or drink, which he always desires and, whenever possible, consumes in copious amounts. If Sasha was born to accept the perfidy of the world, Yakimov was born to ignore it, except in so far as it affects his food supply. His assessment of the Nazis, or the Nasties as he calls them, is that they "seemed to start out all right, but they overdid it somehow. Nobody likes them now" (*BT* 45). And when he complains that he has not been paid (for work that he did not do, incidentally) and might have to move to the Minerva Hotel, Guy reminds him that the Minerva is a German hotel, to which he responds, "Don't mind, dear boy. Poor Yaki's not particular" (*BT* 111), a statement that is borne out when, as the Pringle's guest, he steals Guy's "top secret" plans from Sheppy and then shares them with a Nazi acquaintance.

Perhaps the scene that best typifies Yakimov occurs on Christmas in Dragomir's food store, as the penniless prince wanders through the store admiring the foodstuffs:

> An assistant was shearing off the legs of live frogs, throwing the still palpitating trunks into a dustbin. Yakimov was upset by the sight, but forgot it at once as he peered into a basket of button mushrooms. (*BT* 132)

He does indeed have human feelings, but they do not last long and are easily overcome by his appetites. He recognizes cruelty, and other injustices, but he is adept at ignoring them. In his world, mushrooms outweigh suffering.

Sasha, then, is a tragic figure, fleeing from country to country without a home, facing the scattering of his family and the arrest and death of his father, while Yakimov is a comic figure with tragic overtones. Much of his freeloading would be funny if so much of what he does did not have bad consequences for the people around him. He puts on a mask of innocence, but he is an inveterate schemer, and naturally the person who sees through him most clearly is Harriet. When Guy describes him as a child, Harriet counters that he is

> "A pretty cunning child."
> "He's harmless, anyway. If the world was composed of Yakimovs, there'd be no wars."
> "There'd be no anything." (*BT* 238)

Once again Guy is too charitable in his assessment. Yakimov is not harmless, and he very nearly causes great trouble for Guy; but even if he were harmless, that is, if he took no active part in doing wrong, his pretense of noninvolvement would itself be dangerous. He takes no moral positions, so that he can be free to join whichever side will benefit him the most. It is not coincidence that he has terrific success in Guy's production of *Troilus and Cressida* playing the role of Pandarus. The role requires no acting. He has only to be himself. Like Pinkrose, Gracey, Bella, and so many others who populate these pages, Yakimov operates out of a deep sense of self-interest at everyone else's expense. But then there is a twist.

Most of the purely selfish characters come to some kind of a bad end. Bella remains in Bucharest as the Nazis arrive, Pinkrose is mistaken for a British official named Pinkerton and is shot, and Cookson becomes a pathetic figure. Yakimov, too, becomes pathetic, as his clothing becomes increasingly threadbare and he takes a job as a messenger boy; but in the third volume of *The Balkan Trilogy*, he gains a measure of dignity. The volume opens with Harriet arriving in Athens, having left Guy in Bucharest. She worries about him to the verge of panic and is helped by Yakimov, who knows that she does not like him but who is very solicitous of her. He continues to accept food and drink from her, but at least now he provides something in return.

The Pringles' two boarders, then, Sasha and Yakimov, present different perspectives on the terrible situation that confronts Europe. Sasha, the Jew, belongs nowhere. He cannot adapt, but he can, with some help, survive. Yakimov, half-Russian and half-Irish, seems to adapt to almost anything; but his adaptations involve decline, and ultimately he cannot survive. The last thing he does before he dies is to tell, yet again, the story of his fur coat. His glory is the glory of the past, of a past not even his own. Sasha, tragic figure that he is, will have a future, while Yakimov, with no firm principles, with nothing but the past to cling to, does not survive. They offer an interesting contrast and a commentary on Europe both during the war and twenty years later, when Manning wrote *The Balkan Trilogy*.

And then there are Guy and Simon. They, along with Harriet, are the heroes of these trilogies. I want to avoid calling them "epic heroes" because the connotations of that term might lead us to picture Achilles or Hektor in a work of modern fiction and to end up with comic book characters. These characters are certainly not caricatures. They share the complexity of their epic forebears but in distinctly modern ways. Anthony Burgess has said that Guy Pringle is "one of the most fully created male leads of contemporary fiction.... He is a kind of civilization in himself."[7] That is a fascinatingly misleading statement, not because Guy is not major but because it omits Harriet, through whose eyes we usually see Guy and who does so much to allow Guy to be Guy while trying, not always successfully, to keep him from going too far in being Guy. Because we considered Harriet earlier, it is time now to focus on Guy, whose character is revealed almost entirely in the opening scene of *The Balkan Trilogy*. On the train taking them to Rumania, Guy and Harriet meet a German refugee who claims to have lost his wallet containing his passport and money. Both Pringles, unlike so many of the characters we have seen, are impulsively generous and offer him all of their small funds, but before he can react, the refugee is escorted out of the compartment by the police. Guy worries about him, "frowning like a good-tempered child whose toy has been stolen out of its hands" (*BT* 11). That is Guy. He is a child, not spoiled, not demanding, but a child nevertheless. He is not Achilles pouting in his tent. He is, perhaps, Achilles as a four-year-old.

This characterization is repeated a number of times. For instance, after Inchcape has sized up Harriet and realized that he is dealing with a strong woman, he turns back to Guy: "Guy, it seemed, was not a grown-up; he was a boy—a favoured boy, a senior prefect, perhaps, but still a boy" (*BT* 34); and later, when he has to choose between two activities, he "looked like a baby offered too many toys" (*BT* 149). The only progress he makes, if it is progress, is that in Greece he seems to Harriet like "an adolescent among adolescents" (*BT* 674). What is it that makes Guy seem so childlike? There are several factors. One is his naiveté. He is generous and without guile, and he believes that everyone else shows those same qualities. He is not like Yakimov, who links himself to whoever will benefit him the most. Guy links himself to almost everyone. He is especially partial to those like Phipps who call themselves leftists, but he makes excuses as well for the intolerable behavior of the Pinkroses and Dubedats and other characters of dubious motivation. The only person to whom he shows no warmth at all is Charles, who he fears might be having an affair with Harriet; and the only person to whom he actually stands up is Gracey, for whom he refuses to work until Harriet points out that he has no other options.

Another factor that makes Guy seem childlike is his inability to form deep personal relationships. He has so many friends that when he enters a café, he goes from table to table holding long conversations, or people join him at his table; but those friendships tend to be superficial, and though Guy often makes judgments about which friendships are worth pursuing, he seldom communicates to people what he is thinking. In fact, when he finds himself forced to convey bad news to an acquaintance, he usually avoids the responsibility and manages to convince Harriet to do it. This trait is related to another factor that makes him so childlike, his need to be known and liked. It seems that everyone knows Guy: his companions are fond of telling the story of two strangers who are washed up on a desert island, and although they do not know each other, they both know Guy.

It should be obvious that Guy's childlike demeanor and behavior can be endearing, but they can also be irritating. His inability or his unwillingness to form close relationships extends even to Harriet: "He was one of those harbours that prove to be too shallow: there was no getting into it. For him, personal relationships were incidental. His fulfillment came from the outside world" (*BT* 212). Once again Harriet's assessment is on target, and the more she sees of this trait, the more estranged she becomes, culminating in the episode of the diamond brooch that he takes from her. It means little to her, he asserts, and he can gain credit with it in "the outside world" by giving it to Edwina, who means little to him. His action with the brooch is an egregious example of his behavior; but even in less startling circumstances, Guy is incredibly inconsiderate. He regards Harriet as an extension of himself rather than as an independent person; and because he seems willing to deny himself certain pleasures, he feels justified in denying them to her as well. The truth, of course, is that what she regards as pleasures, he does not, so he is really not denying himself anything. Everything that he does, though he so often seems selfless, contributes to his pleasure. Although he is unfit for military service, for instance, he feels guilty for not being in the army (and for not having fought in Spain). He therefore feels good when he denies himself certain pleasures. He feels as though he is not such a shirker. Similarly, he seems selfless in his devotion to his students, often at Harriet's expense, but he also revels in their adulation.

At the same time, Guy loves Harriet as best he can. He is not intentionally cruel, even in the brooch episode, so much as he is supremely self-centered and inconsiderate. Guy is not like the characters in so many of Manning's other novels who have been neglected as children and are therefore lost in the world as adults. (Actually Harriet is the one who was abandoned by her parents, but the experience seems to have made her into a stronger person, unlike any other character in Manning's works). Guy is simply obtuse and often shallow. For example, when Harriet reappears long after he thinks she drowned at sea,

> She ran to him and he clutched her against his breast and broke into a convulsive sob. Dropping his head down to her head, he wept loudly and wildly while people watched him, amazed. He was known as a good-humoured fellow, a generous and helpful fellow but no one expected him to show any depths of emotion. (*LT* 537)

The fact is that he does show emotion, and he fears losing Harriet again. The problem is that he treats her as though she were part of himself, and Harriet finds that she must, like a colonized nation, insist on her independence. She will not, like Iqal, cut his throat, not even politely; but neither will she continue to function like part of his empire. Paradoxically, it is only by acknowledging her independence that he can remain united with her.

The order of the world is changing, and new perceptions are coming into being, which is why we see Guy, before the production of *Troilus and Cressida* "cutting down Ulysses' speeches" (*BT* 237). Ulysses' most famous speech (1.3), describing universal order, was used by E. M. W. Tillyard as the archetypal example of "the Elizabethan World View;" but it is a speech full of platitudes that no one in the play, and probably in Shakespeare's audience, believes in as anything more than an excuse for maintaining the current hierarchy of power.[8] That Guy cuts these speeches betrays his attitude toward the play he is directing, but it also hints at the rearrangement of power relationships that the trilogies explore on both personal and national levels. Thus, when Guy leaves for a meeting only several pages after having been reunited with Harriet, she is willing to let Guy be Guy, as long as he will let Harriet be Harriet. The string has been untuned, to use Ulysses' image, and the world continues, perhaps in an even healthier way.

It is noteworthy, too, that for all his naive idealism, Guy is hardly capable of action. Harriet knows that "if action had to be taken, she would have to be the one to take it" (*BT* 351). A good example comes when the Pringles, with some of their British friends, are prevented from leaving a hotel by a group of Iron Guardists singing the "Horst Wessel Lied." Harriet removes her brooch (not the one with diamonds) and "thrust the pin into the central backside. Its owner skipped forward with a yelp, leaving a space through which she led her party" (*BT* 376). Still, Guy seems to see himself in heroic terms. So, when he convinces Harriet to leave for Greece while he remains in Rumania,

> the day was one of modest triumph. In sending Harriet [and] Sasha . . . he was not only safeguarding them, but clearing the decks for action in a war he had chosen to wage, the war against despotism. He believed the ultimate engagement was at hand. He could now face it alone. (*BT* 548)

He sounds much like Hektor, preparing to meet Achilles outside the walls of Troy, and we know what Hektor's fate was. Fortunately, Guy does not share that fate. Instead, he, too, escapes to Greece. Nevertheless, he feels heroic, in a more old-fashioned sense of the term than the mid-twentieth century could comfortably bear.

Perhaps the best characterization of Guy is that delivered by Clarence, who tells Harriet, "He may be a sort of saint but he's also a sort of fool" (*BT* 268). Guy is not exactly Prince Myshkin, but in many ways he comes close to being a "holy fool." He means well, but invariably his good intentions cause all sorts of problems, largely because he is willing to initiate projects but leaves the carrying out to others, often to Harriet. Manning makes this point repeatedly with a nice play on words: Guy is unfit for military service because of severe myopia, which is so bad that he often has trouble recognizing people even across a room. Manning frequently refers to his being "short-sighted," as she does when he accidentally buys tickets to a German propaganda concert. That his "short-sightedness" does not refer only to his physical myopia is evident when she cites Harriet's "long sight." In other words, Guy simply does not see much, is not aware of much, certainly not as much as Harriet sees and knows. His shortsightedness often threatens to get them into trouble; her long-sightedness often saves them.[9]

At the same time, Guy does have a duplicitous side. For instance, he tells Harriet that they must take Yakimov into their apartment "'not because he's a good person but because he needs help'" (*BT* 220), which sounds very noble indeed; but later Guy lets slip that he wants Yakimov to be in *Troilus and Cressida*, and the only way to assure his appearance is to give him a place to live. In this case, his shortsightedness applies to his willingness to ignore Harriet's insistence that Yakimov is not welcome in their home. If Guy is a saint, then, he is a flawed one.

Guy's most notable lapse, perhaps aside from those concerning Harriet, comes late in *The Levant Trilogy* and has been referred to already. Aidan Pratt, a troubled young man, has turned to Guy, with Guy's encouragement, as a confidant; but Guy, as is his wont, has begun to tire of him, and when Aidan slights Guy's idealism about the Spanish Civil War, Guy resolves to end the friendship. As Aidan boards his train, he reaches out to Guy for friendship, but Guy rejects him. Guy is not particularly at fault here, as he does have the right to choose his friends, even though this right is not one he has extended to Harriet. Still, he cannot be responsible for everyone, even if he occasionally behaves as though he is; and he surely cannot be held responsible for the fact that Aidan kills himself on the train as a result, partially, of Guy's rejection. He can, however, be held responsible for his reaction to news of Aidan's death: "I'm afraid he was rather a one for dramatic gestures," he says, and the narrative voice tells us that "Guy could feel little more than exasperation at Aidan's death." The problem for Guy is that Aidan's death brings him uncomfortably close to self-realization, the kind of discovery that Guy finds particularly disquieting:

> He remembered that Harriet had accused him of taking up with inadequate people so for the first time they felt understood and appreciated. Then, their dependence becoming tedious, he would leave her to cope with them. She had, apparently, coped with Aidan. Guy, having talked him out of his de-

fences, had become bored with him and wished him away. He had gone, and gone for good. (*LT* 533–34)

Harriet's assessment, of course, is correct. Guy thinks about that assessment, but he never acknowledges its accuracy. To do so would be to engage in a kind of self-scrutiny that he energetically avoids. Truly, he is not at fault if other people are incapable of handling their problems; but he is at fault if he uses their problems to enhance his stature and if he refuses to recognize that he does so.

Guy, then, is partially a saint and partially a fool, if not worse. Early on, Harriet wonders "at the complexity of the apparently simple creature she had married" (*BT* 233). Part of Guy's problem is that it is difficult to be a hero, as we have already seen. Even the greatest heroes of the ancient epics—Achilles, Hektor, Aeneas, Turnus—all have flaws that contrast with their glory. Modern heroes can have the flaws, but they cannot share the glory because modern societies have such different ideas about what constitutes glory. Epics are about pivotal moments, as are Manning's trilogies, but we no longer look for the singular hero who plays a central role in that moment. Neither Winston Churchill nor the character incessantly played by John Wayne could be the hero of a modern epic, so the twentieth-century author has to create extraordinary ordinary people. Guy and Harriet fit that description. Over the course of fifteen hundred pages, through Rumania, Greece, and Egypt, we see their heroic characteristics and their flaws. They are ordinary people—an English teacher and his wife—but they go through extraordinary experiences and behave in extraordinary ways. Their behavior, like that of an Achilles or an Aeneas, is magnified, which makes it subject to additional scrutiny; but it is the events that surround them and the focus on those events that give epic status to the trilogies.

There is one more character who fits into the equation, Simon Boulderstone (a wonderfully tautological name). Simon, unlike Guy, experiences the war directly. He nearly sees his brother's grotesque death in battle, and later he wanders the battlefield like Tolstoy's Pierre at Borodino, not actually fighting but observing the chaos and horror of battle. As Harriet notes, Simon is only a few years younger than the Pringles, but he represents a whole new generation. Guy and Harriet persevere, much like Faulkner's Dilsey. They will be there when the war ends to help pick up the pieces, but it is Simon and his generation, those who actually fight the war, who will come to inhabit the new world. Simon has been dreadfully injured, but he has recovered and yearns to reenter the war. Like Britain itself, he was almost overcome, and his recovery leaves him strong enough to reassess his history. As he leaves Egypt, heading for Greece in a reversal of the Pringles' itinerary, he looks back and says, "Not a lucky place" (*LT* 569), which is, over all, not a bad summary of Britain's history in Egypt. He is on his way to help create a new world and to take part in the disintegration of the old one. Despite his experience, he is still somewhat naive. He has learned a great deal, but he still looks hopefully to the future.

Simon is, in many ways, an ideal character to watch as the disintegration of the old world order continues. We saw memories of the Ottoman Empire early in *The Balkan Trilogy*, and the sense of disintegration continues throughout the six novels. There are the numerous references to the fall of Troy, which is coupled with the fall of Paris. We see Rumania and Greece fall to the Nazis, and we get clear indications that the British Empire is in decline. When Dobson offers his ideas about when "the British Empire began to decay" (*LT* 512), the discussion revolves around his theory, not about his basic premise that the Empire is in decay. That premise is never questioned. Guy, Dobson, and all their friends are part of that old empire. Simon is part of the transition to what will follow the Empire's collapse. His geological last name (and even his first name, with the Simon recalling Simon Peter) indicate a kind of permanence. Conditions, boundaries, and empires will change, but the Simon Boulderstones will weather the changes. Simon recalls the first epilogue of *War and Peace*, with its picture of normalcy after the upheavals of war. *The Levant Trilogy* may not take us quite so far, but it does hold out the promise as Simon leaves for Greece and looks forward, as Guy and Harriet do not, to his return to England.

The Balkan and *Levant Trilogies*, then, constitute not six separate novels or two separate trilogies but a single major work, *The Fortunes of War*, that focuses on a pivotal moment in history, that offers a broad scope, and that considers crucial issues of both personal and national import, issues that intertwine and operate simultaneously on different levels. Olivia Manning was not a particularly adventurous writer—the nearest she comes to innovation is in having so much of the narrative be seen through Harriet's eyes—but she was a skilled writer who showed a keen sense of craftsmanship in her work, as can be seen in the way each of the six novels ends. In *The Balkan Trilogy*, the first book ends with the fall of Paris, the second with Harriet's flight from Rumania, and the third, combining the events of the first two, with the fall of Greece and the Pringles' flight to Egypt. Similarly, the first volume of *The Levant Trilogy* concludes with the death of Hugo, the second with the presumed death of Harriet, and the third with the Pringles united in Alexandria (after Harriet's "resurrection") and with Simon having survived and internalized Hugo's death and having been "reborn" after his own injury, on his way to Greece.

Manning's narrative is tight, her characters are fascinating, and her presentation of the personal and historical stories is perceptive and convincing. *The Balkan* and *Levant Trilogies* are enjoyable to read, and they lend themselves to a Masterpiece Theatre presentation, but they are far more than an idle entertainment. They are a fine mid-twentieth-century epic novel, with all that the label implies.

4
Paul Scott's *Raj Quartet*

In his wonderful, short book *The Hedgehog and the Fox: An Essay on Tolstoy's View of History*, Isaiah Berlin cites a fragment by Archilochus: "The fox knows many things, but the hedgehog knows one big thing."[1] Berlin sees in this opposition a distinction that divides, possibly, all human beings, a distinction between those "who relate everything to a single central vision, one system, less or more coherent or articulate, in terms of which they understand, think and feel . . . and those who pursue many ends, often unrelated and even contradictory, connected, if at all, only in some *de facto* way."[2] Among the former he places Dante, Plato, Hegel, Dostoyevsky, and Proust, among the latter Aristotle, Goethe, Balzac, and Joyce.[3] While acknowledging that these classifications represent an oversimplification, Berlin uses them well to discuss what he sees as a major problem in Tolstoy, that "Tolstoy was by nature a fox, but believed in being a hedgehog; that his gifts and achievement are one thing, and his beliefs, and consequently his interpretation of his own achievement, another."[4]

Berlin focuses particularly on Tolstoy's relation to history, on the apparent paradox that the author of the greatest historical novel of all time displayed a "violently unhistorical and indeed antihistorical rejection of all efforts to explain or justify human action or character in terms of social or individual growth."[5] As readers of *War and Peace* well know, Tolstoy recognized that history is incredibly complex and that historians' attempts to explain history are inevitably condemned to be at best partial and at worst mendacious. "History does not reveal causes; it presents only a blank succession of unexplained events."[6] Historians, for Tolstoy, create the explanations, but those explanations are forever suspect "since no theories can possibly fit the immense variety of possible human behavior."[7]

It is not only historians, however, who are caught in this problem. It afflicts all who think that they can, "by the use of their own resources, understand and control the course of events."[8] High on the list of Tolstoy's targets in *War and Peace*, of course, are the generals, who believe, and who have to make others believe, that they do indeed control the course of events. One of the most amusing scenes in the novel is the strategy meeting at which the European generals debate about tactics—tactics that the historically aware reader knows will be irrelevant—while Kutuzov dozes off. This scene may be profoundly unhistorical in the sense that nothing like it ever took place, but it is emblematic of Tolstoy's historical vision. Nevertheless, Tolstoy knows that people derive great comfort from the illusion that someone is in charge, as Prince Andrei sees in the presence of Prince Bagration:

> Prince Andrei listened carefully to Bagration's colloquies with the commanding officers and to the orders he gave them and remarked to his astonishment that in reality no orders were given but that Prince Bagration merely tried to make it appear as though everything that was being done of necessity, by accident or at the will of individual commanders, was performed if not exactly by his orders at least in accordance with his design. Prince Andrei noticed, however, that though what happened was due to chance and independent of the general's will, the tact shown by Bagration made his presence extremely valuable. Officers who rode up to him with distracted faces regained their composure; soldiers and officers saluted him gaily, recovered their spirits in his presence, and unmistakably took pride in displaying their courage before him.[9]

Prince Bagration is irrelevant to the actual situation. His only value is that his apparent control calms and inspires his subordinates, but his entire status is the product of illusion.

If Prince Bagration's power is illusory, the even greater power of Napoleon is even more illusory. Early in the novel, Pierre declares, "Napoleon is great because he towered above the Revolution, suppressed its abuses, preserving all that was good in it," and Andrei, too, is a devotee of the French general.[10] It is only when Andrei is first wounded that he begins to see things differently: "So trivial seemed to him at that moment all the interests that engrossed Napoleon, so petty did his hero with his paltry vanity and delight in victory appear, compared to that lofty, righteous and kindly sky which he had seen and comprehended, that he could not answer him."[11] Lying on the ground and gazing at the sky, Andrei has seen, if only briefly, something far more important than Napoleon. What that something is, though, will have to wait for elucidation. First, Tolstoy wants us to understand how unimportant, indeed, irrelevant, Napoleon truly is. Tolstoy utterly rejects the notion "that Russia was fashioned by the will of one man, Peter I, or that the French

Empire was created and the war with Russia begun by the will of one man, Napoleon."[12] Thus Tolstoy must reject the contention of so many historians "that the French failed at Borodino because Napoleon had a cold in the head."[13] For Tolstoy, "The course of earthly happenings is predetermined from on high, and depends on the combined volition of all who participate in those events."[14] Tolstoy's point here is not simply that Napoleon is irrelevant because earthly events are divinely ordained. It is that success or failure depends on so many causes that it is impossible to cite one single cause, whether it be Napoleon's strategic genius or his cold:

> And it was not Napoleon who ordained the course of the battle, for no part of his plan was executed and during the engagement he did not know what was going on before him. Therefore the way in which these men slaughtered one another was not decided by Napoleon's will but occurred independently of him, in accord with the will of the hundreds of thousands of individuals who took part in the common action. It *only seemed* to Napoleon that it was all happening because he willed it so. Hence the question whether Napoleon had or had not a cold in the head is of no more interest to history than whether the least of the transport soldiers had a cold or not.[15]

Historians who offer such explanations are mistaken, deceiving themselves and others. Why would "millions of men, renouncing their human feelings and their common sense . . . march from west to east to slay their fellows"?[16] Surely those "millions" did not all have the same reason, any more than all those thousands who fought in the American Civil War had the same reason. In fact, says Tolstoy, there are so many reasons that "we are forced to fall back on fatalism to explain the irrational events of history (that is to say, events the intelligence of which we do not see). The more we strive to account for such events in history rationally, the more irrational and incomprehensible do they become to us."[17]

Pierre is an example of someone who tries to find explanations for everything, an overarching system that will account for all that happens and therefore will guide his actions, but he comes to one dead end after another. As Berlin says about Tolstoy, Pierre, along with Andrei, wants to be a hedgehog. Andrei has had that view of "something," though he has not understood it; and unfortunately he dies before his understanding can ripen. Pierre, however, has a rather different experience. He is much like Koheleth, the speaker of Ecclesiastes, who adopts a succession of approaches—through wisdom, through pleasures, through nihilism—before he discovers what is important in life: to eat, to drink, and to meet one's obligations. Pierre tries dissipation, love, Freemasonry, numerical symbolism, and other paths, but none of them lead him to the truth, which he finally learns from the peasant Karatayev:

> Karatayev had no attachments, friendships or loves, as Pierre understood them; but he felt affection for and lived on sympathetic terms with every creature with whom life brought him in contact, and especially with man—not any particular man but those with whom he happened to be. He loved his dog, loved his comrades and the French, loved Pierre who was his neighbour; but Pierre felt that for all Karatayev's warm-heartedness towards him (thus involuntarily paying tribute to Pierre's spiritual life) he would not suffer a pang if they were parted. And Pierre began to feel the same way about Karatayev.[18]

This philosophy, the understanding that we cannot fully understand but that we can fully live, is the "something" that Andrei glimpsed when he was wounded, when he saw the clouds and realized, "Yes, all is vanity, all is delusion except these infinite heavens."[19] At least Andrei grasps the first part, that we cannot understand. And gradually he begins to understand the second part, though he is cut off before he succeeds at it. But Pierre does reach that understanding, as do a handful of other characters, which helps to explain the seemingly anticlimactic first epilogue.

War and Peace is possibly the second greatest war story ever written (after *The Iliad*), full of vivid scenes of fighting interspersed with astute political maneuverings and peopled by emperors, generals, and noblemen; but it concludes (aside from the long, philosophical second epilogue) with an extended scene of blissful domesticity. After all the turbulence, the wars, the burning of Moscow, the numerous deaths, we end up at home with Pierre and Natasha, Nikolai and Maria. Prokofiev's operatic version of *War and Peace* ends, as I noted earlier, with an embarrassing flourish of patriotic sentiment, no doubt in large part the result of Stalin and the political situation when Prokofiev wrote; but that sentiment, aside from its excessiveness, is not out of place in a work that celebrates the Russian victory over invaders. Tolstoy certainly celebrates the Russian victory, but his concluding domestic scene, in which these characters who suffered through the war have now made a life for themselves, a life of loving and caring, is far more eloquent than Prokofiev's overwrought choruses.

Here, then, is where I disagree with Isaiah Berlin (something I do only with the greatest trepidation). Berlin says that like Pierre, Kutuzov, and Karatayev, Tolstoy

> Knows that the truth is there, and not "here"—not in the regions susceptible to observation, discrimination, constructive imagination, not in the power

of microscopic perception and analysis of which he is so much the greatest master of our time; but he has not, himself, seen it face to face; for he has not, do what he might, a vision of the whole; he is not, he is remote from being, a hedgehog; and what he sees is not the one, but always, with an ever growing minuteness, in all its teeming individuality, with an obsessive, inescapable, incorruptible, all-penetrating lucidity which maddens him, the many.[20]

Tolstoy, I believe, does have a vision of the whole, but that vision is paradoxical. It is a vision, a revelation, that human beings cannot see the "whole." This may not seem like a startling revelation, but as Tolstoy's comments about historians, and as our own tendencies indicate, it is a point that we often ignore. Our vision is limited. We can see pieces of the whole, but if we, like the historians whom Tolstoy criticizes, try to find patterns in those pieces, all we really do is to impose patterns. Most human beings (aside from the novelist) can see only from a human, not a divine, perspective. Tolstoy, like the fox, knows many things; but like the hedgehog, he knows this one big thing. Unlike those other hedgehogs that Berlin cites—Dante, Plato, Hegel, Dostoyevsky, and Proust—Tolstoy's hedgehoggism begins with a negative, with what we cannot know, but it then moves to a positive, to how we can live with that knowledge of our limitations. Dante sees God and understands the universe, but then the medieval synthesis collapses and we can only read Dante with a kind of cosmic nostalgia. However, the more we look at history and try to understand what it means to understand history, the more we can see that Tolstoy did indeed know one big thing.

I have devoted so much space at the beginning of this chapter to Tolstoy because Tolstoy was the founder of the epic novel and because, of all the authors I am considering, Paul Scott is the most Tolstoyan, a point that other readers have also made. K. Bhaskara Rao has called *The Raj Quartet* "an Anglo-Indian *War and Peace*," and M. M. Mahood argues that although the *Quartet* is often considered "popular history in a fictionalized form," he wants to show "that it aspires to be an imaginative creation of Tolstoyan breadth and depth." Karina Petersone sees the *Quartet* as part of a "classical French and Russian prose tradition, with even a Tolstoyan or Proustian scope of vision," and she cites other authors who are part of a "revival of the so-called 'big form' novel which in its best samples strives to investigate and at the same time to renew the ties between man and society, to see man as part of historical processes." Petersone sees this revival as a British rather than an American phenomenon, and the authors she cites in addition to Scott are C. P. Snow, Anthony Powell, Anthony Burgess, and Olivia Manning. And Francine Weinbaum notes that the *Quartet* is "like Tolstoy's *War and Peace*, a world unto itself, a totality."[21] It is worth investigating in some depth what it means to say that *The Raj Quartet* is Tolstoyan.

A good place to begin this investigation is with a statement that Scott himself made: "Here I am using the immensity of India to say something about the littleness of the individual human attempt to make an impression on the world as we know it, and this in turn is meant to say something about the frailty of individual human action in the face of pressures exerted by a collective conscience—what I call the moral drift of history" (*W* 93).[22] Scott does not mention Tolstoy in this passage, but what he describes is clearly Tolstoyan. Tolstoy and Scott, like all epic writers, use the past to talk about both the past and the present, use an immense canvas, question the effectiveness of the individual in the face of history, and deal extensively, as we shall see in Scott's case, with "the moral drift of history."

Scott wrote a series of novels before the *Quartet*, some of them very fine, many of them very Conradian, with intelligent protagonists learning to understand themselves against exotic backgrounds; but if he had only written those novels, he would hardly be known. It is *The Raj Quartet* that makes him a great novelist, and what is astounding is that when he began the first of its four parts, *The Jewel in the Crown*, he had no intention of taking the story beyond that novel. One of his notes reads, "No idea that there would be *four novels* (*W* 214), and in a letter to his biographer Hillary Spurling, he wrote, "I've always sneered at sequences a la Proust, Snow and Durrell."[23] Nevertheless, he wrote one of the best of such sequences. As with almost all of the epic novels I am examining, we can think of the *Quartet* as a series of individual novels—*The Jewel in the Crown* (1966), *The Day of the Scorpion* (1968), *The Towers of Silence* (1971), and *A Division of the Spoils* (1975)—but they are truly, however they may have been conceived, a single long work, an epic novel, or as Allen Boyer says, "a four-volume epic of the final years of British rule in India."[24]

There has, understandably, been a good deal of discussion of the *Quartet*'s genre. Benita Parry calls the work an elegy. Scott, she says, regrets "the doom of an idea."[25] I do not think that Scott saw any possibility that the relationship between the British and the Indians, the occupiers and the occupied, could ever have achieved an ideal level, despite the best intentions of many of the people who were involved. More precisely, as Weinbaum says, citing a letter she received from Scott, "The function of the tragic writer is not to blame but to mourn, and Scott once identified the subject of the *Quartet* as, among other things, his 'sadness that things had to work that way and probably will always have to work that way.'"[26] The *Quartet*, then, is elegiac, but it is not a two-thousand page elegy. It is elegiac the way *The*

Iliad is elegiac or the way that *Beowulf* is elegiac, acknowledging and lamenting "that things had to work that way and probably will always have to work that way," for like *The Iliad* and *Beowulf* and so many other epics, *The Raj Quartet* marks an end, a tragic end, and so lets in Matthew Arnold's "eternal note of sadness."

Weinbaum suggests a number of generic possibilities for the *Quartet*. It is, she says, a "*roman-fleuve*, like Galsworthy's *Forsyte Saga*," a "moral detective story, like Conrad's *Lord Jim*," and "a philosophical tragedy" like "Hardy's novels and has something in common with the vast canvases of Tolstoy and the psychological novels of Henry James."[27] At first this looks like a shopping list of genres, but Weinbaum is ultimately correct in identifying these generic strands. She also, quite correctly, mentions the historical novel. What I want to argue is that the epic, because of its scope and its inclusiveness, subsumes all of these others. A work that is over two thousand pages long, that covers a five-year span in considerable detail but that also extends well beyond that five-year span, that examines several cultures and subcultures, must include a variety of generic approaches, but they are all part of the overall epic quality of the work. Just as *The Iliad* is about the end of Troy, so *The Raj Quartet* is about the end of the raj; and just as *The Iliad* focuses on fifty-four days in the history of that ten-year war and yet ranges from heaven to earth and treats universal issues of human existence, so the *Quartet* treats five years in the history of England's imperial occupation of India and also treats universal issues of human existence. Margaret Scanlan says, "What distinguishes [the *Quartet*] from much historical fiction . . . is the constant tension between its realistic texture and its tendency to turn history into stories and stories into myths that seek to explain history."[28]

These words are true of all these epic novels, but especially of *The Raj Quartet*. Scott, as Spurling indicates in her biography, made himself an expert on Indian history, and he visited India several times, including an extended stay when he was stationed there during the Second World War. Consequently, much of the discussion about the *Quartet* focuses on its historicity. Scott does a remarkable job of fitting his characters into historical situations and of making his descriptions seem to capture the sounds and smells of everyday life in India, whether he is describing life among the British officers' wives or in the Indian section of Mayapore, the Chillianwallah Bagh. Scott is, in these ways, a realist, but his realism has had some strange consequences. Salman Rushdie, for instance, has criticized Scott for focusing on the British in India rather than on India itself, ignoring the fact that this is a work about the end of the raj, not about India.[29] Other historians, like Max Beloff, have written critiques in which they either approve or disapprove of Scott's descriptions of India in the 1940s. Such critiques are interesting and certainly have their place, but we must remember always that *The Raj Quartet* is a work of fiction, peopled by characters who never lived in places that never existed (even if those people and places are based on real-life models). Scott's position is similar to that of Tolstoy, who studied the Napoleonic Wars in depth and who claimed to adhere to the history that he scorned but who clearly adapted the history that he had studied to the needs of his novel. In short, Scott does what Scanlan describes: he uses a "realistic texture" and he turns history into story, story into myth, trying to explain the history. What Scanlan describes is not only the method of *The Raj Quartet*; she describes the epic novel.

Scott himself makes much the same point. He was fond of describing the novel—that is, the generic form of the novel—"as an extended metaphor for its author's view of life," and he explained that he wrote about the end of the raj because "the last days of the British raj are the metaphor I have presently chosen to illustrate my view of life" (*W* 151).[30] We would not read *The Iliad* if we wanted a historical description of Troy, nor would we read *Beowulf* if we wanted to know about daily life among the Danes and the Geats. But those stories, fictionalized, mythic accounts of the past, can tell us a great deal about the societies that created or treasured them, because the story of Troy and the story of Beowulf are the metaphors that their creators chose to illustrate their views of life. As in the *Quartet*, their setting is a pivotal historical moment and their scope is huge. They belong to the same family, a family that uses history, that manipulates history in order to clarify it, as Scott illustrates when he has Guy Perron, himself a historian, discuss the treatment of Merrick and Kumar:

> Place Merrick at home, in England, and Harry Coomer [Hari Kumar's name in England] abroad, in England, and it is Coomer on whom the historian's eye lovingly falls; he is a symbol of our virtue. In England it is Merrick who is invisible. Place them there, in India, and the historian cannot see either of them. They have wandered off the guideline, into the jungle. But throw a spotlight on them and it is Merrick on whom it falls. There he is, the unrecorded man, one of the kind of men we really are (as Sarah would say). Yes, their meeting was logical. And they had met before, countless times. You can say they are meeting, that their meeting reveals the real animus, the one that historians won't recognize, or which we relegate to our margins. (*D* 302)

The historian, he says, is limited. In fact, sounding very much like Tolstoy, he says in the preceding paragraph that historians see history "through the unmapped forests of prejudice and self-interest." In India, the Merricks and the Kumars are invisible, everyday people as opposed to political or military leaders, the "great men" who are supposed to shape history. But those "great men," like Tolstoy's Bagration and Napoleon, are shaped by history at least as much as are the Merricks and Kumars. "Throw a spotlight on them," says Guy. Who throws that spotlight? The novelist. The historian, he implies, may focus on Churchill and Mountbatten, Gandhi and Nehru, but the novelist, throwing the spotlight on Kumar and Merrick (who, it bears repeating, are fictional characters) "reveals the real animus, the one that historians won't recognize." As Scott says elsewhere, "How much of Lord Jim actually happened couldn't matter less. That the book happened is a kind of joy to us" (*W* 143). We can say the same thing about the *Quartet*.

Scott, obviously, was very much concerned with the relationship between history and his work and between the life of a nation and the lives of the individuals who make up that nation.[31] These concerns intertwine throughout the *Quartet*. Scott deals with the end of the raj, but he does so by considering the individuals, just as *The Iliad* deals with the end of Troy through the individuals on both sides of the battle. One problem, however, is that Scott frequently referred to the genesis of his novels in images that he would then have to explicate: "A novel is a sequence of images. In sequence these images tell a story" (*W* 74). So, Weinbaum concludes, "*The Raj Quartet* must be seen . . . as an explication of a single image that creates, by association, multiple images" (82), and Michael Gorra says, "The whole of *The Jewel in the Crown* is an attempt to explain its opening command, to tell its readers how that girl has come to be running in the shadow of that wall."[32] By offering his reader multiple perspectives—the same story is told over and over by different people with different points of view, much like Browning's *The Ring and the Book*—Scott creates the illusion that the story is being told in its entirety. *The Jewel in the Crown* tells various parts of the story from at least nine different perspectives, all under the direction of the Stranger, a person who has come to India many years after the events in order to find the truth about the rape of Daphne Manners. Each new perspective adds to the story, which means that the basic pattern of the work is not the circle, as Tedesco and Popham assert, but the spiral. Each time we come back to the same point, we are at a different level in our understanding, in our ability to see not only the story but the perspective from which it is being told. Nevertheless, as Sister Ludmila says to the Stranger, "'Permit me, too, a further observation? That given the material evidence there is also in you an understanding that a specific historical event has no definite beginning, no satisfactory end?'" (*JC* 119). What she means is that there is so much involved in every event, from conscious to unconscious motivations, from purposeful actions to coincidences, that no cause can ever be isolated.

Sister Ludmila makes this point more clearly a few pages later, when she recalls the initial meeting between Merrick and Kumar at the Sanctuary, a meeting which had terrible consequences for virtually everyone in the novel. Hari Kumar has awakened at the Sanctuary, having been brought there in a drunken stupor during the night. Scott explains in extensive detail why Hari was drunk—having been brought up in England with a fine education at a posh school, Hari has become, as numerous people remark, "one of Macaulay's 'brown-skinned Englishmen'" (*D* 301); but his father's bankruptcy and suicide have forced Kumar to return to India, where his upper-class English education, manners, and accent make him an anomaly, a person who belongs neither to India nor to England and who therefore becomes invisible, even to his best friend from England, who has been stationed in Mayapore and who, either consciously or inadvertently, fails to recognize him. This tangled and tragic situation is described and analyzed from multiple perspectives, until we have the illusion that we understand it. In fact, we do understand large parts of it. We understand the racism that is inherent in the colonial situation and in the British attitude toward their dark-skinned subjects. We understand Hari's initial inability to grasp the racism he confronts and his subsequent reactions to that racism. We understand why his father, with good intentions, formed his son as he did, creating a person whom both the British and the Indians can only regard as monstrous.

Similarly, through the course of the *Quartet*, we come to understand Merrick, an Englishman from a lower class whose accent and manners betray his origins, raised without affection, working as a British policeman in India where the racism inherent in the colonial system automatically gives him a higher status than he could ever have had at home, allowing him to become the District Superintendent. None of this background is obscure; in fact, in Merrick's case it sometimes verges on caricature. The clash between these characters seems inevitable, if they were ever to confront each other. But why should they confront each other at all? We know that Hari is at the Sanctuary because Sister Ludmila rescued him. Merrick is there because he is searching for a suspect, not, apparently, an odd thing for a policeman to do, given Sister Ludmila's reputation as a protector of the downtrodden. All of this is explained, and yet there is a mystery, as Sister Ludmila says: "'But never before had District Superintendant come himself. If he had come the day before, the day after, there might never have been Bibighar'" (*JC* 124).

Herein lies the mystery: There is no way, after all the explanations have been given, to understand why Merrick, on that particular day, decided to come himself to the Sanctuary, why he arrived at that particular moment, just as Hari was washing himself at the pump. We can understand, too, what followed: Merrick questions Hari in Urdu, as Sister Ludmila calls it, "The Englishman's Urdu . . . using the familiar *tum* instead of the polite form" (*JC* 129). Merrick, that is, asserts his racial and political superiority over the Indian. Hari replies, "'What?' . . . And spoke for the first time in my hearing. *In perfect English. Better accented than Merrick's.* 'I'm afraid I don't speak Indian'" (*JC* 129). If Hari is a conundrum to most of the British and the Indians, he is a challenge to Merrick's entire existence, an Indian whose very accent marks him as potentially higher on the social scale than Merrick can ever hope to reach. Sister Ludmila says, "[A]lready the Bibighar affair had gone too far. In those few seconds it had begun and could not be stopped because of what Mr. Merrick was and what young Kumar was. Oh, if they had never met!" (*JC* 130).

We can understand a great deal, then, about the enmity between Merrick and Kumar. We know where it originated and we know, as Sister Ludmila says, where it led, not to the rape of Daphne Manners in the Bibighar Gardens but to Merrick's attempt to implicate Kumar in the rape and all the consequences that followed on Merrick's attempt, consequences that affected himself and virtually every other character in the *Quartet*. But there are still mysteries involved in the story. Why did Merrick himself come to the Sanctuary? Why did he find it necessary to address Kumar at all? On a more basic level, why did Merrick react to his upbringing by becoming a racist rather than by identifying with the downtrodden, and why did Kumar respond to his peculiar situation by rejecting rather than embracing India? We can guess at the answers to such questions, but we simply cannot know if our answers are valid. As Robin White says, in his thoughtful recollections about the political and personal events of 1942 that are the subject of *The Jewel in the Crown*, particularly, at this point, about General Reid's actions in having his troops fire on a mass of unarmed civilians,

> In fact, we are not at all after the blow-by-blow account of the politics that led to the action. Actually any one man would be incapable of giving such an account—if he confined himself to the blows. There were so many blows he would spend more than his lifetime recording them. To make the preparation of any account a reasonable task he would have to adapt an attitude towards the available material. The action of such an attitude is rather like that of a sieve. Only what is relevant to the attitude gets through. The rest gets thrown away. The real relevance and truth of what gets through the

mesh then depends on the relevance and truth of the attitude, doesn't it? If one agrees with that one is at once back on the ground of personal preference—even prejudice—which may or may not have anything to do with "truth," so-called. *(JC 333)*

This passage is very Tolstoyan. First, it repeats Tolstoy's reservations about historians, who have to select from all the evidence available to them that evidence that they find most appropriate; but by selecting, which they must do simply because no one can consider all the evidence, they impose patterns. Tolstoy asks, after one battle, "How could anyone tell in all that confusion what did or did not happen?"[33] We can ask the same question about Reid's action, which is based on the action of General Dyer at the Jallianwallah Bagh in 1919, when his troops fired on a gathering of Indian civilians who could not escape from the trap where they had been caught. About four hundred were killed and about twelve hundred were wounded.[34] We can blame General Dyer (whose name, it is remarked, is almost Reid in reverse [*T* 75]), but again, we would ideally have to consider the complete chain of events that led to every individual, on both sides, being in that square at that moment. Dyer was acclaimed for his action and then was forced to retire, but what about his soldiers? Did any of them doubt the rightness of what they were doing? Did any of them fire over the crowd? Why? "How could anyone tell in all that confusion what did or did not happen?" The novelist can throw the spotlight on areas that the historian cannot see, but even the novelist cannot create order out of all the confusion.

Several of the characters in the *Quartet* do think that they can control history, and they think that way largely because of their limited vision. For instance, General Reid presents an eloquent defense of his actions; and from his point of view, he is correct: "One had only to cross the river into the native town to see that in our cantonments and civil lines we had set an example for others to follow and laid down a design for civilized life that the Indians would one day inherit" *(JC 269)*. Throughout *The Jewel in the Crown*, Scott describes in great detail the differences between the orderly British section and the squalid Indian section of Mayapore. For the Stranger, that contrast points to the repressive measures that the British used to preserve their privileges in the colonial empire, but to Reid it indicates the inherent superiority of British civilization over Indian barbarity, with the implication that after two hundred years of occupation, the Indians have still not learned to be civilized. Then, when Reid quotes Kipling to his troops, we easily see his imperialistic indoctrination. But things are never that simple. We also know that Reid is in Mayapore while his wife is dying of cancer, a complication that could surely cloud his judgment. And we know that his son is a prisoner of the Japanese, which would help to explain his vehement response to Indian leaders' refusal to join wholeheartedly the British war with Japan. The situation is similar again to that of General Dyer. In both *The Towers of Silence* and *A Division of the Spoils*, Scott refers to amoebiasis, an ailment from which Scott himself suffered for many years.[35] It is possible that Dyer suffered from this same ailment, that it affected his thought processes and was at least in part responsible for the massacre at Jallianwallah Bagh. This idea is reminiscent of the view that Martin Luther was moved to begin the Reformation by his problems with constipation, in what has been called "the outhouse theory of history." This point may seem amusing, but it is quite serious as we try to consider how well we can actually know the precise causes of historical events.

Whatever Reid's motivations might be, however, he consistently behaves as though he can control history, that is, history as he defines it. Thus, he refers to the Indian desire for "'freedom'" (*JC* 297; the extra quotation marks are his), implying that the Indians are already free and their demands for independence are mere foolishness. He sees no problem in ordering his men not to use each other's names so that they cannot later be identified, and he exonerates British officers of the charges made against them by blaming their Indian subordinates for their misdeeds (*JC* 308). He is a man of action who has little but scorn for someone like Robin White, who tried to understand the Indian point of view and who also understands that the time of British control over India is almost up.

Reid's greatest disciple—the two men share a mutual admiration—is Ronald Merrick, whose theory of history Kumar recounts to Rowan:

> He said history was a sum of situations whose significance was never seen until long afterwards because people had been afraid to act them out. They couldn't face up to their responsibility for them. They preferred to think of the situation they found themselves in as part of a general drift of events they had no control over. (*S* 297)

Merrick believes that the strong leader, the man who acts out situations and takes responsibility for them, "can stop things drifting in the wrong direction, or an unreal direction" (*S* 297). And of course he pictures himself as such a man. Because he believes that he, almost alone, understands situations, he also believes that he is justified in manipulating those situations to make them fit his theories. Such is the case with Havildar Karim Muzzafir Khan, who is suspected of fighting with the Japanese against the British and whom Merrick humiliates and drives to suicide. For Merrick, the havildar's guilt requires no proof, and he is not interested in the niceties of the moral questions involved. This case stands in clear contrast to the long discussion between Mohammed Ali Kasim and his son Sayed, who is accused of the same crime. MAK (as he is called), like Merrick, feels that joining the Japanese-sponsored Indian National Army was wrong, but he also understands that an Indian young man, devoted to Indian independence, captured by the Japanese, could be tempted to turn against the imperialist masters. He disagrees with his son, but he understands. For Merrick, such understanding is part of the "drift" away from strict, clearly defined moral principles and a doctrinaire view of history.

Perhaps this apparent rigidity is what makes Merrick seem so much like Milton's Satan. During his conversation with Barbie Batchelor, after he quotes Edwina Crane's suicide note, "There is no God. Not even on the road from Dibrapur," We read, "An invisible lightning struck the verandah. The purity of its colourless fire etched shadows on his face. The cross glowed on her breast and then seemed to burn out" (*T* 381); and immediately after this interview and her accident in the tonga, Barbie announces, "I have seen the Devil" (*T* 387). Merrick, in a number of ways, promotes this image of himself, especially after being injured. His burned face and the elaborate rituals he goes through with his prosthetic arm are at best disconcerting, an effect he craves, and at worst fiendish.

As Allen Boyer points out, Merrick is the only major character who appears in all four volumes of the *Quartet*, and yet we are never allowed to see things through his eyes.[36] As always in the *Quartet*, Merrick's motivations are far from simple: there are the circumstances of his childhood, his possible jealousy of Kumar's relationship with Daphne Manners, his overwhelming sense of class consciousness, his latent homosexuality, and his sincere belief in the superiority of the white British over the dark-skinned Indians. Obviously many of these elements are related, but none can be isolated. Weinbaum, for instance, argues that Merrick believes Kumar to be guilty because of his behavior toward him at the Sanctuary, but there are problems in this assertion.[37] We cannot be entirely certain that Merrick truly thinks Kumar is guilty, and we cannot even be clear about what he might think him guilty of. If he thinks Kumar is guilty of raping Daphne, does he think so because there is evidence? Apparently not, since he tries to plant Daphne's bicycle near Kumar's apartment to make Kumar look guilty. Merrick, in fact, probably knows that Kumar is not guilty of the rape; but for Merrick, Kumar, as an Indian—as an uppity Indian—is guilty all the same. There is supposed to be an order in the world, and Kumar's upper-class British accent violates that order, as does Daphne's rejection of Merrick's marriage proposal and her obvious preference for Kumar, which is, for Merrick, both a personal and a cosmic slight. Such matters are further evidence of the moral drift to which he objects.

We also must consider his homosexuality, which appears in a sadistic form in his interrogation of Kumar and in his activities with Indian young men just before he is brutally murdered. Scott, it must be emphasized, is not attacking homosexuality. He himself, as Spurling reports, displayed homosexual tendencies in his youth, and, as Boyer says, there are a number of homosexual characters in the *Quartet* who "understand India, and particularly the reality of imperial rule, far better than the heterosexual characters do."[38] Similarly, most of the characters who question the British role in India are female: Lady Manners, Daphne, Edwina Crane, Sarah and Mabel Layton, and Barbie.[39] In both cases, the women and the homosexuals, we see that those who are powerless understand and sympathize with the powerlessness of an oppressed nation. For Merrick, however, the case is somewhat different. He regards homosexuality as a perversion, as he demonstrates in his treatment of Lance-Corporal Pinker. It is a violation of the rigid order of the world, but it is a violation to which he is prone, which produces possibly a degree of self-disgust but more clearly an even greater degree of rigidity. Rao is correct in pointing out that Merrick, for all his faults, "retains our sympathy because he is a victim of both abnormal ambition and of the English class system"; and it is this sympathy that prevents him from becoming a caricature, even at his most devilish.[40] At the same time, Peter Childs argues that "Scott ensures that Merrick's influence is seen to be symptomatic of the 'dark forces' in the novels and in history."[41] It would be going too far to say that Merrick, like Milton's Satan, is a symbol of Evil, but he is certainly a representative of a "dark force" that informed so much of British behavior in India. Merrick himself would have relished the idea of a force, though he would have denied that it was dark. That force was behind the thinking of General Reid (or Dyer) and of all those men who sought, quite successfully for many years, to impose their wills, their rigid way of seeing the world, on India. It was a force that gradually lost power, resulting, ultimately, in the end of the raj, the subject of Scott's epic novel; but like the background radiation in the universe, it never fully disappeared.

This discussion about forces, dark or otherwise, brings us to one of the most important aspects of the *Quartet*, and incidentally to another area where it is related to *War and Peace*, Scott's view about how history works. We have already seen his attitude toward history as an academic subject, but now we must consider history as a phenomenon. The subject is important not only because Scott raises it to prominence in his text, but also because history is an integral part of the epic, which always deals with historical events. This is not to deny that other literature, even novels that we do not classify as historical novels, have historical dimensions. If we read Jane Austen, for instance, we need to know obvious things about how life was lived in Austen's time. To understand *Pride and Prejudice*, we need to know about the Napoleonic wars and we should certainly realize that so much of the wealth that appears in her novels originated in British colonialism. But historical events are not the subjects of her novels. She does not treat anything like the fall of Troy or the Geats, the founding of Rome, the Fall, or the end of the raj. Scott not only describes historical events, but he forces us to consider what history means, how it operates, in a larger context.

Scott achieves this effect in at least two major ways. First, of course, he expands the apparent time covered by his work. The *Quartet* ostensibly covers events from 1942 to 1947, but Scott's frequent references to both earlier and later events make us see those five years, pivotal though they are, as part of a continuum. Both England and India existed independently, came together, then separated but continued to exist. The *Quartet* examines the separation, but it can only do so in light of earlier and later history. Scott emphasizes this point by incorporating important dates into his text. Mabel Layton dies on 6 June 1944, for example, and Barbie Batchelor dies on 6 August 1945. Both D-Day and the bombing of Hiroshima, though not directly involved with the end of the raj, help to provide a context for the events in India.

The second way in which Scott focuses the reader's attention on history as a phenomenon is by discussing it frequently, or, more precisely, by having his characters discuss it, especially by having them discuss Ralph Waldo Emerson's views of history. He does so by what sounds like a cheap novelistic trick, although it works very well. Barbie goes to the library and picks up the wrong book, a collection of Emerson's essays. She reads the essays, finds them to her liking, and often thinks about them; other characters find the book and eventually several of them refer to Emerson, while Guy, as a historian, already knows his Emerson and also takes part in these discussions. The Emersonian passage that most critics have dealt with is Barbie's favorite: "Man is explicable by nothing less than all his history" (*T* 67). Barbie takes this line seriously and, as she descends into madness, obsessively. After Mabel's death, when she is forced to leave Rose Cottage, she begins to view her trunk, filled with memorials to her past, as her history; and it becomes increasingly important and oppressive to her, until finally she loads it onto a tonga and tries to descend a hill with it. Its weight sends the tonga out of control and it crashes, killing the horse, injuring Barbie, and driving her over the edge into madness. Scott has created here a relatively simple allegory. Barbie, like her acquaintance Edwina Crane, whose story opens the *Quartet*, has devoted her life to an ideal that has proved to be anything but an ideal. In fact, it has been a waste, a fraud. The Indian children whom they were supposedly serving did not need what they were offering; but Barbie and Edwina, having bought into the raj, have persisted with the charade. Edwina kills herself with fire, in the manner of a traditional Indian widow, having recognized that the raj, the system to which she had wed herself, is dead. And Barbie is driven to madness by her past. Both are pathetic, if not tragic, symbols of what the whole imperialistic system has done not only to the colonized but also to the colonizers. Scott's use of Emerson in this way increases our awareness of the importance of history, the burden of history, for all of the characters.

There is, however, another passage from Emerson that comes up a number of times and that is perhaps even more important: "Society is a wave. The wave moves onward, but the water of which it is composed does not. The same particle does not rise from the valley to the ridge. Its unity is only phenomenal. The persons who make up a nation today, next year die, and their experience with them" (*T* 194). This is a wonderful passage that explains a great deal about the function of history in the *Quartet*. Perhaps I can show how it does so by beginning with an analogy. Mozart's Jupiter Symphony is a work of incredible genius. It is still frequently performed, listened to, and enjoyed. But if someone like Mozart were to write a symphony like the Jupiter today, no matter how good it might be, that person would be regarded with suspicion. The time for writing such music has passed, and today composers write differently. Mozart expressed his genius through the medium of eighteenth-century forms and techniques. Had he lived at another time, he would have used the forms and techniques of that time. Why? We might argue that the Jupiter is a work of genius no matter when it was written, but clearly, while we may still like to listen to eighteenth-century music, the time for writing it is gone. Mozart's genius would have emerged in any time, but it would have emerged as an expression of its time. Music is the constant, but it is subject to the action of the wave, of the Zeitgeist, that passes through it.

Society is like that as well. However far we have yet to go to eliminate racism and sexism completely, American society is far less racist and sexist than it was a century ago, not because an individual, a Napoleon, spoke up but because "society is a wave." Rosa Parks, for all her courage, was an expression of her time. (In order not to make this assessment too optimistic, let me add that the wave can move in any direction, not only in the direction that we think of as progressive.) The raj, too, was subject to the wave.

What had seemed fine, noble, and moral even at the beginning of the twentieth century no longer seemed so, even though the material conditions had not changed. The wave, as Emerson indicates, is the energy that moves through the water. The "particles" of water, like the individuals in the society, do not ride the wave; but the wave moves through them. It is one of those scientific phenomena that seems counterintuitive, or as Tolstoy says, "The more we strive to account for [the irrational] events in history, the more irrational and incomprehensible do they become to us."[42]

This "wave theory" is reflected throughout the *Quartet*. Many characters recognize, in one form or another, that the raj has come to its end. They may approve or disapprove of that fact, but they accept it as fact. A few, of course, do not, the Reids and Merricks, who believe not only in their cause but in their own ability to shape that cause. Nevertheless, however much damage such people may do, the wave has passed them by. Barbie sees the truth when she begins to comprehend Mabel Layton's withdrawal from the British society in Pankot:

> The truth could no longer be avoided. [Her withdrawal] had been a criticism of the foundations of the edifice, of the sense of duty which kept alive the senses of pride and loyalty and honour. It drew attention to a situation it was painful to acknowledge; that the god had left the temple, no one knew when, or how, or why. What one was left with were the rites which had once propitiated, once been obligatory but were now meaningless because god was no longer there to receive them. Poor Teddie! His was an end of an expository kind, like a last sacrificial attempt to recall godly favour. If there was still a glow to be had it would have spread from there, but it did not. Nor did it spread from the action of the man Merrick, as an earlier victim of changed circumstances, of the general loss of confidence, the grave shifting of the ground beneath one's feet as the layers of authoritarian support above one's head thinned and those of hostile spirits thickened. (*T* 255)

This long quotation illustrates Emerson's, and Scott's, wave theory. The metaphoric "shifting of the ground beneath one's feet" expresses it perfectly, if we can think of a very slow earthquake sending its waves through the earth. All the changes described in this paragraph are gradual, so gradual that no one notices them happening. People can only notice that they have happened. The "god" has not suddenly stalked out of the temple. No one saw him go, but he is no longer there. Teddie's suicidal act of paternalistic heroism is based on the concept of man-bap—I am your father and your mother. Teddie does not know, cannot grasp, that the situation has changed, that Indians no longer regard the British as their "fathers-mothers." There was not a single moment when the concept changed, but the change is undeniable. Merrick's situation is similar, even though he acknowledges Teddie's foolishness. His conception of the white man's role in India is Kipling's, but Kipling is dead. The British have to cover up Merrick's misdeeds—and virtually everyone in authority knows that they are misdeeds—but those misdeeds are not lionized. Merrick is no one's hero. He may be good at what he does, which is why Count Bronowski cynically hires him to reform the Mirat Police Department, but generally what he does is no longer viewed as desirable. The raj was built on illusions, and that foundation has been revealed to be insubstantial. There is a sadness to the revelation—to the recognition of self-deception based on greed, to the coming to an end of something that for so long was considered fine and noble—which explains the *Quartet*'s elegiac tone, but the wave is inexorable. The raj not only must end, it is in the process of ending.

Not everyone, however, accepts Emerson's wave theory, and the exceptions are interesting, for they are characters whom the reader likes and trusts, Guy Perron and Sarah Layton. Guy, speaking to Rowan, quotes Emerson on the wave and then says, "Emerson failed to see that there were exceptions. People like you and me" (*D* 207), and he adds, "Society is a wave. The wave moves onward. You and I move along with it. Emerson was writing for the Merricks and Purvises of the world. The ones who get drowned" (*D* 208). Perron is a good person and a likable hero in *A Division of the Spoils*, but he is quite mistaken here. To retain the aquatic imagery, he is like a fish that is unaware of water. Perron clearly does not sympathize with the British role in India, nor does he sympathize with the British reliance on class structure. Consequently, he refuses to become an officer, even though as an officer he might be able to stand in the way of someone like Merrick. Still, his refusal to join the officer class despite not only his entitlement to be in it but also despite the good his intelligence and his morality could do can be excused on the grounds of solidarity with the Other Ranks, an admirable trait. But then, when Merrick "chooses" him, as he "chooses" all his victims, Perron plays his trump card. His aunt back in England has connections that she uses to have him released from the service. His solidarity with the Other Ranks and his refusal to be an officer have always been contingent on conditions not being too bad. When they do become too bad, Perron does what Merrick's other victims could never have done: he withdraws. The wave goes through him as much as it does through anyone else, and his thinking that he is above its power is a sign of just how much he is imbued with it. Merrick tries to stop the wave, which is impossible. Perron, in contrast, thinks he is not affected by it, which is equally impossible. Even their names give them away. Merrick tells Edward that "Ronald means the same as Rex or Reginald. It means someone with power who Rules" (*D* 503). That is what Merrick is, or wants to be. Perron, on the other hand, has a wonderfully literary set of names, Guy Lancelot Percival Perron (*D* 38). Lancelot and Percival, along with Guy of Warwick, are romance heroes, individuals who go off on their own adventures. Those adventures may have far wider consequences, but the emphasis is on the self, not on the collective, as it tends to be in epic. Furthermore, despite all their virtues, these romance heroes are all flawed. But also Guy is a guy, one of the people, not one "who Rules."[43] His position is complex, but every decision that he thinks he makes by exercising his free will is directed by the wave. He can opt out of the army, but he cannot escape the effects of the wave.

Somewhat later, Sarah finds Barbie's copy of Emerson: "A quick flip through the pages showed that many of the passages were underlined. I read several of these but found them tiresome and self-righteous" (*D* 382). So much for Emerson. But Sarah, too, despite her kindness and her other good qualities, is unavoidably caught up in the wave, which helps to explain her frequent lack of assertiveness, her willingness to go along with things and so often seem like a victim. She begins to change in the later parts of the *Quartet*, and her letter to Lucy Smalley in *Staying On,* Scott's sequel to the *Quartet*, indicates that she has made progress.

But how can one "make progress" in the face of the wave? The image of society as a wave must also take into account the individuals. In a wave, the individual particles do not move as a result of the wave; but in a real body of water, as Heraclitus knew, the particles are always moving. So, too, in society, and so, too, in a novel that portrays society. When MAK is in prison, he contrasts his perceptions of the British and the Indians: "They act collectively, and so can afford detachment. We react individually, which weakens us. We haven't yet acquired the collective instinct. The English send Kasim to prison. But it is Kasim who goes to prison. The prisoner in the zenana house is a man. But who is his jailer? The jailer is an idea" (*S* 39). MAK's analysis is too simple—at the end of the *Quartet,* as India is being partitioned, the mobs of Muslims and Hindus who slaughter each other are surely behaving as collectives, operating in the service of what might pass as an idea. Nevertheless, MAK's meditation raises an important problem for the *Quartet* and for the epic novel. We can say that in *The Iliad* and *Beowulf,* Hector *is* Troy and Beowulf *is* the Geats in the sense that without these heroes, those civilizations cannot long exist. Similarly, in *The Aeneid,* Aeneas *is* the Romans, who are established on his model. Such heroes are not possible in a modern epic novel that pretends to any kind of verisimilitude. (Such heroes can, however, exist in science fiction epics, which are not held to the same requirements.) How, then, does the individual exist and function in light of the wave theory? Scott himself wrote, "[A] novel is about people, and until you have got the people you haven't, in my opinion, got the novel" (*W* 79). A novel is about people, he says, not about the wave. Of course, as we saw earlier, Scott also said that the novel is "a sequence of images," that the *Quartet* is about the end of the raj as a metaphor to illustrate his view of life, and that he used India "to say something about the littleness of the individual human attempt to make an impression on the world ... in the face of pressures exerted by a collective conscience." If we must ask, in an age of multiple-choice questions, which is the most valid statement about the *Quartet*, the answer is that they all are. The collective does exist and it does influence everyone, but every individual can also try to understand that collective and situate himself or herself in relation to it. Perron, as we saw, is not fully successful at doing so, but he is, after all, a human being and therefore flawed. Nevertheless, the *Quartet* encourages such an approach to the problem. At Susan and Teddie's wedding breakfast, Sarah

> Looked again at the faces in the restaurant—ordinary private faces that seemed constantly to be aware of the need to express something remote, beyond their capacity to imagine—martyrdom in the cause of a power and a responsibility they had not sought individually but had collectively inherited, and the stiffness of a refusal to be intimidated; group expressions arising from group psychology. And yet they were the faces of people whose private consciousness of self was the principal source of their vitality. (*S* 139)

This relation between a public, collective and a private self may be complicated by the requirements of being imperialistic masters, but it is also common to the human situation, a result of our being particles in a universe full of waves. If Merrick, as Childs says, represents a "dark force," it is a force both external and internal, collective and individual, that we have to confront. Childs adds that "for Emerson, the personal and the historical are analogous."[44] So, too, for Scott, who "locates the meaning of public events in the lives and consciousness of single people," just as Tolstoy did.[45] That is how epic novels function, following the lives of individuals as those individuals are swept along in a pivotal historical event.

To return, then, to Isaiah Berlin's fox and hedgehog statement, Tolstoy and Scott both know one big thing, but they can only get at that big thing by considering many things, so many that their vision requires thousands of pages; but everything in those thousands of pages is related to that one big thing. It has long been a tenet of criticism (recently challenged) that a work must be unified, that everything in a work must have a function that contributes to the whole (even if critics disagree about what that contribution may be). In the epic novel, that whole must involve a vision of a society, a nation, a civilization, or even, as in Milton and Dante, the universe. The hedgehog must subsume the fox.

The Raj Quartet, for instance, to repeat the point once more, uses India as a metaphor for Scott's view of the world, and that view has definite moral parameters. We know from Scott's comments, even if it were not totally obvious from his novels, that he had strong views about the moral dimensions of literature. Scott wrote, "Shelley described the poet as the unacknowledged legislator of mankind. Lenin called Tolstoy the mirror of the Russian Revolution. Tolstoy said he was influenced by the work of Charles Dickens. So is it to the author of *Hard Times* that the world owed Joseph Stalin? . . . On the whole I can't help wishing Shelley had kept his mouth shut" (*W* 169–70). Why does Scott wish that Shelley had kept silent? If what he illustrates in the *Quartet* about historical forces and about the infinite number and the unpredictability of individual forces that contribute to historical change is valid, then Stalin is, to some degree, the descendant of Mr. Gradgrind and Mr. McChoakumchild. He is not the inevitable product of *Hard Times*, and we cannot blame Dickens for Stalin; but we may be able to say that Dickens foresaw, in some small way, the possibility of a Stalin. Should Shelley have kept silent? Should—or could—Scott? Not the Scott who wrote, "Nothing is worse for a novel than for the novelist to see all sides of a question and fail to support one. You must commit yourself. . . . Stick your neck out. Your novel will then say something" (*W* 79). Here Scott describes the *Quartet*, which presents the same events from so many different perspectives. It treats all of those perspectives, even those which, like General Reid's, are overtly hateful, with respect and even understanding. Nevertheless, the *Quartet* also takes a clear and definite stand. There is a moral center to the work. Scott does, indeed, commit himself.

Scott's comments on the *Quartet* are often helpful. As Spurling makes clear in her biography, Scott knew he was writing something important. He sacrificed his health and his marriage to the completion of this extraordinary work. Two comments in particular are illustrative of his attitude. "The lasting monument to the perfidy of Albion is, to me, the way we pointed British India towards democracy but preserved through thick and thin the autocracy of the princes . . . feudal islands in a democratic, socialist sea" (*W* 32–33). In these words, Scott deals with a specific historical phenomenon that he treats in some detail in the *Quartet*, with its concern with the princedom of Mirat and the way the British made special arrangements with the princedoms for their own advantage and much to the detriment of India. Like the partition of India and the creation of Pakistan, this strategy was a matter of convenience for the British, who, having seen that their time was finished in India, got out as quickly as they could without trying to clean up the mess they had created, thereby making the mess even messier. But again, this specific historical phenomenon is put to a more universal use. Scott says that he saw India "as the place where the British came to the end of themselves as they were. It was, even more than England was, the scene of the victory of liberal humanism over dying paternal imperialism" (*W* 69). The *Quartet*, as I said earlier, is not ultimately about India. It is about the British in India, what they did there, why they did it, what the Indian experience meant to Britain. In India "the British came to the end of themselves as they were." There is the pivotal historical event, which has both a specific historical reference and a wider, universal resonance. The British withdrawal from India, to an even greater extent than its withdrawal from other areas (Olivia Manning's subject), marked a major change in the way the British regarded themselves as well as a change in the way the British were. Scott may seem a little overoptimistic about "the victory of liberal humanism over dying paternal imperialism," but he was well aware, as his many attacks on Enoch Powell testify, that the victory was incomplete. And he was also aware that liberal humanism had grave flaws. It was liberal humanism, in its rush to get Britain out of India, that made possible the massive slaughters of Muslims and Hindus by each other. That exodus was not a result of sudden, or even gradual enlightenment. Perron's Aunt Charlotte represents all those who voted for liberal humanism on the purely pragmatic basis that "a British presence in India was an economic and administrative burden" (*D* 222). While a majority of the British in India and the British at home recognized that it was time for Britain to leave India, that recognition did not always mark the victory of a philosophical position.

Perron himself has such a position, though as we saw, Perron, too, can be pragmatic as he uses his aunt to get him out of a dangerous and uncomfortable situation; and his frequent references to this hidden advantage by the Wildean term "Bunbury" indicates his lack of recognition of the seriousness of his equivocation. Nevertheless, in regard to the Hindu-Muslim carnage, he says, "I never told Aunt Charlotte that she, as well as I, was responsible for the one-quarter million deaths in the Punjab and elsewhere. But I did once ask her who, in her opinion *was* responsible. She said, '"But that is obvious. The people who attacked and killed each other.' There was no arguing with this, but it confirmed my impression of her historical significance (and mine), of the overwhelming importance of the part that had been played in

British-Indian affairs by the indifference and ignorance of the English at home" (*D* 222). Perron sees himself and Aunt Charlotte, and, by extension, all the British, as responsible for those massacres. Aunt Charlotte, in her pragmatic way, sees the actual perpetrators as responsible, a point that Perron both accepts and dismisses—" There was no arguing with this, but . . ." In fact, both are correct, and here we can see how India does indeed serve as a metaphor for Scott, a metaphor whose historical basis must be taken absolutely seriously but which has ramifications that resonate everywhere. In a world in which society is a wave and individuals are particles, to what extent can we or must we accept responsibility for what happens? If Hutus and Tutsis kill each other in Rwanda, if Albanians and Serbs kill each other in the Balkans, who is responsible? And to pose an even more important question, how do we stop such behavior? Sadly enough, we are asking the same question that Homer asked almost three thousand years ago.

Francine Weinbaum takes a utopian view of the matter when she says that "England's ideal should have ended in the egalitarian union of England and India," but of course "utopia" means "nowhere."[46] For many of the English in the *Quartet*, the ideal is still imperialistic. The Indians are, at best, inefficient and need the British to teach them (even though that education has not worked for two hundred years). Furthermore, there is no obvious reason for the British and the Indians to be together on Indian soil at all. As Dr. Aziz says to Fielding in *A Passage to India*, the British and the Indians can become friends only when the Indians have driven "every blasted Englishmen into the sea."[47] Finally, the "egalitarian union" of England and India is certainly not an Indian ideal.

Of course, Scott's focus is always on the British and on their attitude toward India, and Scott goes into some depth in trying to present and understand that attitude, occasionally in roundabout ways. For example, early in *The Towers of Silence*, an anonymous narrator presents the "standard" British view of Gandhi and his Quit India campaign, his demand, after British India's declaration of war on Japan without any consultation with Indian leaders, that the British leave India immediately. Gandhi, the standard view holds, "obviously expected to make a bargain. Unless you were stupid you did not make bargains with the Japanese but war. Even the liberal American Jew, Roosevelt, had been forced to understand this" (*T* 43). That offhanded, offensive, and inaccurate characterization of Roosevelt exemplifies something about that standard British view, something that we see repeated when we meet Susan Layton's psychiatrist, Captain Samuels, "who was after all a Jew" (*T* 309) and who is referred to several times as "the Jewboy trick cyclist" (*T* 348, 349). It is not only the Indians whom the British regard with suspicion and condescension. They are both literally and metaphorically insular, and they regard anyone who is not like them with suspicion and condescension.

Given such an attitude, it is easy to understand British behavior toward the Indians, summarized so well by the expression "man-bap." Edwina Crane seems like the most inoffensive of women. She cares about the children for whom she is responsible and she cares about the Indians with whom, to whatever limited extent, she interacts. But she, too, reacts negatively to the Quit India movement, which is certainly appropriate for someone in her position. She even takes Gandhi's picture off her wall, a meaningful if futile form of protest. She knows that the Japanese will not treat India any better than Britain has treated it, but her way of putting that idea is significant: if Gandhi "thought that they would be the better masters then she could only assume he was out of his senses" (*JC* 2). Regardless of her kindness or her personal liking for the Indians, she still regards the British as their "masters." It is only later, after Mr. Chaudhuri has sacrificed his life to save hers, urging her to keep driving through the mob by shouting, "Do you only keep promises you make to your own kind?" (*JC* 56) that she stops thinking in terms of masters and underlings. After his death, after the crowd disperses, she goes back to the body. "'It's taken me a long time,' she said, meaning not only Mr. Chaudhuri, 'I'm sorry it was so late'" (*JC* 59). And then, when she regains her health, she sets herself on fire like a traditional Hindu widow. Whose widow is she? Perhaps she is the widow of the ideal of the raj, for that ideal involved bringing "civilization" to India, with the assumption, naturally, that no non-European, non-Christian nation could be civilized.

This theme runs throughout the *Quartet*, helped along by the presence of missionary teachers like Edwina Crane and Barbie Batchelor. Because Christianity is a proseletizing religion, it has often been used, or abused, in the service of imperialism, and so it is in the *Quartet*. One of the best expressions of this point comes in one of Perron's rare visits to church, where he notices the absence of Indians at the service. "In a moment there would be another hymn. I checked the advertised number in the borrowed hymn book. From Greenland's Icy Mountains, From India's coral strand, They call us to deliver, Their land from error's claim" (*D* 326). The British are there to deliver the Indians from error, specifically religious error, but those same Indians are not welcomed into the British churches. Edwina Crane comes to a similar recognition when she hears a group of Indian children singing one of her favorite hymns and she feels "an incongruity, a curious resistance to the idea of subverting these children from worship of their own gods to worship of one she herself had sung to when young but now had no strong faith in" *(JC* 15). She knows that the children are in the church school not because of religious faith, not because Christianity has been properly presented to them. They are there because the school feeds them, and in return for that food they (or their parents) are willing to sing about strange concepts in an alien musical system.

Scott, it should be emphasized, is not attacking Christianity in such passages. He is attacking Christianity when it is used as yet another imperialistic tool. Perhaps the most telling episode involving Christianity happened early in Barbie Batchelor's career, when she discovered one of her pupils giving Jesus "a bright blue complexion because that was the colour of Krishna's face in the picture her parents had at home." After the Krishna episode, she had taken away the blue crayons, and "then the children had no way of coloring the sky" *(T* 9). This episode epitomizes British rule in India. The British have come with the purpose (a rationalization, of course) of civilizing the Indians, but they go about the task by imposing their culture on the Indians, denying the legitimacy of the Indians' own culture, and thereby denying the Indians and themselves any chance of leading natural, normal lives. As we have seen, many characters in the *Quartet* still feel that this way of life is appropriate, while many others, subject to the power of the wave, feel that the time has come for change. Edwina suffers a traumatic change, and the change that Barbie undergoes is only slightly less traumatic.

Barbie is as imbued with British ideology as anyone. Early in the *Quartet,* she considers Daphne Manners' child, the child engendered either by Hari Kumar or by one of the rapists. Barbie shows her "Old Missionary zeal" as she talks about this child not having "been brought to God," by which she means, of course, to *her* God. She thinks about the child having "a heathen name, Parvati (which Barbie remembered because that was the name of Siva's consort), and being dark-skinned into the bargain (so it was said), in witness of the original sin of its conception" (*S* 352). The child has dark skin, naturally, because her father was Indian and her mother British; but if dark skin is the sign "of the original sin of its conception," we must consider the implications for all those millions of dark-skinned Indians. To Barbie's way of thinking—and many others think the way she does—the Indians are visible witnesses to their own sinfulness, their darkness, as opposed to European whiteness, an indelible mark of their spiritual and therefore social status. Such a view, of course, gives the lie to all of the British pretenses about civilizing the Indians. If they are indelibly marked by the color of their skin, they cannot be saved, they cannot be civilized, and the British will have to serve as their fathers and mothers, their masters, forever.

But Barbie changes. As a missionary she was tolerated, but just barely. People who would have ignored her back in England accept her in India because she is one of "us" rather than one of "them." After her retirement, however, she becomes increasingly outcast. She begins to understand what it must be like to be an Indian, a process that undermines her conventional Christian beliefs, until she can say, "Blessed are the insulted and shat upon... For they shall inherit the Kingdom of Heaven, which is currently under offer with vacant possession" (*T* 289). Without knowing it, she has embraced liberation theology, and she continues to express her doubts in conventional theology while embracing a far more radical kind of Christianity. Even a bit earlier she had questioned the kind of love that missionaries had brought to India: "I do not mean pity, I do not mean compassion, I do not mean instruction nor do I mean devotion to the interests either of the child or the institution. Love is what I mean" (*T* 195). What she means is the unconditional, unself-interested love that should be but so often is not the center of religion. She knows that she has never before shown or even felt that love, and though she remains a difficult and meddlesome person, she does begin to feel it now. She shows it, to some extent, in her relationship with Mabel Layton, but she shows it especially in her relationship with Ashok, an Indian orphan whom she accepts on his own terms, whom she loves unconditionally. She may not be good at such love, and she is in the process of losing her mind, but she has come a long distance from her previous way of thinking. In fact, Scott may well be making the point that such unconditional love can come only with insanity. Barbie dies on 6 August 1945, the day of the bombing of Hiroshima, and the last paragraph of *The Towers of Silence* presents one of Scott's few departures from verisimilitude: "They found her thus, eternally alert, in sudden sunshine, her shadow burnt into the wall behind her as if by some distant but terrible fire" (*T* 392). Scott here combines the religious theme that runs through the *Quartet* with a motif from Revelation and the historical event of August 6. This combination of elements, of history, religion, and fiction, is typical of the epic, of its simultaneously specific and general views of history; and Scott's use of religion as an element of power helps to illustrate the British attitude toward India with greater clarity.

The other exemplar of Christian love in the *Quartet* is Sister Ludmila (who was modeled, apparently, on Mother Teresa). Sister Ludmila is not an official member of any church, but she loves and cares for the poor and the downtrodden—and almost everyone thinks that she is crazy.[48]

The target of Scott's analysis, then, is not just the British as they behaved in India. It is the British as a people. Scott is not simply writing a popular historical novel. His work encompasses far more, an analysis of a culture, focusing on a pivotal historical event. Scott looks at every aspect of British life, including the English language, because language, too, is an instrument of power. Duleep Kumar, Hari's father, did everything he could to make himself and especially his son seem British, but even he recognized that the English language "cannot be called truthful because its subtleties are infinite. It is the language of a people who have probably earned their reputation for perfidy and hypocrisy because their language itself is so flexible, so often light-headed with statements which appear to mean one thing one year and quite a different thing the next" (*JC* 198). Ahmed Kasim agrees, as he thinks about the English "who spoke bluntly and could make their most transparent lies look honest as a consequence" (*S* 102). Just as they did with Christianity, the British have imposed their language on the Indians and then manipulated it to their advantage. It becomes part of the imperial power structure, but, for those who see through it, it also becomes a symbol of perfidy. The ability to use language, as well as one's accent in speaking the language, helps to rank people.

Of course, that tendency to use language to signify rank has far-reaching consequences for the *Quartet*. Scott, like Henry Higgins, knows how important accent is. Hari Kumar's upper-class British accent marks him as Merrick's social superior, though his brown skin marks him equally as Merrick's inferior. Such confusion is intolerable to both British and Indian minds, at least to the minds of those who accept the social structure, which is virtually everyone. Very few of the characters state outright the rules that govern the social structure, but everyone knows them and almost everyone obeys them. These rules deal primarily with color and gender, though other factors also complicate the picture.

Merrick is quite explicit about the rules, as he elucidates them for Sarah. The superior qualities are, unsurprisingly, whiteness and maleness. A white man would not be "diminished" by marrying an Indian woman. "He has the dominant role, whatever the colour of his partner's skin," whereas "A dark-skinned man touching a white-skinned woman will always be conscious of the fact that he is—diminishing her. She would be conscious of it too" (*D* 217). Color, then, trumps gender. White men are at the top, with white women following. Darker men, to the extent that anyone sharing Merrick's outlook cares about them, are next, and darker women are at the very bottom. Much of the tragedy in the *Quartet*, as Scott repeatedly indicates, stems from the common acceptance of this scheme. If the scheme were not generally accepted, Daphne Manners' love affair with Hari Kumar would not need to be covered up, he would not have been a suspect, and the real rapists could have been sought; but Daphne knows—and Hari reluctantly agrees—that if she told anyone what had really happened in the Bibighar Gardens, that she and Hari had made love and that she had then been attacked by the rapists, Hari would have been doomed anyhow.

Daphne is quite explicit about this point in a problematic part of her journal:

> I thought that the whole bloody affair of *us* in India had reached flash point. It was bound to because it was based on a violation. Perhaps at one time there was a moral as well as a physical force at work. But the moral thing had gone sour. Has gone sour. Our faces reflect the sourness. The women look worse than the men because consciousness of physical superiority is unnatural to us. A white man in India can feel physically superior without unsexing himself. But what happens to a woman if she tells herself that ninety-nine per cent of the men she sees are not men at all, but creatures of an inferior species whose colour is their main distinguishing mark? What happens when you unsex a nation, treat it like a nation of eunuchs? Because that's what we've done, isn't it? (*JC* 400)

This passage is so problematic because while it questions certain assumptions—Merrick's assumptions about color, for instance—it accepts others. Daphne acknowledges the flaws in using color to determine superiority, but one of her reservations seems to be that doing so allows white women to be superior to Indian men, thereby "unsexing" the men. To Daphne, this situation is as unnatural as Hari Kumar's upper-class accent is to Merrick. Like Merrick, she accepts the concept of a society based on clear, well defined hierarchies. She only objects to defining them by skin color. She has no objection to defining them by gender. She seems to be saying that women, of whatever color, should not be considered superior to men, of whatever color. Otherwise they run the risk of unsexing the men, of making them into eunuchs.

This image of unsexing is interesting, because it intertwines with a number of other images and episodes. We may ask whether the passage we have been considering reflects the thoughts of Daphne Manners or of Paul Scott, since, as we have seen, Scott is a master of presenting a variety of points of view, even those he himself rejects. We could certainly understand Daphne believing in the natural superiority of men, coming, as she does, from a society in which such beliefs were normal. In this case, we might say that Daphne is a more advanced thinker than most of her contemporaries, but she cannot fully escape the beliefs of her society, that there are hierarchies and that men are rightfully in the highest spot. If we can be this sympathetic to Daphne, we ought to be so to Scott as well, because Daphne's "liberalism" in this passage seems to reflect Scott's. *The Raj Quartet* is very sensitively written, but there is one episode that is embarrassing, that seems out of place, or at least outdated. In *The Day of the Scorpion*, after Sarah has visited Merrick in the hospital, she is escorted for a night out by her uncle's protégé Jimmy Clark. Sarah has always had more trouble relating to men than her sister Susan, largely because Sarah is so intelligent and refuses to play the gender games that such relationships so often require. But on this evening, she is vulnerable as a result of fatigue and the mental strain her family has been under and of seeing Merrick so badly injured. And Clark, at least at first, seems to treat her like an intelligent being. Soon, however, it becomes clear that what he wants is a sexual liaison, and Sarah, her defenses weakened, gives in. Today we might be inclined to see sexual harassment or date rape in this episode, and we might even relate it to the rape of Daphne Manners, but Scott treats it quite differently. When Sarah awakens the next morning, she is aware of the "warm quiescence with which her body came back to life and consciousness, flesh to flesh with the body of a man who had penetrated it, liberated it." (*S* 441). And twice, later, she thinks that "she had entered her body's grace" (*D* 443, 458). It seems, then, that Daphne's attitude toward sexual hierarchies coincides with Scott's.

As unfortunate as these passages might be, however, Sarah's experience and its aftermath are important. Daphne is afraid of unsexing the men, and Sarah is brought to sexual awareness, but Sarah also becomes pregnant and has an abortion, which puts her in direct contrast with Daphne, who, despite having been raped, insists on having the baby. Daphne's situation is terribly difficult. Having just made love to Hari and then having been raped, she cannot know whether her baby is a product of love or of violence. Furthermore, whatever it is, the baby will be of mixed race, a class of people who are looked on with favor by neither the British nor the Indians. Nevertheless, Daphne, with the cooperation of her aunt, persists. Out of violence and ugliness, and at the cost of her own life, Daphne produces Parvati, whose charm the Stranger describes. Sarah, on the other hand, may think that "she had entered her body's grace," but the result is abortion and unhappiness. It is only in the sequel to the *Quartet*, in *Staying On*, and only incidentally that we learn that back in England Sarah and Guy have married and produced children.

In fact, sexual relations in India never seem satisfactory. Susan Layton's marriages are strange and strained at best. Her mother, Mildred, has an unfulfilling affair with another officer while her husband is in prison camp. Barbie Batchelor and Edwina Crane are almost defined by their spinsterhood, and Rowan and his wife are unhappy. This inability of the British to form happy, fruitful relationships is emblematic of their existence in India, where they have been anything but happy and fruitful. Boyer quite rightly says, "Throughout the *Quartet*, imperialism's failure is expressed by the motif of thwarted love."[49] Not only have the British unsexed Indian men, they have unsexed themselves.

It is altogether appropriate, then, that the opening and central image of the *Quartet* involves rape, a crime of violence rather than passion. The use of rape as a metaphor for imperialism may seem hackneyed, but Scott uses it extremely well. As was mentioned earlier, Scott claimed that his whole work originated in the image of a running girl, and the whole of *A Jewel in the Crown* (some would say the whole of the *Quartet*) is an attempt to explain why the girl was running. The first paragraph of the *Quartet*, however, is more complex than that image might lead us to think:

> Imagine, then, a flat landscape, dark for the moment, but even so conveying to a girl running in the still deeper shadow cast by the wall of the Bibighar Gardens an idea of immensity, of distance, such as years before Miss Crane had been conscious of standing where a lane ended and cultivation began in a different landscape but also in the alluvial plain between the mountains of the north and the plateau of the south. (*JC* 1)

There is no reason that epics must begin with an imperative, but it is a nice coincidence that Scott's "Imagine" is like Homer's "sing." Homer, however, is addressing the Muse and only indirectly addressing the audience. Scott addresses the audience. He wants that audience to see the image because he wants to convey, in the rest of the work, the significance of that image.

It is important to remember that when Scott began *The Jewel in the Crown*, he had no intention of writing a tetralogy. This single volume was to explain, explore, and expand on that image. It was only later that this first novel grew into the *Quartet*, much the way Wagner found that he had to keep expanding his story, so that *Götterdämmerung* became the *Ring*. Nevertheless, the image that the narrator tells us to imagine, despite what Scott himself may have said, is not the image of a girl running. "Imagine, then, a flat landscape . . . conveying to a girl running . . . an idea of immensity." The girl running is not even part of the image. Rather, we are called on to imagine with her. The image is what she sees. It is a flat landscape, conveying the idea of immensity. It is India that we are to imagine, the site of the story, just as Daphne imagines it. In fact, as we read part seven of *The Jewel in the Crown*, Daphne's journal, we are allowed to fulfill that opening command even further, entering Daphne's mind and sharing her thoughts about India and about the affair that has made her infamous. India, in this image, is a flat landscape, a canvas on which the British and the Indians paint a horrifying picture, a canvas on which the epic writer reproduces salient aspects of that picture, making connections, developing motifs, helping his readers to understand what the depicted events imply for them as historical elements and as elements related to their everyday lives.

Rape is mentioned only in the third paragraph, and there the reference has a wonderful ambiguity:

> This is the story of a rape, of the events that led up to it and followed it and of the place in which it happened. These are the action, the people, and the place; all of which are interrelated but in their totality incommunicable in isolation from the moral continuum of human affairs. (*JC* 1)

Which rape is he talking about? There is the rape of Daphne Manners, that running girl, and there is the rape of India, what he refers to in the next paragraph as the "imperial embrace." A possible problem in seeing one as an analogy for the other is that Daphne is a British girl raped by Indians, whereas the imperial embrace describes India, feminized, being raped by a powerful and brutal Britain. How can such an analogy work?

The analogy works, at least in part, because of what we saw earlier of Scott's concern with individuals and collectives. Daphne is an individual young woman guilty of no crime except that of belonging to an oppressive system. Even though Daphne acts contrary to the rules of that system—she helps Sister Ludmila, she socializes with Hari, she lives with Lady Chatterjee—she can neither change the system nor opt out of it. But because she belongs to that oppressive system, she herself seems to suffer. She is only an individual, politically an insignificant individual, and she cannot help being affected by the forces that control history, the wave. So, too, is it with the imperial embrace. Most of the Indians want Britain out, and few of the British have any ideological motivation to stay, but Britain is more powerful, can exercise control, can insist on the imperial embrace. No individual controls it, but individuals suffer under it. Mildred Layton dislikes the life she is forced to lead as the wife of an officer who is a prisoner of war. She has a belief "that she had been abandoned to cope alone with the problems of a way of life which was under attack from every quarter but in which she had no honourable course but to continue" (*T* 39). She hates everything about her life—she drinks too much, she is having an unsatisfying affair, her daughters disappoint her, she has no affection for her neighbors—but she must keep up that life. She cannot choose not to. She is a victim of inertia, of the wave. So Daphne's rape and the rape of India are both the result of forces over which no one has control.

It does appear that some characters can withdraw from the general situation. Mabel Layton, Sarah's stepgrandmother, is a good example. Mabel has always sympathized with the Indian masses. After General Dyer's massacre of the Indians, he was celebrated but he was also forced to step down from his position. A general collection was taken up to provide him with funds, but Mabel refused to subscribe. Instead, she sent her contribution to the much smaller fund that had been established for General Dyer's victims. Mabel tends to be isolated. She avoids gatherings, has little to do with the social life of Pankot, and spends her time at Rose Cottage tending her roses, the roses that are torn out after her death and replaced by a tennis court. Mabel seems indeed to have opted out of the system, but in fact she has not because she cannot. She still benefits from the position of a British lady in India, and even her roses are somewhat troubling. As beautiful and gentle as they are, they still have a thorn: those roses are not native to India. They must be imported from Britain. For all their beauty, they are yet another British imposition on India, not as offensive as the tennis court, but not indicative of an acceptance of India for itself.

Far more successful at opting out of the system is Lady Manners, Daphne's aunt, who, after Daphne's death in childbirth, persists in raising Parvati. Not only does she raise Parvati, much to the horror of the Anglo-Indian community, but she even puts a birth announcement in the newspaper. The Anglo-Indian community, not knowing what to make of her actions, shuns her. When the Laytons find themselves living near her, only Sarah dares to pay her a visit; and later, when Lady Manners comes to Pankot, she indicates only that she has arrived and that she has left. She has nothing to do with the British, allying herself exclusively with the Indians. And she is instrumental in having Hari removed from prison. In short, Lady Manners makes herself nearly invisible, much to the consternation of her fellow Britishers, the same people who themselves made Hari invisible rather than deal with the implications of what he represented, a dark-skinned Indian who was otherwise as British as themselves. Unable to cope with the possibility that their self-appointed superiority has no basis in reality, they choose to ignore the evidence, while Merrick tries to destroy it. By publishing the birth announcement and by raising Parvati, Lady Manners challenges British assumptions, but she refuses to make Parvati a symbol and instead becomes invisible herself. She challenges the system by stepping out of it.

It is tempting to see Parvati herself as a literary symbol. Benita Parry writes about Parvati, who is of mixed British and Indian parentage, "Perhaps this is Scott's affirmation that whatever the genesis of the raj, whatever its failures and defeats, it did bear fruit which will seed and germinate and be fertile endlessly into the future, an affirmation which many will repudiate and find unacceptable."[50] Would that it were so. When we see Parvati in *The Jewel in the Crown*, she is a happy teenager, but we really know nothing of her fate. We do know that elsewhere in the *Quartet* the lives of mixed race children and adults are not happy, and there is no indication that Parvati's fate will be much different. The *Quartet* focuses on the decline of the raj and the implications of that decline as exemplified in the Hindu-Muslim massacres. That focus makes the work an epic, but it does not look forward to a happy future.

After the completion of the *Quartet*, Scott did write a kind of continuation in the short novel *Staying On*, which is the story of Lucy and Tusker Smalley, two relatively minor characters from the *Quartet* who remained in India after the British withdrawal. Childs compares *Staying On* to a satyr play, commenting that "Scott takes the myths of the raj and his own serious fiction, and leavens them both with ribaldry, bawdy, and farce."[51] *Staying On* is, indeed, a more humorous work than is the *Quartet*, but I do not find it as light and humorous as other readers do. It did win the Booker Prize, but I suspect that it did so as a kind of consolation or a belated recognition of the merits of the *Quartet*. Lucy and Tusker are, despite the elements of farce, pathetic characters, two older people who chose to stay in India but to maintain their British identities. They have never actually reconciled themselves to India, to Indians, or to Indian ways of life; and we learn that their decision to remain was based largely on Tusker's fears over returning to England. When Tusker dies, Lucy is left completely alone, a sad remnant of what had been the raj. They are memorable characters, but they are memorable in much the way that Andromache is memorable in *The Aeneid*, as characters who try to preserve a past that no longer exists.

Many of the other characters in the *Quartet* are memorable as well. Sarah Layton is certainly a great character, intelligent, sensitive, and committed; and the revelation in *Staying On* that she and Guy did eventually marry surely fulfills a romantic ideal. Still, neither Sarah nor Guy can be considered the hero of the *Quartet*, nor can Merrick, in spite of his appearance in all four volumes and his developing devilishness, be considered the villain. There are many characters in the *Quartet* who perform heroic deeds—not in the Homeric sense, of course, but in a more modern sense—and there are many whose behavior is villainous; but there is no single hero. These are people living at a particular time in history, subject to a series of codes that prescribe how they should act, doing their best to deal with difficult circumstances. Given Scott's Tolstoyan bent, a single hero would not be possible.

Weinbaum, searching for a hero, says that the hero of the work is "creative, egalitarian love" and the villain is not Merrick but "the force of insularity which victimizes protagonists . . . and antagonists alike."[52] I would not go so far as to specify love as the protagonist, but I agree that in a very important sense, the hero and the villain of the *Quartet* are forces with which the characters must contend. From this perspective, Michael Gorra's argument that the *Quartet* "appears even in its book to provide not a single story but a collection of them, whose unifying principle seems far from clear" is unjustified.[53] As in Tolstoy, all of those smaller elements are subsumed by a single overwhelming factor. We see a clash of historical forces and the people who must live through that clash, who must live their lives in the midst of that clash, who must, somehow, persevere as a new synthesis comes into being. The *Quartet* is unified, as an epic must be unified, by these larger concerns.

It is almost impossible to consider Scott's accomplishments in the *Quartet* without some mention of E. M. Forster's other Anglo-Indian masterpiece, *A Passage to India*, and the contrast is instructive because there are so many obvious similarities between the two works. Both deal with India, both center on a sexual assault (either real or alleged), both examine the relations between the British and the Indians; even so, they are quite different. *A Passage to India* is a novel. Within the context of the British occupation of India, it establishes a community and explores the relationships among members of that community. It does very little to examine the historical background of the community or the historical implications of its story. This latter point is understandable for at least two reasons. First, it was not what Forster wanted to do. He focuses on the characters as characters, as independent beings living, of course, in a historical context but acting quite independently within the limits set by that context. Scott, the epic novelist, focuses more on the characters as subject to those historical forces we have been examining. His characters are vivid, and the reader—at least this reader—cares about them, but not so much from a psychological as a historical perspective. And the second reason for the differences between the novel and the epic-novel is that Forster wrote while the raj still flourished, whereas Scott wrote after its demise. Forster offers an analysis of life in one small corner of the raj; Scott offers a panoramic picture of the raj at the pivotal moment when it came to an end. The experiences of reading these two works, both excellent examples of their kinds, are startlingly different. One, to return to the beginning of this chapter, is the work of a fox, the other the work of a hedgehog. Forster conveys the sense of day-to-day life and its multiplicities, while Scott, like Tolstoy, includes such things when he has to in order to arrive at his one big thing.

That one big thing might best be exemplified by the picture entitled *The Jewel in her Crown*, which initially belongs to Edwina Crane. It showed "the old Queen . . . surrounded by representative figures of her Indian Empire. . . . The Queen was sitting on a golden throne, under a crimson canopy, attended by her temporal and spiritual aides. . . . Above the clouds flew the prayerful figures of the angels who were the benevolent spectators of the scene below. . . . An Indian prince, attended by native servants, was approaching the throne bearing a velvet cushion on which he offered a large and sparkling gem" (*JC* 18). Although Miss Crane has "mixed feelings" about the picture, she uses it to teach English to her students, thereby also imbuing them with the ideology that it represents, whether she agrees with it or not. The picture is mentioned several times in the course of the *Quartet*, but significantly, its last owner is Merrick, who gets it from Barbie. Barbie is willing to give it away, along with all that it represents. For Merrick, however, its ideology still applies, but the last time the picture is mentioned is when Perron sees it in the room of Merrick's stepson. For Perron, it "was the kind of picture whose awfulness gave it a kind of distinction" (*D* 504). *The Raj Quartet* follows the trajectory of opinions toward this picture, from its beginnings as an idealized version of Britain's overlordship to its last appearance as an object distinguished by its awfulness.

Robin Moore presents a comprehensive overview of the early reviews of the *Quartet*, which were, on the whole, not favorable.[54] One reason for such reviews was undoubtedly sensitivity on the part of the British to the unfavorable views of the raj that pervade the work. Another reason, however, probably has something to do with the *Quartet* as an epic. Each volume of the work was published individually; but, as is the case with every work being considered in this study, it would be impossible to get a true sense of the whole work by considering individual volumes. If reviewers were expecting novels, their expectations were bound to be defeated and their critical views were consequently sure to be negative. There were, to be certain, some readers who saw the *Quartet* in a positive light, many of whom have been cited in previous pages; but it was only when the *Quartet* was filmed that many people began to discover its true worth. Of course, it is easier for many people to watch hours of a film than it would be to read over two thousand pages of text, but for readers who are willing to undertake that project, *The Raj Quartet* offers innumerable rewards. And for anyone who is addicted to *War and Peace*, it is especially rewarding. It is not simply *War and Peace* without the snow, but it belongs to the same epic family tree.

5
Edward Whittemore's *Jerusalem Quartet*

AN INTERESTING ASPECT OF THIS STUDY OF TWENTIETH-CENTURY EPIC novels involves how many of them are set in the Middle East, either in Egypt, like *The Alexandria Quartet* and *The Levant Trilogy*, or in Israel, like Edward Whittemore's *Jerusalem Quartet* (much of which, incidentally, is also set in Egypt). A simple explanation for this phenomenon is that these authors lived in the places they describe, but we cannot always tell whether they used these settings because they knew them so well or whether they lived in those places because they thought there was something special about them. Undoubtedly the answer is some combination of those possibilities. Undoubtedly, too, another reason for those settings is that the civilizations of the Middle East offer, by virtue of their recorded antiquity and their continuing centrality in so much of world history, the kind of temporal scope that so often forms part of the epic background. This last reason is certainly true of Edward Whittemore's work.

I

Edward Whittemore, the author of *Quin's Shanghai Circus* and *The Jerusalem Quartet*, is a little-known novelist who deserves to be better known. Thus far, the only critical attention he has received has been in the form of reviews; and the reviewers have not always treated him kindly. In fact, some of them seem to have set out deliberately to misunderstand him, which is an easy thing to do. Part of the reason for this misunderstanding lies in Whittemore's apparent simplicity. Thomas Pynchon, the writer to whom Whittemore is most frequently compared, is so obviously difficult that readers may immediately be willing to grant him some latitude in his treatment of representational reality, though reading Pynchon criticism often seems like reading the results of a mass Rorschach test, which in many ways is just what Pynchon is after. Whittemore, on the other hand, employs a more deceptive style. His syntax, for instance, is seldom as involved as Pynchon's, so that whereas the complexity of Pynchon's surrealism is matched by the complexity of his language, Whittemore's surrealistic complexity is presented in transparent prose. As I hope to demonstrate, this juxtaposition of the simple and the complex is essential to Whittemore's vision.

The reviewers, however, clamor for representational realism. J. D. O'Hara, trying to find the most insulting thing he can think of, says that Whittemore resembles Pynchon more than Borges, and the three separate reviews of Whittemore's novels in the *Times Literary Supplement* show depths of revulsion that one might suppose should be reserved for child molesters.[1] Nonetheless, Whittemore has his following, among whom are Jim Hougan, who reviewed *Jerusalem Poker* in *Harper's*, and Anthony Heilbut, who reviewed *Sinai Tapestry* in *The Nation*.

Because so little attention has been paid to Whittemore's work, I will begin this chapter by considering his first novel, in which his major concerns are already evident. *Quin's Shanghai Circus* joins such works of self-discovery as book 1 of *The Faerie Queene*, as the hero, in this case Quin, an orphan raised by his aunt, tries to learn about his origins, his roots. But this fictional search for roots is more complex and more mysterious than Alex Haley's genealogical search, for Quin's search moves from Boston to Japan to Shanghai, from 1965 to the thirteenth century to the mists of prehistory, to deal not only with Quin's origins but with the origins and implications of the human situation. And much of what Whittemore has to say verges, at least, on the inexpressible. Again, a comparison with Pynchon may be helpful. In his three earliest novels, Pynchon leaves his readers not with answers or assertions but with questions. In *V.*, has Stencil really found a pattern? Does V have an objective, coherent existence? Or has Stencil, in his paranoia, amassed a body of material upon which he has imposed order and pattern? In *The Crying of Lot 49*, is the Trystero real? Or has Oedipa Maas constructed a paranoid network based on random evidence? And is either alternative satisfying? In *Gravity's Rainbow*, is the Second World War nothing more than an elaborate plot to promote rocket construction and international cartels? Who are the "They" of the novel? Do "They" exist? Or is the "They" locution a sign of our paranoia? Is everything connected or is nothing connected? By forcing us to ask these questions, Pynchon forces us to question our notions of reality and fiction, our relationships to the world, our perceptions. Whittemore deals with similar problems, but in a different way, a way that leads him to the inexpressible.

To clarify what I mean by the inexpressible, it is appropriate, especially with a writer as fascinated with religion as Whittemore is, to go back to St. Augustine. Whittemore is not, like Pynchon, concerned with paranoia. Rather, like Augustine, he believes that the patterns we may see are not always based on arbitrary pieces of evidence that our psyches form into a gestalt, but that the patterns are really there if only we can see and understand them. The issue is not paranoia but blindness. Everything is connected. All the strands in the tapestry have their place, but the tapestry is so vast that we are not always able—or we are seldom able—to see the pattern, to perceive order in the apparent chaos that confronts us. We would require a more cosmic view of the universe than we are generally allowed in order to gain such a perception. Attempting to provide this view is part of the function of Whittemore's work. But such a view, with its overtones of divinity, of omniscience, is inexpressible, more to be felt than stated and analyzed.

St. Augustine, too, was concerned with providing a more cosmic view—in his case, specifically, a divine view—of the universe, but he knew that this view transcended literal human language. The divine mysteries, even if the author had encountered them directly through some mystical experience, could not be directly communicated to an audience. Rather the writer had to rely, as did the authors of the biblical texts, according to Augustine, on various figures of speech, especially allegory. As D. W. Robertson says in discussing Augustine's "assertion that the obscurity of Scripture is both pleasant and useful": "The appeal of the Augustinian comparison lies in an intellectual recognition of an abstraction beneath the surface of the language. . . . Much of the figurative material in medieval writing, and, in fact, much of the symbolism in medieval art, was designed to have exactly this kind of appeal; the function of figurative expression was . . . to encourage the observer to seek an abstract pattern of philosophical significance beneath the symbolic configuration. In this respect . . . medieval art is considerably more objective than modern art, even in those instances where it is least 'realistic.'"[2] Such art deals not with representational reality but with ultimate reality, which cannot be described or discussed in a representational way and which in fact must often undercut attempts at representational reality. Thus, when John Skow deprecatingly notes that Whittemore's "scheme for persuading literature to lurch forward is simply to introduce another freakish impossibility whenever reason's vague outline is sighted through the fog," he is quite right, though obviously for the wrong reasons.[3] Whittemore, in trying to illustrate the order in a seemingly chaotic and fragmented world, cannot write an orderly, realistic, nineteenth-century novel. He cannot, for one thing, make the matter that easy for his audience. We can see this point most clearly, perhaps, in his treatment of ritual, both in religion and in the Nō drama.

Whittemore's novels are full of religious matter. *The Jerusalem Quartet*, for instance, focuses on the discovery of the original manuscript of the Bible, the metaphysical status of Jerusalem, and the relationships between religion and sex. *Quin's Shanghai Circus* begins with two epigraphs, one from the *Tao Te Ching* and one from Ephesians; and among its major characters are a Canadian priest who ran a spy network in Japan before the war, a Japanese baron who converted to Judaism and became an Orthodox rabbi (and was killed during a bombing raid as he worked on his translation of the Talmud into Japanese), a drunken American who constantly quotes the Gospel According to Luke, and a Buddhist madam. In addition, there are numerous references to the Japanese tea ceremony and especially to Nō drama. Whittemore's use of Nō is most revealing.

Nō is an ancient Japanese dramatic form that relies heavily on a set of long-established conventions, incuding scenery, which is minimal, costumes, masks, vocal inflections, and gestures. A person who is unfamiliar with the conventions, the rituals, of Nō may enjoy a performance but will have understood almost none of it. To such a viewer, even if he knew Japanese, the whole performance would be absurdly chaotic. The drama requires a knowledgeable audience, often an audience whose members are themselves amateur Nō players. And the drama requires what we in the West might call a considerable amount of suspension of disbelief. As Ishikawa Jun says,

> Spiritual communication between the stage and the audience, based on a similar understanding of artist and beholder, makes unnecessary, for example, scenery depicting landscapes or buildings. The use of minute gestures to express the perturbations of the emotions also becomes unnecessary. A few steps taken on the level boards of the stage may at times take the actor a hundred leagues to distant mountains and shores. A man's and a woman's sleeves brushing each other lightly as petals will at once signify to the audience that their love has been accomplished.[4]

Similarly, Donald Keene notes that "the purpose of Nō is not to divert on the surface but to move profoundly and ultimately, to transcend the particular and touch the very springs of human emotion."[5] Like figurative language for St. Augustine, Nō is a way of getting beyond the ephemeral elements of life, of expressing the inexpressible. Again Keene notes, in reference to Nō and to the tea ceremony, "These arts are all marked by an economy of means used to achieve a maximum effect, a preference for suggestion rather than representation."⁶ This notion resembles Augustine's famous, or infamous, discussion of a figure from the Song of Songs:

> "Thy teeth are as flocks of sheep, that are shorn, which come up from the washing, all with twins, and there is none barren among them." Does one learn anything else besides that which he learns when he hears the same thought expressed in plain words without this similitude? Nevertheless, in a strange way, I contemplate the saints more pleasantly when I envisage them as the teeth of the Church cutting off men from their errors and transferring them to her body after their hardness has been softened as if by being bitten and chewed. . . .
>
> But why it seems sweeter to me than if no such similitude were offered in the divine books, since the thing perceived is the same, is difficult to say and is a problem for another discussion.⁷

Figures of speech, allegories, like the rituals of Nō, while they make great demands on the audience, help to concretize the abstract, to reach out "towards eternity through beauty and the elimination of the temporal and accidental."⁸ They provide means of discovering—not imposing, but discovering—some of the order that underlies the apparent chaos that we see around us. Similes, metaphors, and allegories reveal the hidden connections in the world, while the rituals of Nō distill experience down to the essentials. As Whittemore's narrator says, "So powerful was the discipline of *Nō* that it could contain any emotion no matter how painful, no matter how seemingly unbearable."⁹ This sentence occurs during an extraordinary scene in which Father Lamereaux and Geraty act out a whole afternoon's conversation just by assuming appropriate Nō poses. In fact, when Father Lamereaux realized that Geraty was a devotee of Nō, he was "amazed and delighted . . . for he knew there was now a way for him to help his tormented friend" (87) and "that evening the two actors broke into tears over the unparalleled performance they had staged together that day. Since early morning neither of them had spoken a word. Instead they had communicated through the abrupt, austere attitudes of their arms, their hands, their bodies. Even without masks they had completely understood each other" (88). The rituals of Nō enable Geraty to confess to a theft and allow the priest to offer absolution, both of which expressions would have been unthinkable in any other medium. But this communication also depends on a complete sympathy between actor and audience, and in this particular conversation those roles keep changing. Having achieved such sympathy, having used the rituals to get beyond surface considerations which would otherwise have made this communication impossible, Father Lamereaux teaches Geraty the line from the Gospel According to Luke that he so often repeats, which allows him to become a kind of confessor to other characters and ultimately to reveal to his nephew Quin the secret of his past: Magnificat anima mea Dominum, my soul doth magnify the Lord. By seeing, and occasionally revealing, the hidden springs of life, by seeing enough order to trace even a few strands in the vast tapestry of history, he does indeed magnify the Lord. In a sense, he carries the end of Job to its logical conclusion, for that difficult book teaches that just as God created the natural order, so he has created a moral order; and the discovery of one level of order therefore necessitates the existence of others.

As may be obvious at this point, religion functions in much the same way as Nō in this novel, though religions, like the book of Job, also teach the limitations of human knowledge. Human beings can only hope to see a very few strands of the world order, and the world never stops to allow a closer look. As Taoism teaches, though, the tao "always seems to be in flux, the balance of its forces is forever the same, so that in a larger sense it is unchanging. And it is absolutely indivisible. Since it is indivisible, it follows that it cannot be described in words or even comprehended by thought."[10] How similar this thought is to what we have seen of Nō or to Maimonides' doctrine that God can only be described in negative terms, or to Spenser's conclusion in the Mutabilitie Cantos! But religion, recognizing human limitations, provides a vantage point onto the ineffable and so offers a glimpse of order through its teachings and its rituals, which often themselves contain order in apparent chaos, like the epigraph from the *Tao Te Ching*, which reads, in part, "To remain whole, be twisted. To become straight, let yourself be bent. . . . The Sage . . . does not define himself, therefore he is distinct." There is order behind this kind of teaching, though it differs considerably from the logical, Aristotelian order of the *Summa Theologica*, which, incidentally, Father Lamereaux memorized in his youth, before his move to Japan. This same point is true of the Talmud, which has its own non-Aristotelian logic and order, which attempts to codify almost every aspect of human existence, and which so appeals to the former Baron Kikuchi, now known as Rabbi Lotmann. It, like Nō, like the tao, like Job, leads the believer beyond superficial chaos to a vision of order.

The other side of this problem is presented in the character of Big Gobi, the developmentally delayed orphan who accompanies Quin to Japan. Gobi's world (like that of Faulkner's Benjy) is completely disordered. Not only is he incapable of seeing order but he is almost obsessed by its opposite. He loves oysters, for instance, "because they were shapeless, because they had no hands" (42). He sees them as just globs of protoplasm, his vision the opposite of that of Mama, who is actually his mother, for whom "the oyster had always been a theological symbol, because it was encapsuled and complex, because it resembled the gray jelly of the brain" (148). It is significant, therefore, that Mama is the one who discovers the relationship between Gobi and the desert after which he is named, a "region of sudden sandstorms . . . and terrifying visions. Rivers disappear overnight. . . . A timeless nonexistent land meant to plague the mind with its mirages" (222) There is always the element of the unknown, no matter how clearly we may think that we see things. This trackless, patternless desert, like the shapeless oysters, presents a real threat to humankind, the threat that the whole world may appear to be trackless, patternless, and shapeless. Nevertheless, Mama also learns that "the Gobi was probably one of the original cradles of the race. Where it all began . . . the origin of man" (224). Furthermore, Gobi is the name given to the spy network organized by Father Lamereaux in Japan which ultimately saved Moscow from the chaos of the Nazis and helped to overcome that outbreak of Gobi-like barbarity that we call World War II. Even these various "Gobis" in the novel, symbols of chaos, eventually create a pattern.

Thus, the multiple uses of the name Gobi point to another factor in the novel that is closely related to the problem of order and chaos, the incredible profusion of coincidences. A summary of *Quin's Shanghai Circus* would be so full of coincidences that it would sound absurd, and yet within the context of the novel the coincidences make good sense. Every character has multiple connections with every other character. Quin, Gobi, and Kikuchi-Lotmann, the gangster foster son of Rabbi Lotmann, turn out, for example, to be half brothers. If such a thing were to happen in Pynchon, it would be evidence of a paranoid plot, but in Whittemore's world it is evidence of order, of a reality that transcends the ephemeral and ties together all aspects of human existence. Thus Geraty, who sets the novel's plot in motion, "wants to assure himself that the insane tale told by the stranger on the beach won't end the way it began. He wants to prove to himself that even an account of history as grotesque as that can have some small measure of order behind it" (280). And he does, for many of the characters, including Quin, Mama, Geraty, and Kikuchi-Lotmann, gain a vision of the order behind the grotesqueries of history.

And certainly the reader gains that vision as well. A novel like *Quin's Shanghai Circus* makes great demands on its readers, for the novel becomes an image of itself. As Keene says about the Nō drama *Okina*, "Before the actor makes his entrance he gazes at his masked face in the mirror, and though until that moment an ordinary man—whether an outcast or a nobleman—he himself becomes as he stares at the mask a reflection."[11] Because of the timeless flux of eternity, the novel's story can be told—must be told—with little regard for chronological order. Because all the strands are intertwined in this tapestry and because no strand can be followed from end to end, though there are certain important stopping points, like the thirteenth century, the story must be told not from beginning to end but in a fragmentary way. It is up to the reader, who may see in the novel a reflection of himself or herself, to reconstruct the chronological order. Similarly, the reader must be able to understand, and to discover, the various relationships that exist in the book. Thus the narrator tells us that during Big Gobi's funeral, "the two surviving half-brothers watched the procession." And he goes on:

> Kikuchi-Lotmann knew now that the woman he had described on the highbar in the abandoned warehouse was indeed his mother, but that his father had not been the circus master of that story but of another, one that began on a houseboat in Shanghai when his father and Quin's father had been introduced to each other by the woman they both loved eight years before their deaths, eight years before the circus and Nanking, eight years before the conception of the third half-brother, whose funeral was now being celebrated in the world's largest city, the cause of the black ring around Tokyo twenty years after the end of the war known only to them and the Kannon Buddha and the aging Emperor who had long ago found homes for the sons of Maeve and Mama. (236)

Not only do we have to keep all this history in mind, but we have to reconstruct all the history that we know surrounds it. And even further, we have to decipher the relationships that make Gobi, Quin, and Kikuchi-Lotmann half brothers. We have to realize that Quin is the son of Maeve Geraty and Quin, Sr., that Gobi is the son of Quin, Sr. and Mama, and that Kikuchi-Lotmann is the son of Maeve and Baron Kikuchi, Mama's lover and Rabbi Lotmann's brother. We also have to realize that Baron Kikuchi, while he was Mama's lover, was the head of the Japanese secret police as well as a member of Father Lamereaux's Gobi spy network, that Mama left Gobi with Father Lamereaux for safekeeping, that Maeve was Geraty's sister, making Quin his nephew. The interweaving goes on and on.

The reader's problem here is not like trying to keep the names straight in a Russian novel. It is, rather, a matter of finding the order beyond the apparently chaotic surface of the action, just as Adzhar collects and indexes, with an elaborate system of cross-referencing, a history of Japanese pornography. And the reader is also obligated to laugh, for the novel is hysterically funny, sometimes with black humor but often with a kind of resignation that sees the humorous aspects of our seemingly chaotic existence. And finally, the reader must also confront the problem of mankind's frequent barbarities, including, in this novel, the Japanese rape of Shanghai and the murderous circus that Quin's father stages. And, of course, the greatest circus of all, World War II.

In short, *Quin's Shanghai Circus*, like so many novels, presents a microcosm; and the reader's task in addressing the novel is like Quin's in addressing his world: they both must move beyond the fragmentary, grotesque, superficial, and most easily accessible levels of experience so that they can get a glimpse of the order, of the reality—even in Platonic terms—which is there and which transcends human understanding. Like the Nō actor, the reader may come to think of himself or herself as a reflection of the novel. And like the Nō drama, like the language and rituals of religion, *Quin's Shanghai Circus* will repay the reader who can transcend and dispose of representational reality. With the insights gained from such an experience, the reader might well repeat Geraty's motto, Magnificat anima mea Dominum.

II

Quin's Shanghai Circus does not stand in the same relationship to *The Jerusalem Quartet* as Virgil's *Eclogues* do to *The Aeneid*, but it is an important introduction to the epic nonetheless. Its use of Nō, for instance, presages not only the *Quartet's* focus on the inefficacy of words but also its reversion to mythic elements. In fact, more than any of the other works I have considered, *The Jerusalem Quartet* employs a structure of myth as a foundation for the rest of the epic. The first volume, *Sinai Tapestry* (1977), is largely the story of Plantagenet Strongbow, a deaf giant of a man, who is an expert botanist, an expert on love (and author of a "gigantic thirty-three volume study [of love], the volumes containing some sixty thousand pages of straight exposition and another twenty thousand pages in fine type listing footnotes and allied contortions [*ST* 81]), the secret owner of the Ottoman Empire, and an Arab holy man.[12] Among the other characters are Skanderberg Wallenstein, who flees to the wilderness, like St. Jerome, to forge the oldest known Bible, and Haj Harun, a gentle old man who has lived in Jerusalem for some three thousand years, defending the Holy City, rather unsuccessfully, against all who have attempted to destroy it. In modern terms, such characters might be thought to belong to the world of fantasy, but, though Strongbow and Wallenstein are born in the nineteenth century, they are mythic, larger than life characters whose lives turn into legends.

Their descendants, like Stern, who finally dominates the third volume, *Nile Shadows* (1983), may live in extraordinary conditions and do extraordinary deeds, but they are tied to verisimilitude, whereas Strongbow, Wallenstein, Haj Harun, the baking priest, and others escape the bonds of verisimilitude and lead lives that never could have been lived. One of Whittemore's great accomplishments in the *Quartet* is the way he ties those mythic and actual worlds together; and while each volume has some of both, there is also a clear progression from *Sinai Tapestry* through *Jerusalem Poker* (1978), *Nile Shadows*, and *Jericho Mosaic* (1987) from the mythic to the actual, from the discovery of the real Sinai Bible to the creation of its forgery, from the legendary hypocrisies of Victorian England to the founding of Israel, the Six Days' War, and beyond. This progression, as well as the intertwining, can be seen in the *Quartet's* closing words, when Tajar says to Anna, "And now, dearest Anna . . . isn't it time for us to make our way up the mountain to our mythical city . . . our beautiful and imaginary and oh-so-real Jerusalem?" (*JM* 374). Jerusalem, the focus, after all, of *The Jerusalem Quartet*, is both imaginary and oh-so-real, like the characters in these books, like the events they describe, like the whole world described in the vast panorama that Whittemore has created.

Edward Whittemore, unfortunately, passed away several years ago, but we can see these aspects of his work still active today, as Moslems and Jews clash over the city's status. What city are they really disputing about? There is the physical city of Jerusalem, composed of houses, streets, utility systems, and all the other things that comprise a modern city; and there is the mythic city, the city where Abraham was supposed to sacrifice Isaac, the city that David conquered and in which Solomon built the Temple, the city where Mohammed began his night journey. (And of course it is also the city of the Crucifixion and the Resurrection.) When one walks the streets of Jerusalem, which Jerusalem does one occupy? Can a person occupy only one? Or are the mythic and the real inseparably intertwined?

Whittemore raises the same kinds of questions about the Bible. The Bible is, in itself, a mythic history, but according to the myth that Whittemore creates in *Sinai Tapestry*, the Bible has an even more tenuous existence than that, for when Skanderberg Wallenstein discovers the oldest Bible in the world, he discovers that "it denied every religious truth ever held by anyone" and that its stories "distorted every event that had taken place over three millennia in the Eastern Mediterranean" (*ST* 32). Finally Wallenstein discovers that this original Bible was the product of a "nameless blind beggar chanting whatever came into his head . . . recorded by an imbecile who saw fit to insert a few shadowy thoughts of his own" (*ST* 38). The Bible as we know it, then, is a parody of the Documentary Hypothesis, is a reworking, a reordering, of that chaotic original. Wallenstein cannot stand this notion, and so he forges the earliest known manuscript of the Bible as we know it. Here again, then, we have the mingling of the actual and the mythical. The original Bible is a myth composed of whatever came into the blind beggar's head, but it is also the actual original. The Bible as we know it, containing the mythic history of Judaism and Christianity, really is a myth, an invented work based on that chaotic original. In the context of the *Quartet*, the actual original manuscript becomes the stuff of myth, as several of the characters expend a great deal of effort and money in attempts to locate and possess it.

If this discussion begins to resemble a snake with its tail in its mouth, it does so not only because the word "myth" is used in a number of different though related ways. It does so because that is the picture that Whittemore develops in his epic novel, spanning fifteen hundred pages and several thousand years of human history. Is there order, and therefore purpose, in the universe, or is there chaos, on which we impose order? Perhaps even more important, how can we tell? If we say there is no order, we might simply have missed it; and if we say there is order, we might just have invented it. There is no way for us to know the truth. Like Wallenstein, we might not be able to cope with chaos, but to assuage ourselves, we might be creating a vast forgery. Whittemore's description of the world presented in that manuscript is particularly striking: "an entire fabric of history was woven in magical confusion, threaded in unexpected knots and colored in reverse patterns, the sacred shadows of belief now lengthened or shortened by a constantly revolving sun and shifting moon. . . . Numbing in its disorder and perplexing to the edge of madness. Circular and unchronicled and calmly contradictory, suggesting infinity" (*ST* 34). This is the image of history that runs throughout the *Quartet*. It controls not only the mythic characters like Strongbow and Wallenstein but also the more realistic characters like Bletchley and Yossi, who are so deeply involved in more historically based espionage. It has often been observed that Edmund Spenser's epic romance *The Faerie Queene* resembles a tapestry. Edward Whittemore's *Jerusalem Quartet* depicts a tapestry, but in this case it is a tapestry seen from behind, a tapestry whose front, one presumes, portrays order. But one cannot be certain.

Whittemore explores this problem, this image, throughout the *Quartet*, and he never settles for easy answers, as we can see in his presentation of Strongbowism, the system presented by Strongbow in his thirty-three-volume opus on love, the result of his brief love affair with a gentle Persian girl who died shortly after they met. Whittemore's narrator presents extensive selections from the work, along with his commentary, and he concludes:

> Strongbowism, it was apparent, ranged wide. It could and did attack every sort of person. And it was especially damaging to those who wanted to believe there was some kind of scheme operating in the universe, preferably an imposing or dramatic scheme that could provide an overall explanation for events either through religion or nature, society or the psyche.
>
> Or at least a partial explanation. And if not daily events then events that occurred once in a lifetime. Or once in a century. Or even once in an epoch.
>
> Or at the very least one reassuring explanation for some event somewhere since the beginning of time, some tiny structure no matter how pathetic. For otherwise what did it all mean?
>
> And here Strongbow appeared to be smiling. Exactly the point, he seemed to be saying.
>
> For nowhere in his thirty-three volumes was there to be found even a nascent conspiracy. Not even that. On the contrary, as seen by Strongbow all yearnings for the existence of a conspiracy in life were hopeless illusions from childhood that surfaced later in idle moments. (*ST* 88)

There is no order, no scheme, he says; nor is there, *pace* Pynchon, "even a nascent conspiracy." What is there? In a footnote to volume thirty-two, Strongbow writes that "men and women fuck right along as they always have and always will, paying no particular attention to kingdoms or dynasties, ignoring the universal theorems that are regularly announced over the ages as applicable to all when they aren't." (*ST* 89). According to Strongbow, then, there is no system, no order, although "*man has always wanted to return to the orderly and ordered conditions of the animal state where he once found contentment*" (*ST* 90). The universe is chaotic, and all the systems that we think we see are our attempts to deny that chaos, to seek comfort by pretending that order exists. "Thus Strongbow's thesis was nothing less than a vicious onslaught on the entire rational world of the nineteenth century. . . . In proof . . . he had offered three hundred million words in thirty-three volumes with no deviations from the facts" (*ST* 91). To prove that order and systems do not exist, Strongbow has invented Strongbowism, a system if ever there was one, complete with critical apparatus.

In fact, Strongbowism is like Wallenstein's great forgery, an attempt—an unavoidable attempt—to see order in the chaos, to guess what the tapestry looks like by gazing at its back. Thus, after twelve years of working on his manuscript, Strongbow finds himself unable to complete the work until Haj Harun understands that the author has left himself out of the work by leaving out his relationship with the gentle Persian girl, a relationship that lasted only weeks, until she died of cholera. That event has become the center of his life, and until he acknowledges that centrality, he cannot go on. There is, therefore, an order. What becomes important in *Sinai Tapestry* and continues to be important in the next three volumes is the way in which people order their lives. That order is neither wholly internal nor wholly external. It grows, as we will see, out of the combination of personality and historical occurrence, but it is an essential part of life. Whittemore describes it by using the image of the haj, the pilgrimage.

Pilgrimage is certainly not a new image for human existence, as generations of Chaucerians can testify. Nevertheless, Whittemore uses the image in striking ways. Father Yakouba, for instance, tells Strongbow that he must make a haj, because "we all make one eventually.... And your destination? Jerusalem? Mecca? Perhaps, but it may also be a simpler place you're looking for.... It's the haj itself that's important, so what you want is a long and unhurried journey" (*ST* 50). This use of the image is quite different from Chaucer's medieval Christian use. For a medieval Christian, the journey was surely important, but it was also clearly secondary to the goal, which was heaven. The journey was important only to the extent that it led to that goal. Chaucer's poem concludes with a sermon, with Canterbury in sight. That goal is central; but for Father Yakouba, the journey is central, and each person has to define his or her own journey. In a world in which the possibility of a heaven is less certain, the goal is displaced by the journey. Whereas at one time the goal provided order and meaning, now those elements must be found in the journey.

The journey, of course, can often be misunderstood. Such, for instance, is the case with Joseph Enda Columbkille Kieran Kevin Brendan O'Sullivan Beare, one of the major characters in the first three volumes. Having fought against the British in Ireland and having been forced to flee in disguise as a Poor Clare, Joe ends up—possibly through divine intervention and possibly not—in Jerusalem. That uncertainty about the terms of his arrival is reflected in the novel: to Joe, it is a far-fetched coincidence; but to the baking priest, who rescues him and who obviously has a stake in the divine, Joe's arrival reveals the order in his own life. Why was he a member of the British army? Why did he survive the Charge of the Light Brigade? Finally, with Joe's arrival, the answers are revealed: so that he can install Joe in the veterans' home and give him the Victoria Cross he won in the Crimea. For the baking priest, every part of Joe's story represents "direct intervention" (*ST* 134).

For Joe, naturally, the answer is somewhat different, but later, when he is despondent, he comes to the wrong conclusion. He remembers the baking priest, who bakes loaves of bread in four shapes—the cross, Ireland, Jerusalem, and the Crimea—and he says, "The baking priest has been baking the four boundaries of his life for sixty years, laying out his map, and sure you've got to do that, sure you've got to find the four walls of your own chances and I've done that now, they include me and no one else, just me" (*ST* 224). Through the rest of his time in the *Quartet*, Joe must learn to redirect his journey, his haj, to move it outward from himself. Toward the end of *Jerusalem Poker*, then, as the twenty-year card game for control of the Holy City comes to its conclusion, Joe tells Munk Szondi, "Peace is the treasure, peace to seek, Melchizedek's gentle dream on the mountain" (*JP* 381), and it seems entirely appropriate that at the end of both *Jerusalem Poker* and *Nile Shadows*, Joe is serving as a holy man among the American Indians.

Joe's partners in the game, Cairo Martyr and Munk, also have to redefine their journeys. Cairo wants to avenge "the injustices suffered by Africans over the centuries, historical crimes he intended to repay in full measure" (*JP* 52). By the end of *Jerusalem Poker*, he, too, has redirected his haj. The case of Munk Szondi is somewhat more complicated, however. As it turns out, Munk and Cairo (and Nubar Wallenstein) are related, another instance of a possibly hidden order in the world, but Szondi's dream lives on, for Munk is a passionate Zionist, having learned his Zionism from, of all people, Baron Kikuchi-Rabbi Lotmann, the only character from *Quin's Shanghai Circus* who reappears in the *Quartet*. Rabbi Lotmann's advice to the young Szondi is like Father Yakouba's to Strongbow (which is hardly a coincidence): "Despite the ultimate mystery of the universe there is still one small truth we can live by. Choice. Never merely to take what we are given or inherit, but to choose. It may not seem like much but it's the difference between meanings and memories that disappear in the sand, and something that doesn't" (*JP* 123). Father Yakouba may talk about haj and Rabbi Lotmann about choice, but they are ultimately talking about the same thing, commitment to something important. Again, the universe may seem chaotic or it may actually be chaotic. The metaphysical problem is interesting but need not be solved; and it is Nubar Wallenstein's attempt, through the medium of alchemy and the help of Paracelsus, to solve it that leads to his madness and his death. The universe may or may not have ultimate meaning, but the individual can make a haj or a choice. Quin did. Strongbow, Szondi, Joe, and Cairo Martyr do. So, indeed, do most of the characters in the *Quartet*, but the one that is explored in most depth is that of Stern, because his is the most complex and the most troubling.

Stern, it must be remembered, is Strongbow's son. Strongbow had set out in the guise of an Arab holy man to find the original Sinai Bible (thinking, perhaps, that such a journey was his haj), but in Yemen he met Ya'qub, "an unlettered Yemeni Jew and shepherd" (*ST* 196), who knew that Strongbow had actually reached the end of his haj: "Don't you know that it was written long ago that this hillside in the Yemen would one day be your home? That what you have been seeking so long is the peacefulness of this very tent?" (*ST* 118). Strongbow makes the choice to stay, and Stern is the result of his union with Ya'qub's daughter. It is hardly a coincidence that "Ya'qub" and "Yakouba" are both forms of "Jacob" and that the biblical Jacob was also named Israel, for the combination represented by those names is fundamental to Stern's haj.

Stern, of course, cannot be the kind of character his father is. Strongbow is mythic and becomes a myth even in his own time, as Helen of Troy did in hers. He is, both physically and by reputation, larger than life. His status is much like that of Homer's heroes when Homer tells us that one of them lifted a rock that was so heavy that ten of the poet's contemporaries could not lift it. Those people—Hektor and Akhilleus and Aias—had incredible, mythic physical prowess, but in fact they faced, and were no better than we are at solving, the basic problems of human existence. So, too, with Stern and Strongbow. Stern must face those problems not from a mythical but from a quotidian perspective. The difference between them can be seen in the way they each quit Europe. Strongbow makes his final break with European civilization in a wonderful telegram that he sends to Queen Victoria:

> MADAME, YOU ARE A SMALL AND SMUG MOTHER RULING A SMALL AND SMUG COUNTRY. CERTAINLY GOD MADE YOU BOTH SMALL, BUT WHOM ARE WE TO BLAME FOR THE SMUGNESS?
>
> IT WOULDN'T SURPRISE ME IF YOUR NAME IN THE FUTURE BECAME SYNONYMOUS WITH UGLY CLUTTER AND DARK PONDEROUS FURNITURE AND HIDDEN EVIL THOUGHTS, WITH ARROGANT POMPOSITY AND CHILD PROSTITUTION AND A WHOLE HOST OF OTHER GROSS PERVERSIONS.
>
> IN SHORT, MADAME, YOUR NAME WILL BE USED TO DESIGNATE THE WORST SORT OF SECRET SEXUAL DISEASE, A PRIM HYPOCRISY INCOMPARABLY RANK BENEATH ITS HEAVY LAVENDER SCENT. (*ST* 106–7)

This is the kind of telegram we might like to send, the kind that tells the truth straight out, that shows well-deserved contempt for its recipient. It is also the kind of telegram that we would generally not dare to send, but that a character like Strongbow, who ends up, after all, owning the Ottoman Empire, would.

Stern, on the other hand, is much more ordinary or, we might say, much more realistically depicted. He spends three sterile years studying in Europe before he realizes that he is in the wrong place, doing the wrong things. Neither his plight nor his reaction to it, smashing the things in his apartment, can be as mythically magnificent as Strongbow's, but that failure does not mean that the younger man, the twentieth-century man, cannot make a choice, adapt a haj. It is in this choice that he shows himself to be Strongbow's son, for his choice is heroic, so heroic that it involves him in innumerable contradictions, and finally overwhelms his life: "The vision burst upon him: *A homeland for all the peoples of his heritage.* One nation embracing Arabs and Christians and Jews" (*ST* 209). Such a vision—and the word "vision" is significant here, recalling, as it does, the visions of Israel's prophets—is not only utopian but messianic.

At this point, it is appropriate to consider the meaning of Stern's name. Whittemore never explains the origin of the name. Stern is the son of Strongbow and Ya'qub's daughter, so the name is clearly not a family name. Nevertheless, it is significant. Stern means, in German, star, and in the second century, the leader of the Jewish rebellion against Rome was Simon Bar Kochba, Simon Son of Star. Although it appears that Simon's name was originally Bar Koziba (Son of a Liar), he was called Bar Kochba by those who saw him filling a messianic role in driving out the Romans and restoring Israel to the Jews. Arthur Cohen used this history in his novel *In the Days of Simon Stern*, in which Simon Stern is indeed based on Simon Bar Kochba; and Whittemore is doing something similar here. In *Jerusalem Poker*, Haj Harun identifies Munk Szondi as Bar Cocheba (Whittemore's own spelling of the name). Munk, like Stern, dreams of founding a country in the Holy Land, though his plan is more strictly Zionist than is Stern's (*JP* 104–5). Though Stern is not so overtly a messianic figure, his dream does have messianic overtones. At the same time, Stern's name and his association with the establishment of a homeland in the Middle East recall the Stern Gang, an infamous and peculiar organization in the history of Israel's establishment. The Stern Gang, led by Avraham Stern, were so anti-British—the British having control over Palestine at the time—that they were willing to deal with the Germans. Whittemore uses this history as well: in *Nile Shadows*, it looks as though Stern has had nefarious dealings with the Nazis. So much does this seem to be the case that even Joe, Stern's closest friend (to the extent that either Joe or Stern can have friends), believes it. Stern, then, at least for a time, seems to have become so fanatical that he resembles Bar Kochba (whom some sources treat as a fanatic) or the members of the Stern Gang (who were certainly fanatics). Of course, nothing in Whittemore is that simple. What appears to be the case almost never is.

III

Stern, in fact, is the central figure of Whittemore's epic, although he never appears in the last volume; and there is, indeed, a pivotal historical event that resonates throughout Stern's life and throughout the twentieth century. *The Jerusalem Quartet* is saturated with history, from the writing of the Bible to the Six Days' War; and a number of historical events are central to the story, events from the early history of Jerusalem, the Irish Uprising, World War I, World War II (especially Rommel's North Africa campaign), the founding of Israel, and subsequent wars in the Middle East. Nevertheless, there is a single event that, like Wallace Stevens's jar, becomes the focus of attention.

This event, strangely enough, is one that is little known or studied in the West, and it involves the war between Greece and Turkey (with reminiscences of the Trojan War). In early September, 1922, the city of Smyrna (or, in Turkish, Izmir) had been held by the Greek army, but later in the month, with the army having abandoned the city, it fell to the Turkish forces of Mustafa Kemal, Ataturk. Here are two contrasting accounts of the events, accounts that appeared almost simultaneously:

> On 9th September the Turks entered Izmir. By the middle of September the Greeks evacuated all Anatolia, thus completing the process of surrender of the *Megali Idea* before the force and determination of the *Misak-i Milli*. This Turkish victory Kemal attributed to the joint efforts of the Turkish people. But its repercussions spread beyond the boundaries of Turkey, throughout the dependent and oppressed countries, which now looked to Kemal for liberation. The Muslims all over the world hailed this Turkish success as "the greatest victory of Islam over Christendom, of the East over the West, of Asia over Europe, and of Nationalist Turkey over Imperialist Britain."[13]

The other account says

> On 8 September Greek headquarters, taking off most of the stores, evacuated Smyrna, which Turkish cavalry entered the following day. On 11 September the Turks massacred many Christians and two days later set fire to the town, destroying all of it except for two or three hundred buildings and the Turkish quarter. Over 25,000 people perished and over 200,000, without food or water, thronged to the shore, crying for help.[14]

These two accounts, in addition to providing the history behind the epic's central event, help to illustrate one of Whittemore's important points. A reader might well ask, "Which of those accounts is accurate?" After all, both were written by British historians about fifty years after the fact and, astoundingly, Sonyel even expresses his "deepest gratitude to Professor D. Dakin, Head of Department of History, Birkbeck College;" and yet their accounts are extraordinarily different.[15] From the chaotic mass of facts and events that comprise history, they have made their selections and have created History. For the winners, the Turks, the capture of Izmir was a great victory, an inspiration to oppressed peoples and a source of pride to millions. For the losers, it was a massacre, an atrocity. Which is accurate? Both are, and therein lies the tragedy. The situation may well remind us of the original Bible manuscript, the arbitrary chanting of a "nameless blind beggar . . . recorded by an imbecile who saw fit to insert a few shadowy thoughts of his own" (*ST* 38). The more orderly Bible, the Bible of our everyday experience, the Bible that Wallenstein forges, resembles, for Whittemore, the accounts of Sonyel and Dakin. It is an attempt to bring order, and every sect, every denomination that has used the Bible to justify its own set of beliefs has gone a step further, attempting, once again, to impose order on what can easily be seen as a chaotic anthology of texts composed over the span of a thousand years or so.

So what really did happen in Smyrna? We may not be able to say, from a global perspective, but we certainly can say from the perspective of *Sinai Tapestry*, in which the events at Smyrna play a key role. Like the terrible scenes of slaughter in Homer, the chapter about Smyrna provides background for everything else in the *Quartet*; and like the Snowden episode in *Catch-22*, it resonates throughout the rest of the novel, even when it is not directly mentioned. It becomes a symbol for the whole of the twentieth century, which may have broken from the hypocrisy of the nineteenth but which developed a horror and a hypocrisy of its own:

> The world of Strongbow and Wallenstein had died in the First World War. It couldn't survive the anonymous machine guns, their world, and the faceless tanks and the skies of poison gas that killed brave men and cowards equally, the strong and the weak all the same, the good and the bad together, so that it no longer mattered who you were, what you were. Yes, their world died and we had to have a new one and we got it, we got our new century in 1918 and Smyrna was its very first act, the prelude to everything. (*ST* 279–80)

Stern, in pursuit of his dream of a homeland for Christians, Jews, and Moslems, has become a gunrunner. At first this undertaking may seem incongruous, but, unfortunately, perhaps, it has a certain historical logic, much like the policy so properly called MAD, mutually assured destruction. Before all of these peoples can feel safe with each other, they need to know not only that they can defend themselves but that they can destroy each other. Clearly this attitude dooms Stern's dream from the start, but Stern is committed to it and cannot see the implications of his activities. And Stern's best gunrunner is Joe, who, since his experience killing British soldiers in Ireland, has foresworn violence. These two unlikely weapons smugglers have come to Smyrna, accompanied by the 3000-year-old Haj Harun, in September of 1922; almost immediately they are caught up in the violence. Their only concern is to escape with their host and his secretary, and ultimately they succeed, though at a price. The price for Sivi, their host, is madness. For them, and perhaps more terribly, the price is a clearer vision of the world, a vision that Haj Harun, thanks to his longevity, appears to have transcended. Thus, when he tells Joe that he had seen Stern once, before the war, Joe asks, "Hold it. Which war would we be talking about? The Mameluke invasion? The Babylonian conquest?" (*ST* 288). Haj Harun, having seen all the wars, recognizes the futility of all of them. He knows that "When you're defending Jerusalem you're always on the losing side" (*ST* 295), but that Jerusalem continues to exist.

Neither Joe nor Stern can share that vision. They are twentieth-century men, trapped in a battle that politically does not concern them, and their only responsibility is to escape. Nevertheless, when Joe tells Stern that he attacked a soldier and took his gun, "Stern looked at him in disgust" (*ST* 288); and when Joe thinks about Stern, he recognizes him as "the bloody fake of an idealist who had been trying to play father confessor to him for the last years when he was smuggling useless rifles to countries that didn't exist and never would" (*ST* 288). The two gunrunners, one a confirmed idealist, the other a lapsed idealist but both working toward that ideal, turn on each other in a moment of actual violence. The tragic irony of the scene is almost overwhelming. While their guns are not being used in this particular confrontation, they have, in the name of peace, been making other such confrontations possible, and they collapse in the crisis.

Whittemore underscores the irony even further by infusing the scene with religious imagery, for Haj Harun has indeed recognized Stern as the being whose flying balloon descended near him in the desert some eight years earlier. Haj Harun has taken Stern for God, who was pleased to grant the old man a vision of himself. Then, as a result of the violence, Haj Harun begins to think of himself as Gabriel, who, Joe mentions, "revealed the Koran to the Prophet" (*ST* 292). And finally, when Joe is attacked by the hysterical secretary, he escapes from her and says simply, "Jaysus," to which Stern replies, "Yes . . . and may it be your first and last time" (*ST* 292). In quick order, in the midst of horrifying violence, we have God, Gabriel, and Jesus, divine beings respectively sacred to the three people that Stern wants to unite. And later, when Smyrna is aflame, "At night the glow of the fires could be seen fifty miles away. During the day the smoke was a vast mountain range that could be seen two hundred miles away" (*ST* 300): a pillar of fire and a cloud of smoke. In the Bible, these elements lead the Ark of the Covenant. In *Sinai Tapestry* they indicate the virtual impossibility of covenants. God, Jesus, and Gabriel can come together symbolically. They cannot, despite Stern's dream, seem to make that union in reality. This is not, it should be noted, the only example of a trinity-like grouping in the *Quartet*. In *Jerusalem Poker*, Nubar, in his mercury-induced delirium, thinks of Strongbow, Stern, and Haj Harun as Father, Son, and Holy Ghost (*JP* 359). Always in the *Quartet* religion is called into doubt and yet lurks in the background. It is consistently rejected and always powerful, either as an active force in the world or as an ordering principle.

Those religious references in the Smyrna chapter are especially telling. Certainly they can be read ironically—amid the slaughter and the mayhem, the presence of the divine is a travesty; the fire and smoke indicate not the presence of the divine over the Ark of the Covenant but the failure of the divine over a burning city. There would be little point, however, in indicating the failure of a transcendent divinity. Those religious references should be read rather differently, as Whittemore demonstrates when he discusses the reaction of other nations to the devastation:

> The English poured scalding water on the swimmers.
> The Italians, anchored much farther out, took on board anyone who could swim that far.
> The French launches coming into the quay took on board anyone who could say in French, no matter how badly, *I'm French, I lost my papers in the fire*. Soon groups of children were huddled around Armenian teachers on the quay learning this magical phrase.
> The captain of an American destroyer turned away children at the quay, shouting *Only Americans*.
> A small Armenian girl from the interior heard the first English words of her life while swimming beside the HMS *Iron Duke*.
> NO NO NO. (*ST* 299–300)

The failure lies not with the divine but with the human, with those who perpetrated the massacre and with those who refused to aid its victims. The religious references stand as symbols that highlight the human failure to live up to human responsibilities. As the American consul in Smyrna is reputed to have said, *"The one impression I brought away from there was utter shame in belonging to the human race"* (*ST* 302).

Of course, not everyone behaved badly. Whittemore also tells the story of Asa Jennings, a Methodist minister who worked at the YMCA and who used a combination of deception and cleverness to raise a fleet with which he rescued fifty-eight thousand refugees, after which the English and American fleets also began an evacuation. Asa Jennings, too, is a symbol of the divine.

If the Smyrna massacre is a pivotal event in the history of the novel—a subject to which we will return—and in the lives of its characters, one brief episode in the massacre becomes absolutely central to Stern's life, and to Joe's as well, and it involves a little girl. Joe sees her first:

> The soft moan, he turned. The fingers were broken, he hadn't seen that before. The hands were smashed and hanging the wrong way, backward. She must have tried to scratch them and they'd beaten her hands with their rifle butts, crushed them on the stones before stabbing her in the chest, stabbing and doing everything else while she was on her back in her black silk dress and her Sunday shoes. (*ST* 298)

Both Stern and Joe know that the little girl will die and that the merciful thing to do would be to kill her, but neither can face the prospect. Finally, after Joe explodes at him, vowing never to take part in killing again, "Stern picked up the knife, Joe watched him do it. He watched him take the little girl by the hair and pull back her head. He saw the thin white neck" (*ST* 299). Stern does the humanitarian thing, but that humanitarian act requires him to kill the girl. We see the same irony that we saw in his running guns to create a peaceable kingdom, but this time the irony is even clearer, so clear that even Stern cannot avoid it. That one act, merciful and terrible simultaneously, reverberates throughout the rest of the *Quartet*, not only when it is explicitly mentioned but even when it is not. When we hear the story for the first time, in *Sinai Tapestry*, Stern is telling it to Maud, almost immediately before his assassination, an episode that becomes the subject of *Nile Shadows*.

Thanks to Whittemore's complex chronological scheme, the Smyrna story is also referred to in *Jerusalem Poker*, before it actually takes place. The novel's omniscient narrator, who throughout the first two volumes foreshadows what will happen, looks ahead to the massacre and its consequences for the characters. It left Stern "a tormented man forever," while for Maud, Smyrna and Jerusalem became the "profane and sacred cities one day to be inextricably entwined in [her] memories" (*JP* 247). The reference to the "profane and sacred cities" might bring to mind St. Augustine's distinction between Rome and Jerusalem, between the city of man and the city of God, between the earthly city of corruption and human failure and the heavenly city of the divine and the ideal. Smyrna and Jerusalem are real cities, but they are also, in accordance with medieval allegorical theory, representations of concepts. Smyrna represents the horror that will not go away; Jerusalem represents the ideal that will not be achieved.

There is one more reference to Stern's killing of the little girl that must be mentioned, this time in *Nile Shadows*. Now Joe, posing as a medicine man on a Hopi reservation, casting spells in Gaelic, recalls the massacre:

> beside Joe, moaning softly, an abandoned little Armenian girl lay ripped and torn and dying in unspeakable pain. . . . Joe unable to touch the knife by his hand and shrieking at Stern in his anger, his pain . . . Stern wild with anguish and violently shaking as he clutched the knife and buried his hand in the little girl's hair and pulled back her head, the tiny throat so white and bare.
>
> . . . the wet knife clattering on the cobblestones and Joe not daring to look up then . . . a night twenty years ago and forever and but a prelude to the century, but a shadow of the far deeper descent into darkness that was yet to come. (*NS* 57–58)

This almost unbearable passage works in at least two ways. In the first, it recalls the *akedah*, the biblical binding of Isaac by Abraham as a prelude to sacrifice. Abraham holds the knife above his son, ready to strike, before a voice from heaven stops him. Usually this story is cited as an example of a test that Abraham passes, showing his unwavering allegiance to God; but another interpretation says that Abraham has failed the test, that he should have refused to sacrifice his son and that he therefore needs to learn the lesson that human sacrifice is unacceptable. Wilfred Owen plays with this idea in his startling poem "The Parable of the Old Man and the Young" when he tells the story of Abraham and concludes

> Behold
> A ram, caught in a thicket by its horns;
> Offer the Ram of Pride instead of him.
> But the old man would not so, but slew his son,
> And half the seed of Europe, one by one.[16]

Stern must kill the little girl to end her suffering, but his doing so is an act that haunts him forever, that destroys his dream, that helps turn him into a morphine addict in his attempt to blunt the horrors of the world.

What Whittemore does so skillfully, however, is to transform this act of individual horror into a symbol of the century. It was "but a shadow of the far deeper descent into darkness that was yet to come." Thus, back at the first mention of the incident in *Sinai Tapestry*, after we read of the horror and of the shameful behavior of other nations in not rescuing the victims, we read, "Or as Hitler said a few days before his panzer divisions stormed into Poland to begin a war, *Who after all speaks today of the annihilation of the Armenians? The world believes in success alone*" (*ST* 302). The death of a single little girl, even under such circumstances, may not seem like a pivotal moment, but the death of this little girl comes to represent all the similar deaths in the century, and they are many indeed. Because of the way he treats that little girl's death, Whittemore does not have to focus on the Holocaust, though that mass killing is in many ways central to the *Quartet*. The death of that little girl, in the first of the century's holocausts, both personalizes and typifies the mass slaughters that were to come. Whittemore does refer twice to the Holocaust, once in *Nile Shadows* when Joe mentions Stern's contention that "there are whole communities of Jews disappearing in Europe . . . And he says the Allies are doing nothing about it because the evidence isn't conclusive enough for them yet" (*NS* 190), and once in *Jericho Mosaic* when, after the Six Days' War, Tajar thinks bitterly that "the whole world applauds as if history had suddenly reversed the evil of the holocaust, easing everyone's conscience a bit" (*JM* 105). The little girl's death is "but a shadow" of what is to come, a foreshadowing, but it was the deaths of the Armenians, about which no one cared, that allowed Hitler to go even further. That shadow, then, most certainly is a pivotal moment, for the individual characters and for the world. Most of the events that form the direct subject of the *Quartet*, from the hypocritical behaviors of Victorian England through the First World War, the collapse of the Ottoman Empire, the Second World War, and the wars in Israel, center on that little girl. They either lead to that death or they are consequences of what that death represents.

Once again, we must return to a controlling image of the *Quartet*, the tapestry seen from the back. There are connections and coincidences everywhere—characters are related, people appear unexpectedly. We know there is a pattern, a design, to the tapestry. We simply cannot see it. People, individuals, create patterns and then behave as though those patterns were real, but what set Strongbow apart from everyone else was his conscious decision "to enter confusion and not let destiny rest" (*ST* 9). This phrase does not mean that he adopted anarchy. In fact he becomes a world-famous botanist, which means that he is very much involved with detailed classification. The phrase does mean that he tries not to impose a vision on the world, even though, as we saw in the case of Strongbowism, such an imposition cannot be avoided. These statements may sound confused, even self-contradictory. Ordinarily we might, thinking that we see and understand patterns, reject such statements. It is only if we can remember always that what we see is the back of the tapestry that we can understand why these statements can all be accurate. They may be contradictory, but they are, as Whittemore says, "calmly contradictory" (*ST* 34).

The whole structure of the *Quartet* illustrates this principle, but perhaps Joe's son, Bernini, best expresses the underlying reality after he responds to Joe's "Quick, what's five plus eight?" by saying, "Eleven or twelve." As he explains, "At different times, to me different numbers answer better. When I have a feeling about one, I use it," to which Joe answers, "And it strikes me you just might be a poet. . . . In poetry all things skip and slide, just as they do when you're hearing the whispers of the *little people*, and knowing they're behind the wall all right, but not seeing them" (*JP* 393–94). It is not that poetry is imprecise or merely impressionistic. Poetry can express what is otherwise inexpressible; it can try to discern the pattern of the tapestry.

Nile Shadows, too, illustrates the principle. *Sinai Tapestry* begins with Strongbow's childhood and ends with a brief account of Stern's death in a Cairo bar in 1942. *Jerusalem Poker* is concerned with the twenty-year poker game played by Joe, Munk Szondi, and Cairo Martyr for control of Jerusalem. Stern, of course, is part of the story, but his death is not alluded to. *Nile Shadows* begins with a more detailed account of Stern's death, but then the novel explores the background of that death, presenting pattern after pattern to explain what is going on. Toward the end, as the novel increasingly takes on the air of a spy thriller, the overarching pattern has become quite clear, and Joe, who has been brought back to Egypt from the Hopi Reservation ostensibly to save Stern, thinks he understands what his friend has been doing, and a nasty piece of business it is, involving collaboration with the Nazis. But suddenly Joe realizes that he has put the pieces together incorrectly, that the pattern that he thought he saw was an illusion, created both by himself and by others with more nefarious motives; and he tries to save Stern. Thus, at the novel's end, we go through Stern's death scene yet one more time, only this time we have a sense that we truly do understand it, as we may when we replay a scene over and over in our imaginations. We can make some sense out of the "magical confusion" (*ST* 34) that is the back of the tapestry. Nonetheless, all of the loose ends (by which I refer to the loose ends of the story and of the tapestry) are not tied up. The British, of course, fighting against the Nazis, are the good guys; but it is the good guys who try, because of the patterns that they see (or think they see), to kill Joe and do kill Stern, Liffy, and others. It is simply not possible to make sense out of the whole story, to have every detail clearly explained, as might be the case in a typical thriller or a typical Victorian novel. Whittemore's *Quartet*, as absurd as it seems, is too realistic to make that kind of sense, because true verisimilitude would demand a certain level of chaos.

Whittemore develops this point when Joe explains to Cohen why, when we look through the wrong end of a spyglass, the world looks neat and tidy:

> Because small things always look tidy. That's why we try so hard to reduce things and put them in categories and give them labels, so we can pretend we know them and they won't bother us. . . . So we have this little game we play, rather like children lining up their toys on a rainy afternoon and giving each toy a name, and then calling them by these made-up names and telling them what they are and why. . . . And sometimes we pretend we can do that with life, lining up people as it suits us and telling ourselves what they do and calling it history. (*NS* 226–27)

Studying history is like looking through the wrong end of a spyglass. It allows us to categorize, to order, but, as Professors Sonyel and Dakin showed in their analysis of Smyrna, we can look through that spyglass and still see very different things. Poetry, however, which in Philip Sidney's sense would include fiction, operates otherwise. It never lies because it never pretends to tell the truth. It is fiction, but underneath that fiction is a greater truth. Thus Jesus told parables and reprimanded the disciples by saying, "He that hath ears to hear, let him hear" (Mark 4:9). Listen, in other words, to what is beneath the surface. Again, Joe and Bernini clarify this point. Bernini says, "'I thought kings and parliaments and presidents ran countries,'" and Joe says, "'So it seems from afar, but that's only for the sake of appearances, only on the surface of things. In actual fact the *little people* are in charge, always have been and always will be'" (*JP* 391). Of course, Joe's answer, like all answers, is insufficient, because he means something by "the *little people*" that others may not mean, since we all order the world differently. Stern, for instance, makes his first arms shipment on "the first day of 1914 or 5674 or 1292, depending on the prophet quoted" (*ST* 213). There seems to be order, but all orders are constructs. That is not only Stern's story. That is everyone's story.

IV

The reader may have noticed that the last volume of the *Quartet*, *Jericho Mosaic*, has barely been mentioned. There is a reason for that near-omission.

The first three novels, as I have already indicated, form a close unit, centering on a particular theme and focusing on Stern and, to a lesser extent, Joe. *Jericho Mosaic* could, conceivably, be read as a completely independent novel. Of course, Jerusalem is central to this novel, as it is to the others, but there are many independent novels about Jerusalem. Only two characters are carried over from the previous novels. One is Anna, David Cohen's sister, who plays a small but important role in *Nile Shadows*. The other is Bletchley, whose role in *Nile Shadows* is much larger and is related to some of Whittemore's major themes.

In the earlier novel, Bletchley is in charge of England's secret operations in Egypt, but he plays the role of a minor functionary. It takes Joe quite a while before he comprehends Bletchley's importance to the British war effort and to Stern's life, since Stern is so deeply involved in that effort. Once again, then, Joe thinks that he sees order, that he understands what is happening, when the actuality, the real order (to the extent that a real order exists) is very different. Furthermore, as a result of an injury, Bletchley's face is grotesquely distorted, making him unable to produce normal facial gestures. Early in their acquaintance, Joe tends to misunderstand what Bletchley says, because he reads what Bletchley says in conjunction with what appear to be inappropriate physical expressions. Once Joe understands, decodes, what those gestures actually mean, he is able to understand and communicate on deeper levels with Bletchley. It is as though someone said to him, "Those who have eyes, let them see." His ability to decode, to see beneath the superficial (or superfacial) meaning allows him to establish a meaningful relationship with the enigmatic spy.

In *Jericho Mosaic*, the war is over, and Bletchley, now a retired spy who goes by the name of Bell, takes up residence in Jericho, not far from Jerusalem physically, to be sure, but a great distance away culturally and politically, for the historical background of the novel is the history of Israel, from its early days until the early 1980s. This novel adopts a far greater sense of conventional verisimilitude, much greater even than *Nile Shadows*, which has its own share of the fantastic. In this sense, *Jericho Mosaic* is a much more traditional novel. In fact, it represents yet another step from the mythic that we saw in *Sinai Tapestry* and *Jerusalem Poker*. There are no Strongbows and Wallensteins in *Jericho Mosaic*, just ordinary people trying to live their lives. Nevertheless, Whittemore still manages to include mythic elements. Jericho itself is one. Jerusalem, the eponym of the *Quartet*, is clearly a mythic city, layer upon layer of civilization, of sacred history. One of the strange things about Jerusalem's history, however, is how unstrategic the city is. It has no particular natural resources or military value, but people have fought over it for three millennia, and they continue to fight over it. Jericho, however, is even older, a point that is made several times in the novel. It is often considered, rightly or wrongly, the oldest city in the world. It, too, has a significant history, including the biblical myth about its tumbling walls, but it has not been the subject of nearly so much conflict as its near neighbor. In the context of the novel, covering, as it does, the history of Israel, Jerusalem is the city of the Jews and Jericho is the city of the Arabs, so close to each other and yet so distant.

Another mythic element in *Jericho Mosaic* involves characters, particularly Abu Musa, the Moslem Arab, and Moses the Ethiopian Christian. They, along with Bell, form yet another of the *Quartet*'s many trinities. We have already seen the Stern-Joe-Haj Harun grouping in the first two novels, while the mercury-crazed Nubar Wallenstein reflects on a Strongbow-Stern-Haj trinity (*JP* 359), and in the same novel we have the three card players, Joe-Cairo Martyr-Munk Szondi. In *Nile Shadows* we have a Strongbow-Menelik-old Cohen grouping, which is reflected later in the novel in a Stern-Ahmed-young Cohen grouping. These trinities—and I use the word because they are occasionally referred to in terms of the Trinity and because each grouping reflects the kind of religious diversity that underlay Stern's dream—make an important point. They all represent a yoking together of disparate elements. Whether the world is truly chaotic or only appears so from the back of the tapestry, these unlikely groupings, all of them presented as somehow special, demonstrate the power of human choice, taking us back, again, to Rabbi Lotmann's advice to Munk that choice is "the difference between meanings and memories that disappear in the sand, and something that doesn't" (*JP* 123) and, finally, back to the idea of the haj that we must all make.

Naturally, then, *Jericho Mosaic* also has its trinity, Bell-Abu Musa-Moses the Ethiopian, representing three different religions and three different cultures. Like the cardplayers of *Jerusalem Poker*, Abu Musa and Moses the Ethiopian are engaged in an ongoing game, backgammon; but there is something else that ties them together: Musa is the Arabic form of Moses, and both of those names are drawn from the Hebrew "Moshe." Not only do they reflect their Christian and Moslem traditions in both being derived from the Hebraic, but, despite the superficial difference, the two names are the same. Once again, the back of the tapestry differs from the actual pattern on the front, which can only be glimpsed, if it can be glimpsed at all, with great difficulty. Furthermore, the connotations of the names are significant, for it was Moshe who, by transmitting the Torah, gave its central text to Judaism, from which sprang Christianity and Islam. Whether Moses was a historical figure or not, he has taken on a mythic dimension, which is brought to this seemingly historical novel by his two namesakes.

These themes, the whole complex of ideas related to the tapestry, along with the coexistence of the mundane and the mythic, have run through the first three books of the *Quartet*, and they control the fourth as well, for *Jericho Mosaic* is largely the story of Yossi, an Iraqi Jew, now an Israeli, who marries Anna Cohen. But Yossi cannot adapt to ordinary life in Israel and so is recruited by Tajar, yet another spy, for undercover work in Syria. Yossi, of course, is the perfect candidate for the job, since he speaks Arabic and looks like an Arab; and he does the job extremely well for many years. But an interesting thing happens to him during those years. He does not simply change, becoming more sympathetic to the Arabs among whom he lives. Instead, he becomes, in effect, two people, Yossi the Israeli and Halim the Syrian, and he gains the kind of double perspective that is often so difficult for other people to attain. He never betrays Israel, but he also helps Syria. Thus

> when he met with his new Palestinian contacts and talked about their humiliation and anger and their national destiny, their fight for a homeland, his own childhood dreams fired his words with a passion no one could mistake. I know *exactly* how you feel, Halim told them, and the depth of his feelings could not help but make a powerful impression upon his listeners. Indeed, it was the intensity of Halim's vision that set him apart. (*JM* 42)

He does know exactly how they feel, and in his role as Halim, he can give voice to his sympathies. He is not locked into a single perspective. He can be an Israeli patriot and still speak sincerely about Palestinian suffering. (It must be remembered that *Jericho Mosaic* was published in 1987, before such feelings became more common.)

Even more striking is what happens after the Six Days' War, when Yossi "had no choice but to become Halim, a man who was as much a Syrian in his complex way as Ziad" (*JM* 233). After the Six Days' War, which, according to the novel, Yossi helped Israel win, his relation to his two roles changes. No longer is he one man playing two roles, even if those two roles are played sincerely. Now he must *become* Halim, not play at being Halim, but even this shift does not mean that he has abandoned his Israeli identity. Instead, he recognizes that what is best for Syria is also best for Israel, that the opposition between them is based on superficialities and that what they have in common is more fundamental, just as the not-so-obvious relationship between Abu Musa and Moses is more fundamental than the superficial differences. In a novel that has three major characters—Yossi, Tajar, and Bell—who are spies, this theme takes on great significance. What is the true identity of a spy? Is he the person he pretends to be or is he the person pretending to be someone else? Is it possible to tell? Perhaps most important is the notion of pretense. So many of Whittemore's characters, from *Quin's Shanghai Circus* through the *Quartet*, engage in an almost conscious process of self-fashioning, locking themselves into clearly defined roles, roles that then dictate actions. Thus the British and the Irish kill each other (and it is no coincidence that "Yossi" means "Joe"), the Turks and the Greeks and the Armenians kill each other, and the Israelis and the Arabs kill each other, always fruitlessly, never really gaining anything.

The first three books of the *Quartet*, somewhat like the Synoptic Gospels, tell the same story from different but related perspectives, the story, basically, of Plantagenet Strongbow and his son Stern and all the people they come in contact with. *Jericho Mosaic*, like the Gospel According to John, strikes out in a new direction. These books show many of the same concerns, but *Jericho Mosaic* makes them seem more immediate, dealing, as it does, with a conflict that shows no signs of being settled. Jerusalem—"our beautiful and imaginary and oh-so-real Jerusalem" (*JM* 374)—is one of the major foci of the *Quartet*, and we see it in all the permutations of those views, beautiful, imaginary, and real, just as it has existed throughout its long history. But always in the background is that little girl killed in Smyrna, that innocent child who represents the millions of innocents killed during the twentieth century by people who have tried to impose their perspectives on others, who have been incapable of distinguishing the real from the imaginary. The Israeli-Arab wars described in *Jericho Mosaic* are only the latest manifestation of this confusion. As Yossi says, and Anna repeats, "*so seldom do we know the worlds where we walk*" (*JM* 356).

V

I will discuss shortly the more specifically epic aspects of *The Jerusalem Quartet*, but first I should point out that Whittemore himself seemed to think that the *Quartet* belonged to a particular class of literary works, at least judging by his allusions. Some of these allusions, of course, are more pointed than others. For instance, in *Jerusalem Poker* we read, "At the time Nubar was fascinated with bad Albanian poetry as a result of having met a man named Arnauti, a young French national of Albanian descent who had shown him a battered yellow volume of his poems while passing through the country on his way to Alexandria" (216). Who is Arnauti? He is a character from *The Alexandria Quartet*, a poet, and the lover of Justine. We could go even further and suppose that the end of this description contains a critical view of Durrell himself: "The poems were grossly sentimental, but they had beguiled Nubar and he was now writing poems himself, imitating Arnauti by cramming his verses with the names of rare minerals and semiprecious stones, a device Arnauti had developed to make commonplace colors seem exotic" (216). Durrell certainly made his language sound exotic, though we might not concur with the overall judgment of his work. Whether we do or not, the name Arnauti in this context hardly seems accidental, especially when we consider a passage two pages later: "Accordingly, the next morning, he donned his white duster and racing goggles and set off through the mountains in his Hispano-Suiza." (*JP* 218–19). Again, it hardly seems coincidental that in *The Levant Trilogy*, Yakimov's car is an Hispano-Suiza. Whittemore apparently recognized his quartet's kinship with these other works. Similarly, Joe's question in *Nile Shadows*—"'What can I tell you about Ahmad or the Hotel Babylon or the music of time?'" (147) is a clear reference to Anthony Powell's *A Dance to the Music of Time*.

But Whittemore includes allusions not only to contemporary epic novels. There are also plentiful allusions to older works that are generally accepted as epics. Thus, one of Nubar's agents, writing from the Dead Sea, refers to "*the shores of what has been referred to, in an important piece of literature, as* the dried cunt of the world" (*JP* 330). *Ulysses* is one of the more generally accepted epics of the twentieth century, and Whittemore's reference to it indicates, perhaps, a sense of family resemblance. Nor is this the only reference to Joyce, for in *Nile Shadows*, Liffy (and the name itself is an allusion to *Finnegans Wake*) tells Joe, "I was given intensive training in silence and exile and cunning, and a quick course in forgery with emphasis on forging the uncreated conscience of the race" (68). Liffy is citing Stephen Daedalus's words from Joyce's *Portrait of the Artist as a Young Man*, of course, and Stephen is one of the major characters in *Ulysses*. Similarly, the reference to "this Alexandrian rag" is an allusion to another twentieth-century epic, Eliot's *The Waste Land*.

These references may still be taken as circumstantial evidence that Whittemore thought of his work, like the works of Durrell and Manning, as being related to epic, but there is even more to consider. One of the funniest scenes in *Jerusalem Poker* involves an extended look at the poker game, during which each of the major characters—Joe, Cairo Martyr, and Munk Szondi—slips out of the room and returns in an absolutely transparent disguise; and the three of them proceed to win fortunes from the other characters who are sitting in on the game and who are incapable of seeing through those transparent disguises. The Libyan rug merchant describes his losses: his rugs, his shop, his villas, his wives, his children, his servants, his greyhound, and finally his freedom (*JP* 163). This is a scene straight out of the Indian epic *The Mahabharata*, in which Yudhisthira wagers and loses all that he owns in a famous dice game. His losses include the freedom of himself and his brothers and that of his wife, though it is quickly discovered that he wagered his wife's freedom after he had lost his own and so was not free to make the wager at all. And when the king cancels the whole dice match, one more wager is made that results in the Pandavas being banished to the forest for ten years, just as the Libyan rug merchant is banished to serve as a goatherd.

There is also an important and obvious reference in *Nile Shadows* to the greatest of all medieval epics, *The Divine Comedy*. As Joe and Ahmad enter Ahmad's closet, Ahmad says, "Abandon hope, all ye who enter here. . . . The descent into the underworld begins" (*NS* 166). And if anyone doubts that Whittemore saw himself operating in an epic mode, there are at least two significant references to Homer, one brief and one lengthy. In *Jericho Mosaic*, Tajar, the character who sees more deeply than any of the others, is, as the narrator says, a cripple, having been injured in an accident. "While recuperating, he pursued a childhood dream by teaching himself ancient Greek in order to hear the words of Homer" (*JM* 9). Tajar's vision, in the conflict between Israelis and Arabs is indeed Homeric, as he recognizes the merit of both sides, the need for one to be victorious, and the ultimate senselessness of the conflict. There is also a clear connection between Tajar's love of Homer, his ability to see so clearly, and Whittemore's own powers as an epic novelist, as Joe learns just as he is on the verge of finally understanding what Stern is about and why Stern's life is in great danger. Belle, one of the sisters who helps Joe solve the mystery, says to him

> By chance, we know the name of their first great teller of tales, don't we? Or at least time and tradition have assigned a name to this blind man who would otherwise be anonymous, who must have sat in the dust of some wayside recounting what he had overheard from the din raised by those who passed him by, or what he imagined he had overheard. And curiously enough, since you mention Smyrna, it was that very same ancient Greek city in Asia Minor where this obscure blind man was said to have been born. Blind Homer seeing deeply behind his dead eyes, seeing brilliantly . . . where others passed him by on their journeys, passed him by while imagining they sailed and strived in the clear white light of their days. When in fact he was the one who saw the journey, not them, because he was blind and they had only lived it. (*NS* 290)

Once again, Whittemore returns to his main theme, tying together everything in the tetralogy. When Belle says, "To recite a tale . . . was to speak darkly because the essentials forever lay just beyond the clear light of the mind" (290), she returns us to the idea of the tapestry. We can see the back of the tapestry, not its actual pattern. We tell a tale, and we can sense its essentials even though we can never clearly make them out. Even what she says about Homer exemplifies this point, because, while we have the Homeric poems, Homer himself is a legend, the subject of a tale. Belle says that we know his name, and then she turns that assertion into a question: "don't we?" Then she retreats further, saying that we know the legend, the tradition, of blind Homer who sat in the dust recording stories, just like the blind storyteller who sat in the dust and created the Sinai Bible, the original Bible. And Homer, the epic poet, came from Smyrna, the center of this epic, bringing epic tradition full circle. Other people thought they could see, but only blind Homer (like Sophocles' Oedipus or like Tiresias) could truly see. Others had lived the journey, but living does not necessitate understanding. Homer had seen, and he conveyed his vision in those remarkable poems of his. The blind writer of the Sinai Bible, with his imbecile companion, had seen. And by implication, Edward Whittemore, author of the chaotic epic *The Jerusalem Quartet*, has seen the pattern of the tapestry, or at least the fact that there is a pattern.

Whittemore, then, has tied together Homer, the Bible (which has at least epic components), and his own work, as well as those works that have already been mentioned, *The Mahabharata, The Divine Comedy, Ulysses, The Alexandria Quartet, The Fortunes of War*. Different though they may be in so many respects, these works belong to a family. They meet the qualifications for epic, with their consciousness of pivotal moments and of the relationship between individuals and social history, with their scope, with their larger view that makes them relevant for their immediate time and for an extended time, with their view of the dignity, or the potential dignity, of humankind. They embody truths but their power remains an enigma "untouched by millennia, no less of a truth today and yet no more resolvable than it was then, three thousand years ago" (*NS* 290). Literature—tales—has this mysterious power, a power that will remain mysterious no matter how much theorizing we do about it; and epic uses this power in special ways, ways that Whittemore, through Belle, says allow it to transcend time. The power of epic, whether we read epic from ancient Greece or India, Africa, or Ireland, makes it always relevant, because it is always about a specific historical situation *and* a universal one. It makes no difference whether that little girl in Smyrna died in 1922 or in 1200 BCE. Her story is emblematic of the twentieth century, of a particular historical atrocity, but it is also emblematic of all human atrocity, of our collective human errors on the wrong side of the tapestry. Epic's power is indeed enigmatic, as Belle says several times, thereby commenting on the fictional work in which she appears and simultaneously providing the key to Stern's behavior.

Stern's enigmatic behavior, Joe suddenly realizes, has nothing to do with nefarious deals made with the Nazis. It has to do with Enigma, the German code machine. Stern is one of the few people who know about that machine, and the British, wanting to keep their knowledge about Enigma a secret, are eliminating everyone who shares that knowledge. Thanks to Enigma, Stern's behavior now makes sense, and Joe realizes that the pattern he thought he had seen, implying Stern's guilt, was completely mistaken. One small section of the tapestry has become clear, though it is still an Enigma. (Such wordplay, incidentally, is not out of place in a novel that also makes a link between the Nazi myth of Aryan supremacy and the early Christian Arian heresy.)

The Jerusalem Quartet may well be the last epic novel written in the twentieth century. Many works are described as unjustly neglected, but that description applies perfectly to Whittemore's work, an epic novel that so perfectly captures so many aspects of the twentieth century in the three-thousand-year-old voice of epic. When Yossi thinks back to his youth in the days just before the Israeli War of Independence, he adds, "How pure the dream had seemed to them then, how simple and right and good" (JM 308). But as epic always shows, tying together the personal and the historical, human existence is neither pure nor simple. As in a tapestry, everything is joined together in hidden ways. Epic can bring us close to sensing the essentials of the tale that is human history, and therein lies its greatest value.

6
Lawrence Durrell's *Alexandria Quartet*

THROUGHOUT THIS STUDY, I HAVE DEFINED EPIC AS A WORK THAT FOCUSES on a pivotal moment in the history of a nation or a people utilizing a wide—or cosmic—perspective. To conclude, I will consider a work that only partially meets those criteria but that is, nevertheless, a work of epic scope, Lawrence Durrell's *Alexandria Quartet*. While the Second World War occurs during the course of this tetralogy and is mentioned prominently, no one could argue that the war is the focus in any of the novels. No nation or people is shown being born or declining or facing a political or historical crisis. What, then, makes it an epic and why should it be included in this study?

For the answers to those questions, I will go back some seven hundred years, to Dante. I will not claim that Durrell used Dante's works as a direct model, though I will present evidence that links Durrell to Dante. A more important point, however, is that there is a resemblance—a family resemblance—between Durrell's *Quartet* and Dante's best known works, the *Vita Nuova* and the *Comedy*.

Opinions differ on whether the *Comedy* actually is an epic. Although critics often refer to the poem as an epic, they might be doing so in the offhanded way in which that term is so often used. Ingrid Rowland, for example, refers to the *Comedy* as "the epic poem (completed circa 1321) by a Florentine exile that granted consolation on a cosmic scale for temporal woes."[1] Ernst Robert Curtius, on the other hand, talks about "the literary form which Dante created in his *Commedia*. That form itself can be assigned to no genre. If it is commonly classed as 'epic,' that can be ascribed only to the inanity which thinks that the *Iliad* and *The Forsyte Saga* are to be spoken of in the same breath."[2] This is indeed an odd comment from a great scholar, for if the *Iliad* is the archetypal epic, Curtius seems to be implying that the *Comedy* is no more like it than is *The Forsyte Saga*, a position that is difficult to accept.

In fact, Curtius undercuts that position himself when he points out resemblances between the *Comedy* and Alan of Lille's twelfth-century poem the *Anticlaudianus*, in whose prologue, according to Curtius, "we have the program for a new poetic genre, the philosophical-theological epic. It is distinguished from the scientific or philosophical didactic poem by the fact that the ascent of reason to the 'regions where the pure forms dwell' [Goethe] is accomplished under the guidance of an epic action. Hence Alan is obliged to reject the mythological and historical epic, which was being contemporaneously revived by Joseph of Exeter (*De bello Troiano*) and Walter of Châtillon (*Alexandreis*)."[3] What Curtius means here is that in the twelfth century, concurrent with the rise of medieval romance, there were attempts to revive the classical epic. There were several problems with those attempts, however. One was that the twelfth century had no access to the Greek epics. Readers and writers formed their opinions about the Greek epics from the versions of the Troy story by Dares and Dictys, versions that were closer to Greek romance than they were to the *Iliad*.

The twelfth century did, of course, have access to Virgil and Statius, but that access also involved problems. For one, Virgil was always seen through the lens created by Servius and a host of other commentators who viewed the *Aeneid* as a vast and elaborate allegory of the soul's progress from the City of Man to the City of God. For some readers, actually, such allegorizing would carry great weight and would reduce the poem's battles or the love of Dido and Aeneas to static symbols. For other readers, however, those stories retained their excitement, despite the allegorical baggage. Writers who chose the former path created works like the *De bello Troiano* or the *Alexandreis*, cited by Curtius, that virtually no one reads anymore and that had few successors. Writers who chose the latter path created works like the *Eneas*, a retelling of the *Aeneid* as, to use the subtitle of John Yunck's translation, "A Twelfth-Century French Romance." The *Eneas* is much more closely related to the romances of Chrétien de Troyes than it is to Virgil's poem. As Yunck says, "The romance is fundamentally a narrative of a knight's fulfillment of himself, the realization of his potentialities, the accomplishment of his secular pilgrimage, his achievement of *joi* through love and war—a pattern later to be made familiar in a far more complex and sensitive manner by Chrétien de Troyes."[4]

As Curtius indicates, Alan of Lille chose to write neither an old-fashioned epic, aping the classics, nor a new-fashioned romance. Instead he created "the philosophical-theological epic," the progenitor of what was to be a very small family. Two members of that family are Dante's *Comedy* and Durrell's *Alexandria Quartet*, works that focus not precisely on a single pivotal moment in history but that take, in their own different ways, a cosmic view of the universe, a phrase that is not tautological. Dante literally presents the whole of the universe as it was known in the early fourteenth century; and Durrell, though his use of multiple perspectives and his reliance on an Einsteinian scheme of space and time, achieves something similar, as we will see.

Despite Curtius's objections, Dante himself seems to have considered the *Comedy* in epic terms, for at the beginning of "Purgatory" he invokes his muse:

> Here let death's poetry arise to life,
>   O Muses sacrosanct whose liege I am!
>   And let Calliope rise up and play
> her sweet accompaniment in the same strain
>   that pierced the wretched magpies with the truth
>   of unforgivable presumptuousness.
>
> (1:7–12)

This invocation to Calliope, the muse of epic poetry, reflects Dante's attitude toward the poem's genre. Of course, Dante could have been mistaken, as we saw that Asch was when he subtitled *Kiddush Ha-Shem* "an epic of 1648," but seven centuries of readers have tended to agree with him. The reasons are not hard to find. Dante, in his tour of the universe, deals with some of the fundamental problems of human existence, problems that we might classify as psychological, artistic, historical, and religious. He treats them from multiple perspectives by having a large variety of characters comment on them in hell, purgatory, and heaven. His poem is encyclopedic, noble, and ennobling. It takes the classical epic, represented by Dante's guide Virgil, as it was refracted through thirteen hundred years of pagan and Christian criticism, and gives it a fourteenth-century complexion. Toward the end of "Purgatory," Virgil disappears. The primary reason for his disappearance is that he, as a pagan, cannot go beyond the limits of purgatory; but his disappearance and his replacement by Beatrice may also represent the limitations of the classical epic for Dante and the necessity he feels to go beyond those limitations, to write the monumental Christian epic that is *The Divine Comedy*.

One factor that we must recognize in relating the *Comedy* to the *Quartet* is the primacy of love in both works. Dante, in his letter to Can Grande della Scala (if that letter is authentic), said that the subject of the *Comedy* is "the state of souls after death, pure and simple," which is rather like saying that the subject of *War and Peace* is Russia.[5] The central factor in determining the state of those souls is love, which is also, therefore, the central factor in the *Comedy* as well as in the *Vita Nuova*. That early work shows Dante falling in love with Beatrice, and with other women, without understanding what love means. He treats it, as did his contemporaries, as a matter of physical attraction, as an excuse for philosophical explorations, and as a game played between men and women; but at the end of the *Vita Nuova*, with Beatrice dead and himself confused, he is metaphorically lost in the woods, which is where he literally is at the beginning of the *Comedy*. As he learns through the course of that work, it is love that has rescued him, and it is true love, divine love, that orders both the physical and human universes and that determines the state of souls after death.

What, then, constitutes divine love? The answer goes back to St. Augustine (though he would cite biblical precedents). For Augustine, there is the kind of love that characterizes the City of Man, *cupiditas*, and there is the love that characterizes the City of God, *caritas*. The former is a selfish love. We love things for what they offer to us, whether it be wealth or status or physical pleasure. This kind of love, which obviously is not a real love, is a love for the things of this world. The other kind of love is quite different. In that kind of love, we acknowledge the otherness of the beloved object. We love it either for its own sake or, most properly, for the sake of God who created it. Such love, as we see throughout Dante's "Paradise," is unconditional and completely unselfish. The problem is that it is often difficult to determine which kind of love we see or feel. In Canto V of the "Inferno," for instance, we see Dante speaking to Francesca da Rimini, who describes her love affair with her brother-in-law Paolo. Her story is superficially very romantic and touching, and when she finishes, Dante faints, largely out of pity. He needs to learn that the kind of love Francesca describes is sinful. He needs to see beneath the surface of that superficial love and not be moved by mere sentimentality. He needs to understand that if divine justice has put Francesca and Paolo into hell, they must belong there.

On the other hand, "Paradise," especially the last several cantos, is a paean to divine love. After his lessons in hell and purgatory, Dante the pilgrim understands his love for Beatrice and sees the love that suffuses the universe, indicating that such love shares in and contributes to the unity of the universe. It is only after Dante has been through this experience, after his extraordinary journey, that he can go back and write the *Comedy*. Throughout the poem, Dante, as pilgrim, raises numerous questions with his interlocutors, and he is constantly learning and sharing his learning with his readers. At the poem's end, however, the pilgrim is still trying to understand rationally things that surpass rational understanding, specifically the nature of God:

> As the geometer who tries so hard
>> to square the circle, but cannot discover,
>> think as he may, the principle involved,
> so did I strive with this new mystery:
>> I yearned to know how could our image fit
>> into that circle, how could it conform;
> but my own wings could not take me so high—
>> then a great flash of understanding struck
>> my mind, and suddenly its wish was granted.
> At this point power failed high fantasy
>> but, like a wheel in perfect balance turning,
>> I felt my will and my desire impelled
> by the Love that moves the sun and the other stars.[6]

There can be no rational understanding of God, just as the circle cannot be squared, but Dante can have an experience of God, an epiphany, in which he feels at one with the universe and with the divine will that suffuses the universe with Love. After that epiphany, all the rest of his experiences in hell, purgatory, and heaven make sense and Dante can begin to write the *Comedy*.

The *Comedy* in many ways is the culmination of the Middle Ages. Not only does it deal brilliantly with many of the social, political, and theological questions of the period, but its very structure is significant. Medieval writers were as concerned with structure as writers in any other era, but their interest had its own basis, the medieval concern with seeing and establishing the idea of order in the universe. This concern finds its source in the first chapters of Genesis and it manifests itself in many different ways. Augustine, for instance, concludes his *Confessions*, his spiritual autobiography, with long chapters exploring the Creation story. Medieval ideas about allegory and about hierarchies of all kinds are related to this passion for order. So, too, is Gothic architecture, which viewed the cathedral as an earthly representation of the universe, full of allegorical significances (starting with the cruciform structure), embedded patterns, devices to control the diffusion of light, and, of course, providing a feeling of monumentality.

The *Comedy* is analogous to a cathedral in numerous ways, but perhaps the most striking resemblance lies in its allegorical structure. "Inferno" consists of thirty-four cantos, while "Purgatory" and "Paradise" both have thirty-three, for a total of one hundred. If we see the very first canto as an introduction, however, each of the canticles then has thirty-three cantos. Dante takes advantage of this structure by making connections between corresponding cantos. Thus, a theme that is raised in canto 15 of the "Inferno" might appear again in canto 14 of the "Purgatory" and of the "Paradise." Furthermore, each of the canticles concludes with the same word, "stele," stars. The *Comedy*, then, is a perfect synthesis of its age both in what it says and in how it says it.

So, too is *The Alexandria Quartet*, and for many of the same reasons. Darley, as both author and character, is much like Dante; and their experiences, whose completion allows them to understand both those experiences and themselves and consequently allows them to begin writing, are also similar. But what they have most in common is the subject of love treated on a cosmic scale. What Dante learns about love is truly cosmic: he learns about divine love, the love that medieval Christianity would have seen as holding the universe together. This examination of love is presented in combination with Florentine and European political problems, thereby tying together the human and the divine, attempting to make the human more divine.

Durrell, in his introductory note to *Balthazar*, talks about the *Quartet* in terms of "modern love"—"the central topic of the book is an investigation of modern love." Alan Friedman cleverly uses a quotation from George Meredith's *Modern Love* as an epigraph for one of his chapters, but I suspect that Durrell was not only thinking of Meredith but was contrasting "modern love" to earlier love, perhaps to the kind of purely spiritual, uncarnal love that Dante, as a good medieval, advocated.[7] It is interesting to note how many of Durrell's readers have assumed that Durrell is speaking here of erotic, sexual love—critics are just like men, except that some of those readers have been women! Friedman, for instance, says that by defining his subject as "an investigation of modern love," Durrell "immediately invoked echoes of De Sade, George Meredith, and Kinsey," a trio who beg the question of what "modern" means and who tend to deal more specifically with sex than they do with love.[8] Carl Bode is even more direct when he says that the "central subject of the *Quartet* is sex. . . . In kind the sex ranges from incest to nymphomania."[9] Sex is certainly part of Durrell's exploration, but it is only part, because he is exploring multiple facets of modern love, the whole spectrum, from the carnal to the spiritual, which explains why the range is far wider than "from incest to nymphomania," a range that even limits the carnal and omits the spiritual entirely.

Of course, Dante also explored the carnal: he just put it in hell. Durrell is not particularly concerned with heaven and hell, nor does he necessarily make judgments about the many facets of modern love that he includes. He is exploring modern love in its earthly manifestations but still as a universal, if not a cosmic, force. As he said when he was asked if his claim to be pursuing an "investigation of modern love" was serious, "Yes, it is a serious claim,

I suppose—love as the *point faible* of the human psyche; human and divine love." He went on to say, "The French recognize that love is a form of metaphysical inquiry. The English imagine it has something to do with the plumbing."[10] Durrell, then, is interested in "divine love" and love as "a form of metaphysical inquiry." This notion helps us to understand Durrell's exact words in the introductory note: "The central topic of the book is an investigation of modern love." The central topic is not precisely "modern love." It is an *investigation* of modern love, an investigation that makes progress but remains unfinished at the end of *Clea*. Dante had to find his way out of the woods and back to the path so that he could, among other things, write the *Comedy*. Darley must learn what love means and how to be in love in order to become a writer and a human being. In both cases, the process, the investigation, the metaphysical inquiry, is vital.[11]

Dante, whether he knew it or not—and one supposes he did—wrote at a significant historical juncture, and his work marks simultaneously the culmination and the end of the Middle Ages, at least in Italy. Durrell, too, wrote at a significant historical juncture, and we can be sure that he knew it because he tells us so. Not only was he writing after the Second World War, itself a historical juncture that figures in a number of these twentieth-century epic novels, but more than any of the other authors we have considered, he is aware of the psychological and especially the scientific changes that helped to revolutionize the century. Again, the introductory note to *Balthazar* is revealing:

> *Modern literature offers us no Unities, so I have turned to science and am trying to complete a four-decker novel whose form is based on the relativity proposition.*
>
> *Three sides of space and one of time constitute the soup-mix recipe of a continuum. The four novels follow this pattern.*
>
> *The first three parts, however, are to be deployed spatially (hence the use of "sibling" and not "sequel") and are not linked in serial form. They interlap, interweave, in a purely spatial relation. Time is stayed. The fourth part alone will represent time and be a true sequel.*
>
> *The subject-object relation is so important to relativity that I have tried to turn the novel through both subjective and objective modes.*

Critics may argue about the extent to which Durrell succeeded in writing an Einsteinian novel—it might be argued, for instance, that his three spatial novels are simply collections of various memories that precede the action of *Clea* and are therefore similar to Proust's work—but we must see that Durrell was quite serious in making his claim. We might remember that Dante provided an up-to-date medieval explanation for the shades of light on the moon and that several centuries later Milton offered a very out-of-date explanation for the same phenomenon, but Durrell is one of the few writers who has ever consciously tried to incorporate recent scientific discoveries—pivotal discoveries—in his work. The *Quartet* may share a number of characteristics with Cubist painting, but it is doubtful that the Cubists understood as much about Einsteinian time and space as Durrell did. The Cubists may well embody that scientific revolution, but one of the things that helps make Durrell's work epic is that he both embodies and consciously explores the implications of that revolution, of that critical moment in human history.

Just as Dante, then, synthesizes a medieval view of the universe, so Durrell synthesizes a modern view. J. B. Hainsworth says about the *Comedy*, "It has the vision and function of an epic poem in that it expresses in canonical form the medieval idea of the destiny of the human race, and in that sense it is an epic. It is, however, innocent of the form of an epic poem in the classical tradition; it has no hero, that is, a central figure by or to whom deeds are done, nor is it heroic in any sense."[12] Perhaps we could agree that Dante is the hero, though he is certainly not heroic in any traditional sense; and the same can be said of Darley, who, like Dante, struggles to understand things that can only be felt.

The Alexandria Quartet also shares the *Comedy*'s sense of structure. While almost no other work of literature is as highly structured as the *Comedy*, the *Quartet* does imitate (whether consciously or not) some of Dante's techniques. Dante's poem, of course, is heavily based on numerological allegory, particularly on the number three and on its square, nine. Each canticle, for instance, has those thirty-three cantos (with the introductory canto in the first), and the whole poem is made up of three-line stanzas (Dante's *terza rima*). Durrell's structures are not nearly so elaborate. Nonetheless, in terms of his Einsteinian orientation, we can easily see the first three novels, those "deployed spatially," as representatives of the three dimensions, width, height, and depth. *Justine* presents a developed, complete story, the story of Darley's relationships with Melissa and Justine. Darley himself believes that it is complete when he gives it to Balthazar; but Balthazar replies with the "interlinear," implying that the first volume is one-dimensional. That volume prompts the second volume, supposedly a corrective to Darley's first version of the story. Balthazar's version of events, however, is as one-dimensional as Darley's, though his dimension differs from Darley's: what Balthazar proposes as a correction, as the truth, is just as mistaken as what Darley had written. The third volume, *Mountolive* is very cleverly written from a third-person point of view, thereby giving at least the illusion that what it says is more objective, closer to the reality of what happened, and therefore that it goes into greater depth. And finally *Clea*, which begins after the story has been told three times in the first three volumes, exists in the fourth dimension of time. (A case could also be made, incidentally, that the *Quartet*, like so many epics, begins *in medias res*. Darley is on his island in the present, thinking about all the events that brought him there. He goes back, through memory, in the first two volumes, abetted by the narrator of the third, until the "present" action resumes in the fourth.)

Again, while Durrell's work is not nearly so symmetrical as Dante's, there are clear correspondences among the volumes. For example, each volume begins with a reference to one of the four traditional elements. These references are especially obvious in Darley's three volumes: "The sea is high again today" (*J* 13), "Landscape-tones" (*B* 13), "The oranges . . . glowed in their arbours of burnished green leaf like lanterns, flickering up there among the sunny woods" (*C* 11).[13] Water, earth, fire. The reference to air in *Mountolive* is there, but not as overtly: "the Egyptian night fell—quivering here and there with water-mirages from the rising damps, expanding and contracting horizons, until one thought of the world as being mirrored in a soap-bubble trembling on the edge of disappearance" (*M* 11). This inclusion of the four elements suits well the notion of the *Quartet*'s universality, as it seeks to investigate modern love, a universal phenomenon.

Similarly, each volume includes, near its conclusion, a violent event that seems to happen almost arbitrarily. Toward the end of *Justine*, Capodistria is shot during the duck hunt. (Of course, Capodistria is not really shot, but the reader of *Justine* has no way of knowing the secret.) Toward the end of *Balthazar*, Toto de Brunel is killed during the carnival. *Mountolive* ends with the death and funeral of Narouz. And toward the end of *Clea*, Clea is shot with the harpoon gun and nearly dies. Each of the novels is structured to lead up to those late crescendos, and of course, each reaches a different kind of decrescendo. Nevertheless, as there are in Dante's three canticles, there are correspondences among Durrell's four volumes.

Yet another more specifically epic technique that Durrell uses involves his manipulations of myth and of literary references. Many readers have felt the mythic underpinning of the *Quartet*. Christopher Middleton, for instance, believes that Durrell combined the *Odyssey* and the *Aeneid*, Odysseus and Aeneas, both of whom he says react to Aphrodite.[14] Actually Odysseus does not react to Aphrodite, but Middleton is correct in sensing the presence of mythic elements and in declaring that Durrell explores the "no-man's land [a nice Odyssean touch] between the frontiers of psychology and myth."[15] Similarly, Warren Wedin describes Darley's "final breakthrough" as the realization "that the individual life, with its conglomeration of relative facts and truths, can also have mythic or archetypic significance."[16] And Carol Peirce, in many of her articles on the *Quartet*, shows keen awareness of the mythic elements in Durrell, at one point noting that "Durrell's mystic rose ironically reflects the Dante of the *Paradise*, as Eliot's had the Dante of the *Inferno*."[17] She also calls attention to the way that both "Scobie and Balthazar [both of whom she identifies with Tiresias] belong to the Otherworld of myth existing in and behind the *Quartet* and are guides who give supernatural aid."[18] Durrell, in relying on this mythic substratum, is following established epic tradition. Early epics, like the *Iliad* and the *Mahabharata*, are overtly mythic; and later epics tended to establish their epic identities and cosmic implications by drawing on myth, as Milton does in *Paradise Lost*.

Durrell also makes occasional references to specific epic myths. There are brief references such as this one from *Justine*: "A taxi brayed once in the distance, and from the harbor, like the stifled roar of a minotaur, came a single dark whiff of sound from a siren" (*J* 85). In *Clea*, we learn that Capodistria is living in "a handsomely converted Martello tower" (*C* 73), a phrase that surely recalls the most famous Martello tower in all of literature, the one occupied by Stephen Bloom in *Ulysses*. And later, when Darley is working in the war effort, he refers to "the Homeric Cycle, so to speak, of office life" (156), a wonderful phrase that, in the manner of Joyce, reveals the mythic in the mundane. Durrell also uses longer mythic scenes. In *Balthazar*, for instance, Narouz subdues a wild horse, what the narrator calls a "mythical creature" (*B* 89), in a scene that resembles one of Homer's heroic digressions; and Narouz's funeral at the end of *Mountolive* recalls the elaborate funerals of the *Iliad* or the *Aeneid*.

Similarly, there are numerous oblique references to Dante in the course of the *Quartet*. Some of them are brief, like the mention of the Underworld (*C* 11) or of Paradise (*C* 70), but others are more notable, like Clea's statement, "There are only three things to be done with a woman . . . You can love her, suffer for her, or turn her into literature" (*J* 22). No woman has ever been turned into literature the way Beatrice was (I have often wondered what Dante's wife thought about his obsession) and Darley, writing in ignorance through his first two volumes, seeks to do the same for Justine. He tries to idealize her, and he succeeds in presenting her as a sort of transcendent being, a woman who somehow stands above everyday concerns. Of course, as he later learns, Justine has been using him, using Pursewarden, using virtually everyone with whom she comes in contact for her own goals, however ambiguous those goals might be. Her love is not the *caritas* of a Beatrice but the *cupiditas* of a Francesca. Thus, when Darley sees her again in *Clea*, he finds her pathetic: "The once magnificent image of my love lay now in the hollow of my arm, defenceless as a patient on an operating table.... She had become a woman at last, lying there soiled and tattered.... I could hardly wait to be gone" (*C* 61–62). Dante learns in the course of his journey that Beatrice is divine, that his previous way of thinking about her, as a mortal woman, as an object of his human love, has been incorrect. He must become aware of her divine nature and learn the meaning of divine love. Darley's case is rather different, because, as Durrell says, Darley is part of an investigation of *modern* love. Dante expounds the ideals of medieval love, ideals that Darley tried to imitate in his worship of Justine; but such ideals are no longer relevant. What Darley must learn, and what he eventually does learn, is that Justine is a mortal woman and that his idealization of her was foolish and shortsighted. To put the case somewhat differently, what Darley, like every other man in the *Quartet*, must learn is how to deal with women as real live human beings, not as elements of his fancy, not as Dantean creatures who will bring him salvation.

After Darley's experience with Justine, he is partway to this goal. The next morning, he feels, he says, "like the Adam of the mediaeval legends" (*C* 63). He has become a new man, reborn, as it were. He is like Adam, alone in the Garden of Eden, awaiting, though he does not know it, his Other. By the end of *Clea*, in a movement that we will examine later, he find that Other in Clea herself. The *Quartet*, by examining so many variations on the theme of love and by following Darley through his relationships with Melissa, Justine, and Clea, is indeed an examination of modern love, an examination with a happy ending.

At the same time, the *Quartet* is very much a literary construct that shows an awareness of its literariness. Its very first line has a literary resonance: "The sea is high again today" (*J* 13) immediately calls to mind the opening of Matthew Arnold's "Dover Beach": "The sea is calm tonight." This echo does not occur by accident, for Arnold's poem, especially its last stanza, could serve as an outline for the *Quartet*:

> Ah, love, let us be true
> To one another! for the world, which seems
> To lie before us like a land of dreams,
> So various, so beautiful, so new,
> Hath really neither joy, nor love, nor light,
> Nor certitude, nor peace, nor help for pain;
> And we are here as on a darkling plain
> Swept with confused alarms of struggle and flight,
> Where ignorant armies clash by night.

The love that Arnold describes is not Dantean, not *caritas* in a universe of Christian certainties. It is what two people can give each other in a world of uncertainties, in a world that seeks to crush and destroy, a world in which Scobie can become a Moslem saint or Pombal's mistress can be killed in a freak accident or Clea can be harpooned. It is modern love.

Similarly, and still on the first page of text in *Justine*, Darley says, "At night when the wind roars and the child sleeps quietly in its wooden cot by the echoing chimney-piece" (*J* 13). In these words he recalls Coleridge's "Frost at Midnight," in which Coleridge, also alone at night with a sleeping child, thinks about the hidden connections in the universe, connections that Darley, at the beginning of *Justine*, cannot see. But like Coleridge, he enjoys the solitude "which suits/Abstruser musings," and he thinks of the past—"I return link by link along the iron chains of memory" (*J* 13). Like Coleridge, Darley is obsessed with memory. Coleridge, however, at the end of his poem can turn to the child and think of its future. Darley, on the other hand, is so trapped by memory that he cannot yet look forward. He cares deeply about the child, but he has no friend with whom to share his life. Then he says about Alexandria, "Five races, five languages, a dozen creeds: five fleets" (*J* 14), recalling Wordsworth's "Five years have past; five summers, with the length/Of five long winters!" in "Tintern Abbey." Wordsworth, too, is transfixed by memory, but he has his Friend, his sister, who helps give meaning to the place. Darley has only his memories, bitter memories, and the sleeping child. He tries to create meaning, but thus far he cannot, haunted as he is by Alexandria and his experiences there. "You would never mistake it for a happy place. The symbolic lovers of the free Hellenic world are replaced here by something different, something subtly androgynous, inverted upon itself" (*J* 14). Given the references to Wordsworth and Coleridge, we can see here an oblique reference to the "happy happy" loves of Keats's "Ode on a Grecian Urn." They are happy because their love, though never consummated, is always young, always hopeful. Alexandria, which, as we shall see, is also symbolic, has none of that hope or the freshness that Keats describes. The city, says Darley, is "inverted upon itself," but the problem is not the city. The problem is Darley, who is "inverted upon" himself.

This notion helps to explain these early poetic references, especially those to the romantic poets. Dante is often thought to have been part of a movement known as the *dolce stil nuovo*, but the ideas espoused by the *stilnovisti* led him from the path until he was lost in the woods. Darley, in the middle of the twentieth century, envisions himself as one of the early nineteenth-century romantics, though he is actually something of a parody of those figures. Judging from the first two volumes, he seems to think of nothing but himself and his success with women, though his treatment of Melissa while he is being manipulated by Justine is shameful. Certainly Darley shows his innate virtue by caring for Melissa's child after her death, but at the same time there is a large area of ambiguity about the child's father. When Darley learns that Melissa has had an affair with Nessim, a sort of vengeance for Darley's affair with Justine, he assumes that the child is Nessim's. He never seems to contemplate the possibility that the child is his, and he has no hesitation about giving the child to Nessim and Justine (surely an inappropriate mother to any child) when he returns to Alexandria.

Darley, then, sees himself as part of a literary tradition, but it is a tradition that is more than a century old and that he seems to misunderstand. Darley thinks that his writing is about him and that love is about him. Balthazar's interlinear therefore comes as a shock to him, because it opens up the possibility that he has been wrong, or at least limited, in his views. Although Balthazar is also wrong in many ways, he makes Darley aware of other perspectives. It was consequently a brilliant move by Durrell to narrate the third volume through an objective narrator, for that narrator moves the *Quartet* in the direction that Darley must take, from pure subjectivity to a greater objectivity. But at the end of *Mountolive*, Darley is not yet ready to be the writer he aspires to be, just as Dante is not prepared to write the *Comedy* at the end of "Purgatory." Dante must go through "Paradise," and Darley must go through the experiences of *Clea*. Then they will be writers. Dante has to have the experience of God, of divine love; and Darley must have the analogous experience in its twentieth-century form.

Dante's readers must always be careful, as Mark Musa often points out in his translation, to differentiate between Dante the character in the poem and Dante the author of the poem, who already knows everything that he shows Dante the character in the process of learning. Similarly, Durrell's readers must differentiate between Darley, the character whose learning experience we follow, and Durrell, the author who knows everything that Darley must discover. *Justine*, then, must be read with deep suspicion, because it is written by a Darley who relies on nothing but his own perceptions. Of course, the first-time reader cannot be aware of this situation and naturally trusts Darley, so that with Balthazar's revelations in the second volume, the reader is as surprised as Darley. The reader, in fact, accompanies Darley on his learning process, in this and subsequent volumes. (Durrell used a similar technique in his later *Avignon Quintet*, in which the first volume turns out to be the beginning of a novel written by one of the characters in later volumes. In both cases, the first volume of a multivolume work is far different from what it initially seems to be.)

"If the romantic poets are at one extreme in Darley's view of the universe, at the other extreme is T. S. Eliot's poem (an anti-epic, perhaps) *The Waste Land*. In *A Key to Modern British Poetry*, Durrell wrote, "in 1922 we stumble upon The Waste Land of T. S. Eliot, which altered the whole face of poetry, and *Ulysses* by James Joyce, whose technical innovations were to alter the face of prose—in neither case, however, for the better."[19] What could he have meant? To answer briefly, he meant that Eliot and Joyce had made what he calls "technical innovations" but did not fully acknowledge the developments, psychological and scientific, that Durrell highlights in the *Key*, with the result that both works present the kind of monocular vision that Durrell would have considered ruinous to Western civilization (a point that he belabors in the *Quintet*). Such a view would be fair to neither Eliot nor Joyce, nor would it be accurate; but it would be normal for an artist working in the shadow of such giants to try to differentiate their work from his own.

Nevertheless, or perhaps consequently, *The Waste Land* is a very real presence in the *Quartet*. As Eleanor Hutchens noted, "It may almost be said that *The Waste Land* has been imported bag and baggage into *The Quartet*," and she adds that the *Quartet* offers a different answer to that poem than does Eliot's own later work.[20] I would go even further and argue that the *Quartet* is a rejection of *The Waste Land*. "Unreal City," says Eliot, and Durrell counters, "Only the city is real" (Note to *Justine*), and "The characters and situations in this novel . . . are entirely imaginary. . . . Nor could the city be less unreal" (Note to *Balthazar*).[21] Durrell's Alexandria, that microcosm of the social, political, psychological, and scientific worlds in the middle of the twentieth century, is indeed real. The problem, in a postmodern world, is to know what "real" (or "less unreal") means. And of course one point of the *Quartet* is that we can never finally answer that question. Nothing—not rationalism nor nationalism nor religion nor even the Kabbalah so beloved of Balthazar—can answer that question, and yet because we are human we must keep trying to find the answer. The scientific revolution, represented by Einstein, and the psychological revolution, represented by Freud and (for Durrell) Groddeck, have led to revolutions in every other facet of human activity. Dante might well have said that the subject of the *Comedy* is "the state of souls after death, pure and simple," because the world seemed that straightforward; but in a world that operates according to Einsteinian relativity, a world in which electrons are sometimes particles and sometimes waves, a world in which atoms, and therefore all matter, are mostly empty space, no matter how solid they feel, things are not so straightforward. Hence the multiple perspectives that pervade the *Quartet* (as they pervaded Scott's *Raj Quartet*). For Durrell, so much depends not just on a red wheelbarrow but on where the viewer stands in relation to it, in both physical and nonphysical terms.

Durrell wrote that "The Waste Land is a jeremiad against a civilization that values knowledge above wisdom, words above The Word. If the keynote is disillusion and negation, as critics have said, it is because we recognize that the cap fits." How, then, can modern man organize all our knowledge "in such a way as to give life meaning? The problem was urgent in 1922. It became still more urgent in the decade that followed. Today it is the only serious problem facing us."[22] Eliot, Durrell notes, resolved the poetic struggle of *The Waste Land* in the *Four Quartets*: "The poet and the man have come to terms, have accepted a creative compromise which enriches both the work and the values it depends upon."[23] Clearly Durrell felt that the question of how modern man gives life meaning was still pressing in his time and that while Eliot had found a compromise solution that worked for him, it did not work for Durrell. *The Alexandria Quartet*, then, is his attempt to work out another. If Eliot's city was "unreal," Durrell would offer a city that could not be "less unreal." Of course, the *Quartet* is not a guidebook to Alexandria, neither a Baedeker nor a literary guidebook, the way *Ulysses* incorporates the actual city of Dublin. Like Paul Scott, Durrell does not focus on the indigenous population. His focus is on Europeans, mostly British, and on a few marginalized Egyptians, chiefly Copts. Nevertheless, the city that he creates, a literary construct, is central to the *Quartet*.

In his poem "Deus Loci," Durrell says (in words that recall the end of the "Ode on a Grecian Urn")

> All our religions founder, you
> remain, small sunburnt *deus loci* . . .

And in the *Key*, he writes, "In all religions the mystical objective is the same one—the gnosis or understanding of the mystery of man's essential being."[24] In all of his works, though especially in *The Avignon Quintet*, Durrell evinced both an interest in and an impatience with religion, particularly with what he regarded as the monocular visions of Judaism and Christianity. He seems to have desired a more mystical view in order to understand "the mystery of man's essential being." An aspect of that mystical view is contained in the "*deus loci*," the god or spirit of place, a concept that pervades Durrell's novels, his poems, and, obviously, his travel books. Durrell's Alexandria, too has a *deus loci*, a spirit that affects and transforms the many aliens who inhabit the city, something like Emerson's wave that Scott used in the *Raj Quartet*. Alan Friedman argues that place is important in Durrell but not central, that Alexandria is a metaphor, "a touchstone for the Künstlerroman treatment of the frustrated, isolated individual maturing into someone capable of meaningful human involvement."[25] Richard Pine, on the other hand, says that, "The central 'event' of the *Quartet* is not a political or social occasion so much as a 'characteristic,' Alexandria as a 'personality' or state of mind."[26] Friedman is certainly correct about the metaphoric nature of Durrell's Alexandria (which is still a real city), but Pine is equally correct about the centrality of that metaphor. Durrell, like Scott, Manning, Asch, Whittemore, Tolstoy, Homer, and others, has created a metaphorical universe in which he can examine questions of cosmic importance. Durrell, in an interview, said, "Define Man? How can I? How can you? An Eros-breath if you like; *amo ergo sum, sed cogito*," to which Durrell's biographer Ian MacNiven adds, "Larry's rephrasing of Descartes could serve as an epigram for that 'Investigation of Modern Love,' the *Quartet*, and it would echo throughout his fiction to come."[27] Alexandria is the world of that new *cogito*.

Durrell thus saw the "mystical objective" of religion as the "understanding of the mystery of man's essential being," which he expressed in the Cartesian *amo ergo sum, sed cogito*. Love, therefore, is the means of achieving that mystical objective; and while "All our religions founder," the *deus loci* remains, intimately bound up with that quest for understanding. Alexandria, then, is a city in Egypt, a city that comes under siege during the War, but it is also a metaphor for the world, for the universe, in which both love and parodies of love manifest themselves. It contains, in a manner of speaking, the hell, purgatory, and heaven that Darley must negotiate in order to become a writer, a person; and as those cosmic territories exist in Dante's memory, Alexandria exists in Darley's, as Darley so often points out: "I return link by link along the iron chains of memory to the city which we inhabited so briefly together: the city which used us as its flora" (*J* 13). The city "used us." The characters, in other words, became subject to the *deus loci*. The city itself has "power" (*J* 27) and a life of its own, which Darley seems to see when he looks at it through Nessim's telescope: "Despite the firm stone base on which the tripod stood the high magnification of the lens and the heat haze between them contributed a feathery vibration to the image which gave the landscape the appearance of breathing softly and irregularly" (*J* 169). Throughout the *Quartet*, Durrell emphasizes the power of the city, the environment inhabited by his characters, to influence those characters.

That Alexandria is a great mixture of peoples: "Fragments of every language—Armenian, Greek, Amharic, Moroccan Arabic; Jews from Asia Minor, Pontus, Georgia; mothers born in Greek settlements on the Black Sea; communities cut down like the branches of trees, lacking a parent body, dreaming of Eden. These are the poor quarters of the white city" (*J* 62). This city "moves not only backwards into our history . . . but also back and forth in the living present, so to speak—among its contemporary faiths and races; the hundred little spheres which religion or love creates and which cohere softly together like cells to form the great sprawling jellyfish which is Alexandria today" (*B* 151). Alexandria, that force, that organism, that place with its own *deus*, where Darley and others try to understand love, and thereby themselves, becomes a microcosm of the world. It is the universe we inhabit, not as orderly as Dante's, perhaps, but with similar pitfalls and rewards; and when Mahmoud Manzaloui objects to Durrell's inaccuracies about the city and his omission of Egyptians, he misses the point.[28] As Darley puts it,

> I see all of us not as men and women any longer, identities swollen with their acts of forgetfulness, follies, and deceits—but as beings unconsciously made part of place, buried to the waist among the ruins of a single city, steeped in its values. . . . All members of a city whose actions lay just outside the scope of the plotting or conniving spirit: Alexandrians. (*B* 225)

We are created by the world we live in, and the reference to our being "buried to the waist" recalls the image of Satan in the middle of Dante's hell, buried to his waist in ice. One of the things that will ultimately free Darley (and Clea) as artists will be the recognition that Alexandria is a place not only of memory but of imagination as well. When he can exert control over memory through imagination, can, as Clea puts it, step "across the threshold into the kingdom of your imagination, to take possession of it once and for all" (*C* 281), only then can he write the "Once upon a time . . ." (*C* 282) that will make him the artist he desires to be.

It is no wonder, then, that one of the memorable minor characters in the *Quartet* is the dwarf Mnemjian, whose name shares the same root as Mnemosyne, goddess of memory and mother of the Muses, those goddesses of the arts that preserve, in history, poetry, music, and dance, the histories of civilizations. Mnemjian "is the Memory man, the archives of the city." And because he barbers both the living and the dead, he "embraces the two worlds" (*J* 36). He is, therefore, a valuable person to know, but at the same time, it turns out, he is a spy. His "shop was a clearing-post for general intelligence concerning the city. . . . [I]t was disheartening to learn much later on that he patiently copied out his intelligence summaries in triplicate and sold copies to various other intelligence services" (*J* 170). Such is memory! Left to itself, without the shaping force of imagination, it is undiscriminating and unreliable, as Proust had shown earlier in the century. Thus, *Justine*, however enjoyable it may be to read, is completely mistaken and misleading. To the extent that Darley conceives of memory being composed of "iron chains" (*J* 13), he is trapped by it and, like Mnemjian, it will betray him.

Another point that must be noticed here is Durrell's technique in presenting Mnemjian, which is no less allegorical than Spenser's description of the mind in book 2, canto 10 of *The Faerie Queene*. Mentioning Durrell and Spenser at the same time is not as shocking as it may seem at first glance, for the *Quartet* has a number of lapses from strict verisimilitude. For instance, it is unlikely that Clea could really read the lips of Liza Pursewarden through a telescope (*C* 117). And the conclusion of the *Quartet*, with Clea shot through the hand by a harpoon gun in a lagoon guarded by dead sailors, necessitating the amputation of the hand and the discovery that she can now paint better with an artificial hand, would be absurd if it did not all fit thematically, and allegorically, into the context of the *Quartet* as a whole.

So, too, the city is allegorical, which means not that it is unreal but rather that it is real on numerous levels. At one point, as Justine talks about the city, Darley thinks of its founders, "the soldier-God in his glass coffin, the youthful body lapped in silver, riding down the river towards his tomb. Or that great square Negro head reverberating with a concept of God conceived in the spirit of pure intellectual play—Plotinus" (*J* 39). From its very foundation the city has contained all of these extremes, from the Greek soldier who saw himself as a god to the philosopher who saw God entirely in terms of intellect. Hence the work is *The Alexandria Quartet*, not the *Love Quartet* or the *Story of Darley*, just as Homer's poem is the *Iliad*, not the *Achilleid*.

Recognizing this allegorical aspect of the *Quartet*, part of its epic heritage, changes the way we might regard some of its qualities. For instance, in an early review of *Clea*, Kenneth Rexroth objected strongly to Durrell's creation of a plot involving Copts, Jews, and Nazis against Arabs and the British. This, he says, is "the kind of yarn we associate with Talbot Mundy, not with a serious writer. . . . The word for it is cheap—as well as dangerous. One step more and the word is malicious."[29] Not only has Rexroth overstated the complicity of the Copts and the Jews with the Nazis, but he has made the mistake of treating the novel as history, which it is not. It is a work, like other epics (as well as like historical novels) that uses history, but it is a work of imagination; the plot device that joins Copts and Jews together offers one explanation for the peculiar marriage of Nessim and Justine. Durrell is not pretending to write history. Whether the Copts and the Jews ever joined forces against the British is as irrelevant as whether there was an actual Aeneas or Beowulf. The real question is whether the plot device works. If Durrell had made more of it, if he had exploited it and tried to write a thriller, the answer might be no. But he did not. He uses it as yet one more complication in the tangle of personal and political relationships that make the *Quartet* so complex, and in that context it works well indeed.

Another area that is affected by this manner of reading the *Quartet* involves the work's characters. Alan Friedmen offers a good discussion of critical reactions to Durrell's characters, but the upshot is that some readers like the characters and find them believable while others do not.[30] On one level, of course, no literary character is anything more than a collection of words, and to speak of them as real or believable makes no more sense than putting flowers on wallpaper makes for Dickens's Mr. Gradgrind. Fortunately, most readers are not like Mr. Gradgrind and do seek verisimilitude in characters. Do Durrell's characters achieve believability? Should they? On this subject, Pine quotes Durrell's notes: "It must be made clear that these are not 'characters': a character is an integer in a temporal series: whereas these are personalities embodied by reminiscence."[31] Durrell's answers, then, would be no and no, they are not believable and they are not meant to be. He makes that point because, despite the multiple perspectives from which we see so many of them, we can never see their full complexity as characters. We always see them from points of view. And as I shall argue, there is another reason for answering those questions negatively.

Balthazar is a particularly fascinating figure. He is apparently liked and respected by everyone else in the *Quartet*. He is regarded as a wise and knowledgeable person. Darley trusts him enough to give him the manuscript of *Justine*, and he is surprised and impressed with Balthazar's careful response to that work, though, as we have seen, Balthazar is as mistaken as Darley on some key points. Furthermore, it is Balthazar who quite stupidly shoots Clea with the harpoon gun when everyone (except perhaps Charlton Heston) knows that he should not be touching it. And Balthazar's Cabal is just another attempt to grasp an ungraspable reality, while his cryptic notes, if they use nothing more than *boustrophedon*, can hardly be as cryptic as everyone makes them out to be.

Those notes using boustrophedon, however, are a key to Balthazar, for "Balthazar" is the form used in Greek and Roman Bibles for the name Belshazzar in Daniel 5. It was Belshazzar, or Balthazar, to whom the handwriting on the wall appeared, handwriting that no one but Daniel could make out because, like boustrophedon, it required reading in a different direction than normal writing. The biblical Balthazar is a ruler who cannot foresee his own destruction, who literally cannot read the handwriting on the wall. Durrell's Balthazar can read the writing, but, for all his good intentions, he cannot understand it. In the interlinear he writes, "Thank God I have never 'loved', wise one, and never will! Thank God!" (*B* 128); but later he does indeed fall in love, with a Greek actor who looks "like a god" but who is "simply a small-spirited, dirty, venal and empty personage" (*C* 68). As a result, Balthazar becomes an alcoholic, nearly loses his medical practice, and almost loses his life. In short, Balthazar, like Belshazzar, is a disaster. It is not accidental that Darley lives with Pombal "in the Rue Nebi Daniel" (*J* 21), the street of the prophet Daniel, since it is Daniel who must interpret things for Belshazzar, not the other way round.

On the other hand, for all of his errors, Balthazar remains a likable and important character; and there is biblical precedent for that aspect of him as well. Traditionally, one of the wise men or wizards who came to pay tribute to the Christ child was named Balthazar. This Balthazar was divinely led to Jesus in defiance of the king's commands. Like him, Durrell's Balthazar is a wise man, in some ways a wizard, who tries to achieve the good even if he often does not succeed. He almost sees the truth, although he never quite gets it.

Balthazar, then, is as allegorical a figure as Mnemjian, though, through his greater exposure, we see more of his personality. Nevertheless, it is clear that he serves a largely symbolic function throughout the four novels. Similarly symbolic is Mountolive. Surely no one can look at his name without thinking of the Mount of Olives, the place where the Messiah is supposed to appear, the place where Jesus spent the night before his arrest. Can it be only coincidence that Mountolive loves Leila, whose name in Arabic means "night"? In this epic about love, their relationship may not be the oddest one, but it has its own peculiarities. Leila loves him because "what she saw in him was something like a prototype of a nation which existed now only in her imagination"(*M* 29). Given her position as a woman in Egypt, her response to him is understandable. The only escape she has is through her imaginary projections on him. His case, however, is somewhat different. Throughout the long years of his career, he thinks only of her; but he never thinks of the reality of her, of her age, for instance, or of the implications of her perception of him. As much as she views him as an ideal, so he views her as an ideal; but that view prevents him from forming a lasting relationship with any other person until he meets Liza Pursewarden. And when he finally does meet Leila again, after so many years, he discovers that she is really an old woman, now scarred by smallpox.

Their images of each other, then, are based on mutual self-delusions. Mountolive especially has played a dangerous and self-defeating game. He has maintained a kind of idealized love for Leila, and that love has complicated his work as a diplomat when he learned of Nessim's anti-British activities. When those activities were revealed to him, "Mountolive felt himself colouring slightly. 'In matters of business, a diplomat has no friends,' he said stiffly, feeling that he spoke in the very accents of Pontius Pilate" (*M* 188). He is Christ-like in his love for Leila, maintained over time and distance, but he is like Pilate in dealing with her sons until the two of them meet again, at which point he "suddenly realized that the precious image which had inhabited his heart for so long had now been dissolved, completely wiped out" (*M* 281). It may seem that he has betrayed, or at least lost, his ideal, but in fact he has finally stopped hiding behind that ideal and joined the world of other people, with all its complications. Mountolive, in fact, is very much like Darley. His mistaken romantic idealizing traps him, and he cannot be a full human being until he abandons that mode for another that allows him to participate actively in the world. He cannot be Jesus, who transcends the world after that night on the Mount of Olives. He cannot be Pilate, who washes his hands of worldly involvement. Like Darley, he has to become truly involved.

Perhaps we can see more clearly what this involvement entails by examining one of the most troubling, and troublesome, characters in the *Quartet*, Pursewarden. A number of respected readers regard Pursewarden as not only an admirable character but as something more than that. Pine, for example, calls him "Darley's ebullient *alter ego*" and then adds that Pursewarden is "more Durrell's own *alter ego* than Darley's."[32] Pursewarden, then, speaks directly for Durrell, which means that readers must take what he says very seriously indeed. Carol Peirce does not go quite so far, but she does say that Darley must claim his heritage from Pursewarden "in order to rise above his old self and find his inner being and ability;" and Frank Kermode, writing after only three volumes had been published, says that Durrell "absolutely must agree about all the important aesthetic issues with Pursewarden."[33]

Such views of Pursewarden are not unanimous, however. Henry Miller, in a letter to Durrell, wrote, "To be frank, of all the characters in the quartet Pursewarden is the least interesting to me. . . . I never get the conviction that he was the great writer you wish him to seem. . . . Too much persiflage. . . . What I mean more precisely, is that one is not sure at times whether the author is taking his double-faced protagonist seriously or ironically."[34] Alan Friedman, in a charitable vein, writes, "Doubtless Durrell did not feel that Pursewarden was as much a failure as he seems to many readers."[35] While I would agree that Pursewarden is a failure, I also want to draw an important distinction: he is a failure as a person, not as a character. As a character, he has an important role to play, a role that is indeed central in Darley's emergence as a writer, a lover, and a human being.

We have already seen that many of the names in the *Quartet*—Mnemjian, Balthazar, Mountolive, Leila—were chosen for their meanings. So, too, with Pursewarden, though some readers may object to the wordplay. Iago says, "He who steals my purse steals trash," which makes the guardian of the purse, the pursewarden, a guardian of rubbish. That wordplay seems to be a key in understanding Pursewarden. Far from serving as Darley's or Durrell's *alter ego*, he is a failure in all the areas in which Darley needs to succeed. He is, perhaps, a negative *alter ego*, a person who is wrong about almost everything, though he is clever enough to make his errors sound right. Darley, in order to succeed, must be the opposite of Pursewarden.

It is astonishing that Kermode, having written positively about Pursewarden after the publication of *Mountolive*, continued, after *Clea* appeared, by saying that "the suicide of the novelist Pursewarden is fully accounted for."[36] Pursewarden's suicide is never fully accounted for because, as is the case with so much else in the *Quartet*, human motivations are never that simple. But more important, Pursewarden's suicide negates almost everything else that he says or does in the *Quartet*. His suicide, unlike almost everything else in the *Quartet*, is regarded as an absolute wrong. This view is not simply a statement of conventional morality. It is a recognition that in a work that examines modern love and that has an important secondary theme dealing with the development of the writer, suicide is literally a dead end, a negation of both love and the responsibilities of the writer. Whatever Pursewarden's motivations may be, his actions, which may have seemed romantic to him, represent an evasion, a refusal to face himself or his duties. As Cecily Mackworth says, Pursewarden "remains detached, an outsider. He watches Humanity and despises it, instead of steeping himself in it."[37] Pursewarden finds it easy to be critical of everyone else, to tell them how they should behave as lovers and as writers, but he demonstrates little self-awareness and we never see any evidence that he is a great writer. People, including Darley, say that he is, but their saying so is not evidence; and Darley's opinions are particularly suspect. More reliable is the opinion of the anonymous narrator of *Mountolive*, who refers to "Pursewarden's solitary act of cowardice" (*M* 213).

In fact, Pursewarden recognizes his resemblance to Darley, whom he describes as a "fellow-romantic" (*M* 110). Darley, too, seems aware of the resemblance. As Clea tells Darley the story of Amaril and Semira, a romantic love story marred only by Amaril's insistence that Semira needs to be given a new nose, Darley writes, "Romantic love! Pursewarden used to call it 'The Comic Demon'" (*C* 91). Darley truly likes the romantic story, just as he is moved later by Pombal's love story. Pursewarden, on the other hand, only mocks love; but of course, Pursewarden's relationship with his sister is another indication of his emotional sterility. He might well regard romantic love as a "Comic Demon" because he is so clearly incapable of it, making it entirely plausible that he kills himself because he realizes that Justine has been using him no less than she used Darley. Equally plausible, of course, are the other explanations that characters advance, such as his attempt to free Liza or his discovery that Nessim has been involved in a political plot.

Whatever explanation we accept, Pursewarden's major problem is that he is trapped in himself. Darley recalls him saying, "There is no Other; there is only oneself facing forever the problem of one's self discovery!" (*C* 99). This attitude is obvious in his inscription in a book that he gave to Balthazar:

> *Pursewarden on Life*
> N.B. Food is for eating
> Art is for arting
> Women for _____
> Finish
> RIP
>
> (*J* 207)

Perhaps the best picture he gives of himself comes in his "Conversations with Brother Ass," where he writes,

> *Disguised as an eiron, why who should it be*
> *But tuft-hunting, dram-drinking, toad-eating me!*
>
> (*C* 129)

Pursewarden, then, is very much like the Darley of *Justine*, wallowing in self-pity, not recognizing the Other, regarding other human beings as objects that exist for his use; but the resemblance is superficial. At the end of *Justine*, Darley is beginning his recovery, like Dante at the beginning of the *Comedy*. He has taken Melissa's child, whoever its father may be, a selfless and caring act. The island to which he exiles himself may be an escape, as Pine says, but it is also a place where he can think about himself and about others, as he cares for the child.[38] As he writes *Justine*, his first reference to Pursewarden is revealing: "I disliked this literary figure for the contrast he offered to his own work—poetry and prose of real grace" (*J* 54). Darley accepts the romantic notion that identifies the writer with the writing, but he is perceptive enough even at this early stage to dislike Pursewarden, as does Balthazar, who calls him a "simpleton" (*B* 109).

John Weigel makes an excellent point when he analyzes one of the aphorisms on which Pursewarden seems to have established his reputation:

Pursewarden is the specialist in paradox: "Words being what they are, people being what they are, perhaps it would be better always to say the opposite of what one means" (*C* 134). And, when Pursewarden practices this theory, what he means is the opposite of what he says, and thus he does not mean the theory at all. If God Himself is an Ironist, there is no way out of this big-scale joke. The theory of relativity becomes the laughter of God. Reality is a joke.[39]

But of course, reality is not a joke. We can only see it as a joke if we disregard the feelings, the sufferings, of others, as Pursewarden consistently does. But even Pursewarden cannot regard reality entirely as a joke. If he did, he could not have killed himself in the shabby way he did. His suicide is an admission of his failure, his bankruptcy, his sterility. Darley, to grow into himself as an author, must grow beyond Pursewarden.

It is significant, then, to note that Pursewarden is a friend of D. H. Lawrence, to whom he bears some resemblance, but whereas Lawrence views sex as an integral component of love, Pursewarden views it as a solitary activity, something he does *to* rather than *with* an Other. And Lawrence is not the only twentieth-century writer who appeals to Pursewarden. Pursewarden also regards himself as a Joycean. His nickname for Darley, for example, is "Lineaments of Gratified Desire" (*B* 110), based, as Balthazar points out, on Darley's initials, just as Joyce creates phrases in *Finnegans Wake* based on his characters' initials ("Haveth Childers Everywhere"); and he signs his long letter to Darley "Earwig van Beetfield" (*M* 128), another reference to that hero, Humphrey Chimpden Earwicker.[40] But in what sense is Pursewarden Joycean? He seems to see himself in Stephen Daedalus's description of the artist in *Portrait of the Artist*: "The artist, like the God of the creation, remains within or behind or beyond or above his handiwork, invisible, refined out of existence, indifferent, paring his fingernails."[41] Pursewarden never realizes that the Stephen of *Ulysses* finally outgrows that view. Stephen leaves his isolation and achieves a profound sort of communication with Bloom. Pursewarden shows no such growth. Instead he kills himself.

Pursewarden, in fact fills the role in the novels that Durrell described for the author of each novel's epigraphs, the Marquis de Sade. At first, Durrell's use of Sade may seem repulsive, but Durrell's own comments help to change that impression:

> The quotations from Sade? In a sense he is the most typical figure of our century, with his ignorance and cruelty. I regard him as both a hero and a pygmy.... He couldn't find the key, and convert his energy into laughter or rapture. He is the champion whiner of all time; yes, infantile as modern man

is: cruel, hysterical, stupid, and self-destructive—just like us all. He is our spiritual malady personified.[42]

Durrell does not approve of Sade, but he sees Sade as emblematic of the century. That may not make him a hero in the Greek sense, but it does make him a hero as a central figure in this investigation of modern love, a field in which he is simultaneously a hero and a pygmy. And everything that Durrell says about Sade could be said about Pursewarden, who is neither Darley's nor Durrell's *alter ego*. More accurately, and in keeping with Durrell's interesting physics, he is their antiparticle.

Pursewarden's objectification of people, and especially of women, raises another problem, Durrell's own treatment of women. Jane Pinchin is quite properly troubled by what she takes to be Durrell's attitude, that women function as a tool that men use for self-discovery, among other things.[43] The *Quartet* certainly seems to treat women that way, but, without arguing that Durrell was a feminist, I would like to suggest another approach. Of course, the use of women as tools for self-discovery has a long history, and perhaps no one illustrates that tradition better than Dante. The historical Beatrice would surely have been completely bewildered by what Dante did with her; and Dante himself, in modern terms, might well qualify as a stalker. Nevertheless, perhaps because he wrote in the fourteenth century or perhaps because of the *Comedy*'s spiritual nature, we tend not to think badly of the Florentine poet. Many of Durrell's characters, however, go well beyond Dante's stance in their thinking about women. Darley himself puts the matter rather crudely when he refers to "the whole portentous scrimmage of sex itself, the act of penetration which could lead a man to despair for the sake of a creature with two breasts and *le croissant* as the picturesque Levant slang has it" (*J* 185). Here Darley reduces women first to creatures and then to comestibles, to be used and devoured by men. In the same vein, he shortly after describes Justine as "a walking abstract of the writers and thinkers whom she had loved or admired—but what clever woman is more?" (*J* 203). Woman, that is, is man's moon, reflecting his light, if she is lucky enough to be clever.

This image is repeated and developed much later, after Darley has returned to Alexandria and seen what has happened to his beloved Justine. Now he thinks that he understands:

> Nymph? Goddess? Vampire? Yes, she was all of these, and none of them. She was like every woman, everything that the mind of a man (let us define "man" as a poet perpetually conspiring against himself)—that the mind of man wished to imagine. She was there forever, and she had never existed!

> Under all these masks there was only another woman, every woman, like a lay figure in a dressmaker's shop, waiting for the poet to clothe her, breathe life into her. In understanding all this for the first time I began to realize with awe the enormous reflexive power of woman—the fecund passivity with which, like the moon, she borrows her second-hand light from the male sun. (*C* 56)

Of course, Darley understands nothing. He continues to think of Woman instead of women, and consequently all he can come up with are generalizations and half-truths that support his traditional male point of view, the point of view to which Pinchin objects.

The problem with Pinchin's objections, however, is that what she says about women's objectification in these books applies to Darley and Pursewarden and Nessim and other men, but it does not apply to Durrell. Until well into *Clea*, we see virtually everything from a male perspective. Certainly, as we learn, Justine herself wrote much of what was passed off as Arnauti's, which makes her sections into a parody of the male perspective, a perspective that too often does regard women as objects to be used, whether physically or spiritually. The first indication in the *Quartet* that there might actually be a female perspective comes near the beginning of *Clea*, when Clea says to Darley, "You men are the strangest creatures" (*C* 78). At first it appears that she makes the same mistake that Darley made earlier: she refers to men as "creatures" and she generalizes. The reader, however, who by this point has read about nine hundred pages from the male perspective, might well share her exasperation, while acknowledging her flippant tone. Much more serious is Clea's later analysis of sex and love, an analysis that differs considerably from so much that has come before:

> Sexual love *is* knowledge, both in etymology and in cold fact; "he knew her" as the Bible says! Sex is the joint or coupling which unites the male and female ends of knowledge merely—a cloud of unknowing! When a culture goes bad in its sex all knowledge is impeded. We women know that. (*C* 113)

Her description of sex and love differs radically from so much that we have seen. There is none of the selfishness, the objectification, the desire for domination, or the hopeless, whining idealism that has pervaded the *Quartet* in her description. She considers sex an expression of love, which is a commonplace enough idea but an idea that has appeared rarely in the *Quartet*. For her, sex is the physical manifestation of a spiritual—perhaps Platonic—idea of love. Most important, it is mutual. This ideal heterosexual love involves knowledge, thought, and the unity of two fully independent human beings, and thus it differs from every other affair in the *Quartet*.

Clea, in explaining this view of love to Darley, is much like Beatrice explaining divine love to Dante; and the love that Clea describes is, with certain modifications that would classify it as "modern," very similar to the kind of love that Beatrice describes, even to Augustinian *caritas*. Darley, unfortunately but understandably, is not yet capable of internalizing Clea's lesson, but by the end of the novel he will be. His development helps to explain that conclusion which, in terms of simple verisimilitude, verges on the silly: Clea has lost her hand in a horrible accident, but she discovers that she can paint better than before with her prosthetic hand. In her letter to Darley, she writes of her discovery that "IT can *paint*!" and then she goes on: "I have crossed the border and entered into the possession of my kingdom, thanks to the Hand" (*C* 278). Rather than allowing herself to become an object, she has made that object, the Hand, part of herself. She is in control—not of other people but of herself—and she is a painter. When Darley, thanks to her lesson, achieves a similar control, he becomes a writer; and though he and Clea are not physically together at the end of the *Quartet,* they are spiritually together, tied by the most profound love in the epic-novel.

Clea, therefore, is the key to the *Quartet.* Lionel Trilling wrote, "If the love that Mr. Durrell describes is indeed to be called modern, it is so by reason of its affinity to love as Proust represents it. That is to say, it is obsessive, corrosive, desperate, highly psychologized."[44] What Trilling said was correct, but only because he said it before the publication of *Clea*. The notion of Clea as the key to the tetralogy must be taken seriously. Not only is Durrell obviously intrigued by the image of keys—he wrote *The Key to Modern British Poetry* and remarked that Sade "couldn't find the key"—but the name Clea itself derives from the Greek *kleis,* key. In an important sense, *The Alexandria Quartet,* like *The Divine Comedy,* is, in Pursewarden's words, "an ordinary Girl Meets Boy story" (*C* 136), but Durrell, like Dante, has transformed that most basic of stories into a complex investigation of modern love, and Clea is indeed the key.

What, then, of Justine, who seems so fascinating through so much of the *Quartet?* It is no accident that her name is prominent in Sade, for she inhabits a universe that Sade could have imagined. She is incapable of "laughter or rapture" because her only mode is to use people. She is "like some powerful engine of destruction" (*C* 280). She knows well how to play the traditional male-female game, the one that pervades the *Quartet.* Thus Nessim believes that an oriental woman's "true obsessions are power, politics and possessions," which is surely an accurate summary of Justine's interests. Nevertheless, in staring at Justine, he sees in her "the perfect submissiveness of the oriental spirit—the absolute feminine submissiveness which is one of the strongest forces in the world" (*M* 201). Justine understand the male perspective, and she knows how to manipulate it, how to make herself the kind of object that the men desire, beautiful, submissive, seemingly without a will of her own, there to be used. She adopts that pose so skillfully that she manages to use each of the men in her life. She is as much a spiritual bankrupt as they are, but she illustrates perfectly the paradoxical way in which "absolute feminine submissiveness . . . is one of the strongest forces in the world."

Durrell's treatment of women is thus much more complex than it at first appears. Women do tend to be viewed through much of the *Quartet* as tools, as sexual objects, as less human than men; but when we consider the men who see them that way, Pursewarden, the immature Darley, the playboy Pombal, the self-deceived wise man Balthazar, we must see that what is being examined is not the nature of women so much as the shallowness of the men. They, like the women who play their game, represent the "spiritual malady" that Durrell saw in Sade, the malady that Darley, with the help of Clea, finally transcends, thereby achieving something that might truly be called love and in the process becoming a writer.

This merging of love and writing has also posed a problem for Durrell's readers. Eugene Hollahan has remarked, "Critics have generally agreed that Durrell developed some single major theme in *The Alexandria Quartet*, but in general they have disagreed as to its exact nature."[45] This disagreement brings us back to Durrell's statement prefacing *Balthazar*: "The central topic of the book is an investigation of modern love." What may at first seem like a simple, straightforward statement actually expresses the complexity of Durrell's achievement. Thus far in this discussion, I, like many other readers have treated this statement as though it said that the subject of the book was modern love, and from one perspective it does mean that. From a different perspective, however, it says that the central topic of the book is an investigation, whose own subject is modern love. On one level, the importance of the *Quartet* lies in what it says about modern love; but on another level its importance focuses on the investigation, which consists of the four novels, the narrator of at least three of them, and the effect of the investigation on that narrator, who, as a result of his investigation and thanks, as we have seen, to Clea and to his own receptivity, grows into a writer. So the theme of love and the theme of writing, or art in general, are intertwined throughout the *Quartet*. Again, the analogy with Dante is instructive. Dante must complete his journey before he can write about it, and throughout the *Comedy*, using allusion and autobiography, Dante calls attention to himself as writer, pilgrim, and lover in a cosmic context. So, too, with Darley, for whom love and art are inextricably linked, if only he can learn how to manage them.

This intertwining of themes also involves Durrell's use of multiple perspectives in the *Quartet*. *Justine* is written by an immature, love-smitten young man; *Balthazar* comments on *Justine* from the perspective of an older, wiser man, whose corrections are often as mistaken as the points they correct; *Mountolive* is written from an impersonal, third-person point of view; and *Clea* is the work of that immature young man reaching maturity.[46] Furthermore, as every reader quickly sees, the *Quartet* is full of letters, diaries, and parts of other books that all contribute other perspectives. Lee Lemon says that "In Durrell's world, as in Derrida's, alternate explanations are simply alternate readings of the text of reality," which returns us to the question of whether there is a reality.[47] In *Tunc*, Count Banubula says, "Haven't you noticed . . . that most things in life happen just outside one's range of vision? One has to see them out of the corner of one's eye."[48] This statement implies that there is a reality but that we can only see it indirectly. In the *Quartet*, for instance, Pursewarden's suicide is a reality; but as we see, each character not only reacts to it differently but gives a different explanation for it. So why did he kill himself? We cannot know what his final motivation was. Neither human motives nor human perceptions are clear enough for us to give a definitive answer. Again in *Tunc* we read, "I realized that any explanation would do, and that all would forever remain merely provisional. Was this perhaps true for all of us, for all our actions? Yes, yes."[49] It is certainly true for the characters in the *Quartet*.

Durrell made this same important point many times in his career, and it appears repeatedly in the *Key*:

> In the last analysis great poetry reflects an unknown in the interpretation and understanding of which all knowledge is refunded into ignorance. It points toward a Something which itself subsists without distinction. In this sense, then, art is useless though in others it has its definite uses. A good poem is a congeries of symbols which transforms an enigmatic knowledge to the reader.[50]

We can only see the truth indirectly. Dante, writing out of his medieval synthesis, could see Truth, could see God, but we cannot. The best we can do is look in the direction of a Something. George Steiner is therefore quite right when he says that Durrell's style "carries the heart of his meaning: 'the world cannot be penetrated by force of reason.'"[51] As Durrell himself put it, "Wilde says somewhere that one of the most effective ways of hating art is to admire it rationally," which, as a dutiful critic, is what I am trying to do.[52] Such are the problems of being a critic in a postmodern world.

The Alexandria Quartet, then, does not follow precisely the pattern for epic that I have laid out in the earlier sections of this book, thus emphasizing the idea that epic is not, and has never been, a single thing. Most epics do indeed follow that pattern, as long works focusing on a pivotal moment in history and having what I call cosmic implications. The *Quartet*, like the *Comedy*, is certainly a long work with cosmic implications. Whether either work can be said to focus on a pivotal historical moment is more problematic. Dante thought that he was living close to the end of time, which is arguably a pivotal moment, though that approaching Apocalypse does not make his work epic. Durrell, though he mentions the Second World War, does not focus on any moment or event that we could call pivotal. Nonetheless, the love that he is investigating in such depth is pivotal and of both personal and cosmic importance. Even so, it is clear that Durrell's twentieth-century epic novel is somewhat different from the others. It is far closer to Dante's. If we think of the *Comedy* as an epic, perhaps as a "philosophical-theological" epic, in Curtius's words, we can also think of *The Alexandria Quartet* as a philosophical epic, a long work that examines in great detail a pivotal concept—or *the* pivotal concept.

Perhaps the best description of the *Quartet* can be found, strangely enough, in the words of Pursewarden, who gives this choice to Darley:

> No, but seriously, if you wished to be—I do not say original but merely contemporary—you might try a four-card trick in the form of a novel; passing a common axis through four stories, say, and dedicating each to one of the four winds of heaven. A continuum, forsooth, embodying not a *temps retrouvé* but a *temps deliver*. The curvature of space itself would give you stereoscopic narrative, while human personality seen across a continuum would perhaps become prismatic? Who can say? I throw the idea out. I can imagine a form which, if satisfied, might raise in human terms the problems of causality or indeterminacy. . . . And nothing very *recherché* either. Just an ordinary Girl Meets Boy story. But tackled in this way you would not, like most of your contemporaries, be drowsily cutting along a dotted line! (*C* 135–36)

This passage describes precisely what Durrell has done: he has told an ordinary story in an extraordinary way, combining space, time, love, and literary artistry. Labels perhaps do not matter a great deal, but if we want to label what Durrell has done here, we must call it epic.

Notes

Chapter 1: Approaching the Epic

1. Frye, *Anatomy*, 312.
2. Colie, *Resources of Kind*, 1.
3. Ibid., 15.
4. Derrida, "Law of Genre," 56, 81.
5. See also Klein, *Exemplary Sidney*.
6. Fowler, *Kinds of Literature*, 265.
7. Le Bossu, *Treatise of the Epick Poem*, 154.
8. I had a teacher who lectured our class on the ten characteristics of Baroque art. This teacher then showed us the "perfect Baroque painting," a monstrosity that he had commissioned himself because none of the Baroque masters had ever painted a "perfect Baroque painting," that is, a painting that utilized all ten of his characteristics. Thomas Greene's comment on epic is appropriate: the historian "knows that in any exact sense a pure epic has never been written" (*Descent from Heaven*, 9).
9. Colie, *Resources of Kind*, 113–14.
10. Maskell, *Historical Epic in France*, 2.
11. Lukács, *Theory of the Novel*, 30.
12. Quint, *Epic and Empire*, 360.
13. Maresca, *Epic to Novel*, 183.
14. Greene, *Descent from Heaven*, 4
15. Javitch, "Italian Epic Theory," 211.
16. Voltaire, *Essay . . . upon the Epick Poetry*, 16. Maurice Bowra points out that even Virgil adapted the Homeric model to the needs of his time and place (*Virgil to Milton*, 10). Fowler discusses "the continual process whereby change in the population of an individual genre gradually alters its character. Epic was not quite the same after Blackmore's *Prince Arthur* and by no means the same after *Paradise Lost*" (*Kinds of Literature*, 11).
17. Kazantzakis, *Odyssey*, xii. On the same page, Kazantzakis also wrote, "Historians of literature come only after the artist has passed; they hold measuring rods, they take measurements and construct useful laws for their science, but these are useless for the creator because he has the right and strength—this is what creation means—to break them by creating new ones." Voltaire, also commenting on critics, felt the same way: "We have in every Art more Rules than Example, for Men are more fond of teaching, than able to perform" (*Essay . . . upon the Epick Poetry*, 37).

18. Javitch, "Italian Epic Theory," 210.

19. "There is no doubt but that the signal event in the history of literary criticism in the Italian Renaissance was the discovery of Aristotle's *Poetics* and its incorporation into the critical tradition" (Weinberg, *History of Literary Criticism,* 349). Still, as John Newman says about the *Poetics*, "Sharing the fate of the rest of his work, it has become over the centuries a repository of authoritarian doctrine which has been more often used to bludgeon originality than to encourage it" (*Classical Epic Tradition,* 37).

20. See Erickson, *Mapping The Faerie Queene* for an analysis of epic and romance elements in Spenser's poem.

21. "Epic theory [in the Renaissance] is best viewed as a genre in its own right. It had its own topoi, its own forms. Writers of epic treatises were less concerned with influencing writers of epic than with constructing imposing and rational edifices" (Maskell, *Historical Epic in France,* 17).

22. Scholler, *Epic in Medieval Society,* ix–x.

23. Safer, *Contemporary American Comic Epic,* 13–14.

24. Tom Winnifrith says that Northrop Frye provides several categories of epic, but they all come down to being encyclopedic or having "wholeness" ("Postscript," 117). Frye does say that the "epic differs from the narrative in the encyclopaedic range of its theme, from heaven to the underworld, and over an enormous mass of traditions" (*Anatomy,* 318).

25. McWilliams, *American Epic,* 3.

26. Sheridan, *Anticladianus,* 28.

27. Keith, *Engendering Epic* 2. All quotations from the *Iliad* and the *Odyssey* are from the translations by Richmond Lattimore.

28. Bowra, *Virgil to Milton,* 1.

29. Winnifrith, "Postscript," 109–10. Some of the works to which Winnifrith alludes will be addressed later in this chapter. *The Divine Comedy* will be discussed in chapter 6.

30. See Wilkie, *Romantic Poets and Epic Tradition.* Clearly works like *The Prelude* and *Hyperion* are not epics according to the terms of this study.

31. Duncan Kennedy gives a good idea of what I am trying to avoid: "Any attempt, by poet or literary historian, to conceptualise genre by narrativising it, by offering a historical overview, will inevitably offer a framework teleologically directed by and towards a particular characterizing, typifying work (e.g., a 'martial' tradition of epic characterized by Homer or an aetiological tradition characterized by Ovid's *Metamophoses*" ("Virgilian Epic," 152).

32. Le Bossu, *Treatise of the Epick Poem,* 6. Sir Philip Sidney would have agreed. He says about "heroicall" poetry, "For as the image of each action styrreth and instructeth the mind, so the loftie image of such Worthies most inflameth the mind with desire to be worthy, and informes with counsel how to be worthy" ("Apology," 179).

33. Voltaire, *Essay . . . upon the Epick Poetry,* 40–41; Merchant, "Children of Homer," 91.

34. Bowra, *Virgil to Milton,* 1.

35. Mori, *Epic Grandeur,* 47ff.

36. Greene, *Descent from Heaven,* 15.

37. The editors of *Epic Traditions in the Contemporary World* offer as their working definition of epic that "the epic is defined here as a poetic narrative of length and complexity that centers around deeds of significance to the community. These deeds are usually presented as deeds of grandeur or heroism, often narrated from within a verisimilitudinous frame of reference" (Beissinger, et al. 2). William Calin provides a long list of epic features, among which he includes a concentration "on a single central hero or event of national sig-

nificance" (*Muse for Heroes*, 5). I would argue that the hero rises out of the event. James Nohrnberg says that one of the two requirements of the epic is that it have "a nearly determinative relation to a culture . . . [t]he epic shows a tendency to become a 'scripture' of its culture. . . . Such an epic is one of the things that a culture, in its quest for self-definition, *intends*" (*"The Iliad,"* 4). And Philip Hardie writes, "From its beginnings, the epic's central subject may be construed as the continuity or discontinuity of social and political structures" (*Epic Successors of Virgil*, 88).

38. Spencer, *Quest for Nationality*, 58.

39. It is not accidental that Maurice Bowra wrote one book called *Heroic Poetry* and another called *From Virgil to Milton*. The works treated in the latter are also dealt with in the former, but most of the works in the former are absent from the latter.

40. Charles Moorman (*Kings and Captains*) includes in his study the *Iliad*, the *Odyssey*, *Beowulf*, the *Song of Roland*, the *Nibelungenlied*, the Icelandic sagas, and Arthurian romances; but he carefully refrains from referring to them as epics. His is a study of heroic literature.

41. Bowra, *Heroic Poetry*, 15.

42. Harrison, "Some Views of the *Aeneid*," 9.

43. Newman, *Classical Epic Tradition*, 32.

44. Winnifrith perhaps goes too far when he says, "Heroes do not make an epic poem, and the great epic poems succeed in spite rather than because of their heroes" ("Postscript," 114). The hero is an integral part of the work, though not as he has usually been considered. Lukács is more accurate: "The epic hero is, strictly speaking, never an individual. It is traditionally thought that one of the essential characteristics of the epic is that its theme is not a personal testing but the destiny of a community" (*Theory of the Novel*, 166). In contrast, Quint refers to the reader's enjoyment of "the sheer athleticism of warfare celebrated throughout the *Iliad*" (*Epic and Empire*, 3). Many readers undoubtedly have enjoyed that aspect of the poem, without thinking about the escalating brutality of the fighting or the ignobility of Hektor's death or Achilleus' gratuitous cruelty. Even the reader who enjoys the athleticism should be expected to become increasingly disenchanted with or even disgusted at the fighting. Quint also cites Vives' comment that "The name of Achilles enflamed Alexander, Alexander Caesar, Caesar many others: Caesar killed in various wars 192,000 men, not counting the civil wars" (*Epic and Empire*, 5). This statement is not necessarily a positive recommendation for the value of epic. Of course, Quint also argues that "When Achilles returns to battle, he reinstates heroism" (*Epic and Empire*, 48). What Achilleus brings to the battle hardly deserves the name of heroism.

45. Keith, *Engendering Epic*, 5.

46. Quotations from *Beowulf* are from the translation of E. Talbot Donaldson (*Beowulf: A New Translation*).

47. A rather different view of this subject can be found in Mihoko Suzuki's *Metamorphoses of Helen*: "I use theories of sacrifice and scapegoating in order to elucidate the contradictions *within* these texts—between the dominant patriarchal perspective and that of the female scapegoat" (3). See also Robinson, *Monstrous Regiment*.

48. See Bakhtin, "Epic and Novel." Wofford, *Choice of Achilles*, 2.

49. See Quint, (*Epic and Empire*, chapter 9) for a good summary of how epic came to be viewed as a statement of nationalist sentiment in the eighteenth and nineteenth centuries. Notice Quint's warning (359) that viewing many of these works, like the *Nibelungenlied*, as expressions of national pride requires considerable imagination.

50. Bellamy, *Translations of Power*, 23.

51. Quint, *Epic and Empire*, 7.

52. Wofford sensibly says that "epic poetry should not be ceded to interpretations that are univocal or idealizing" (*Choice of Achilles*, 8).

53. For example, Ernst Robert Curtius calls him "lifeless" (*European Literature*, 174).

54. Harrison's survey of Virgil criticism illustrates the perspectives from which the *Aeneid* has been viewed. Thus, against the traditional view of Aeneas as the upholder of civilization, the Harvard school (Adam Parry, Wendell Clausen, and Michael Putnam) "tended to hold that the poem presented a pessimistic view alongside the surface glory of Aeneas and Rome" and Harrison refers to "the dark side of political success and the cost of imperialism" ("Some Views of the *Aeneid*," 5).

55. Winnifrith, "Postscript," 112–13.

56. The translation is mine, with the help of Clark Zlotchew.

57. Pound, *ABC of Reading*, 46.

58. Bellamy, *Translations of Power*, 3.

59. *Sundiata*, 1.

60. Frank Cross writes that "the epic form, designed to recreate and give meaning to the historical experiences of a people or nation, is not merely or simply historical" (*Canaanite Myth*, viii).

61. Hardie, *Epic Successor of Virgil*, 107.

62. Routh, *God, Man, and Epic Poetry*, 255.

63. Robert Morris refers to *A Dance to the Music of Time* as "a comic epic on time, history, and change" (*Continuance and Change*, 23), but I regard that statement as relying on a very loose definition of "epic." More pertinently, Morris recognizes that in Powell's work "global tragedy provides only the backdrop for the personal one" (141).

64. Hegel, *Aesthetics*, 1045.

65. As Frye puts it, the *Odyssey* "is a romance of a hero escaping safely from incredible perils" (*Anatomy*, 319). It is far more like *David of Sassoun* or the *Adventures of Sayf ben Dhi Yazan* than it is like the *Iliad*.

66. Colie points out that for Renaissance theorists, Homer had written one epic, the *Iliad*, that "gave rise to the tragic genre, but also he had written an epic from which comedy sprang in the *Odyssey*; from comedy to romance was but a short step" (*Resources of Kind*, 23).

67. Bellamy, *Translations of Power*, 27.

68. Maskell, *Historical Epic in France*, 181–82.

69. Bloomfield, "Episodic Motivation," 97.

70. Hans-Erich Keller says that "it is clear that after 1150, although the *chanson de geste* will still remain alive for another century at least, it had lost its intrinsic function, namely the appeal to the *sainte mellee* (the holy medley) and to the perpetual military pilgrimage in the cause of Christendom. The tastes of the audience now required that the poet praise not so much heroes with extraordinary physical force and endurance in the service of France and Christianity but heroes without ties to their own period, incorporating the virtues defined by the new type of knight and courtly society" ("Changes in Old French Epic Poetry," 173).

71. Parker, *Inescapable Romance*, 5.

72. Bowra, *Heroic Poetry*, 545.

73. Fielding, *Joseph Andrews*, 4. I ran into a friend, a Miltonist, as I was working on this book in the British Library. When I told her that I was working on twentieth-century epic-novels, she immediately responded, "No one has written an epic since Milton."

74. Fielding, *Joseph Andrews*, 3.

75. Morson, *Mikhail Bakhtin*, 318.
76. Lukács, *Theory of the Novel*, 41, 88.
77. Obviously Tolstoy differs here from Apollonius of Rhodes: The *Argonautica* is an epic in search of a hero. This seems to have characterized all epics of that period" (Beye, *The Iliad*, 210). Tolstoy has a hero, but his hero is not an individual.
78. Lukács, *Theory of the Novel*, 145–46.
79. James, *Tragic Muse*, x.
80. The Yiddish title of the trilogy is actually *Farn Mabul, Before the Flood*, but the city-names of the individual volumes are the same.
81. I might refer to this phenomenon as a locus-focus, but I will not. Rather I will point out that some works with similar titles are not epic. Naghib Mahfouz' *Cairo Trilogy*, for example, is an important work, but its focus is not on a pivotal historical moment.

Chapter 2. Sholem Asch's *Three Cities*

1. Maurice Bowra refers also to the heroic *Tale of Lenin* by Marfa Kryukova, in which Lenin and Stalin take on the guise of traditional warrior heroes (*Heroic Poetry*, 116).
2. Solzhenitsyn, *August 1914*, 24.
3. There is a good deal of confusion about the English title of Sholokhov's novel. Ermolaev calls it *The Quiet Don*, while the recent translation by Robert Daglish calls it *Quiet Flows the Don*. Simply because that is the translation on which I have relied, I use that title. Ermolaev, *Mikhail Sholokhov*, 118.
4. Ibid., 90.
5. Murphy, "Introduction," x.
6. Ermolaev, *Mikhail Sholokhov*, 45.
7. Ibid., 88.
8. Solzhenitsyn, *November 1916*, "Author's Note."
9. All dates are from Siegel's chronology (*Controversial Sholem Asch*, 299–304).
10. Unless otherwise noted, all quotations are from *Three Cities: A Trilogy*, (New York: G. P. Putnam's Sons, 1933).
11. In the Yiddish, that rhythm is called a "gemara nigundl," a little Gemara tune, a phrase that would have numerous connotations involving Talmud study for a Yiddish-speaking audience.
12. Madison, *Yiddish Literature*, 225.
13. In fairness to Misha, later on he abandons the Bolsheviks when he sees through their deceptions, and he does his best to protect his father as they try to escape from Russia
14. Another picture of Lodz, not part of an epic but part of a family chronicle, can be found in I. J. Singer's novel *The Family Moskat*.
15. Joyce, *Ulysses*, 35.
16. Kaun, *Soviet Poets and Poetry*, 188.
17. In the English translation, the question is rendered, "Tell me, who are these Bolsheviks," but that translation does not convey the real confusion that Vassily and others feel about the people who are threatening their way of life.
18. Madison, *Yiddish Literature*, 240.
19. Siegel, *Controversial Sholem Asch*, 88.
20. Madison, *Yiddish Literature*, 241.
21. Liptzin, *History of Yiddish Literature*, 147.

22. I have provided my own translation because the English translation—"It was a flight from himself—for in that familiar circle he felt quite different, quite well, as if in another world" (236)—misses the essential tone of the passage.

23. It is interesting that Zachary greets Chomsky in the English translation, "Oh it's you Herr Chomsky" (270), giving the old man a German, secular title. In the Yiddish the text reads, "Oh, it's you, Reb Baruch" (306). The differences are significant. First, Chomsky's identity as a religious Jew underlies the following conversation, so the secular form of address is inappropriate. And second, his name, Baruch, means "blessed," which, in his role with Zachary, he certainly is.

24. The English translation, using the language of the time, calls the land Palestine, but Asch uses the more evocative Hebrew term.

25. Siegel, *Controversial Sholem Asch*, 94.

CHAPTER 3. OLIVIA MANNING'S *FORTUNES OF WAR*

1. For example, Ian MacNiven, in his biography of Lawrence Durrell, reports that Durrell "did not find attractive Olivia's tubular figure and oval face—set, typically under a turban—and still less did he like her sharp, critical manner. In this, his opinion was shared by most people who knew her in Cairo" (*Lawrence Durrell*, 242).

2. All quotations from the trilogies are from *The Balkan Trilogy* (New York: Penguin, 1981) and *The Levant Trilogy* (New York: Penguin, 1982).

3. Robert Morris says that "the relationship between Guy and Harriet, one of the major threads of the trilogy, [is] often hard to unravel and often lost in the rich fabric of external events in Bucharest and Athens" ("Olivia Manning," 46).

4. Bellamy, *Translations of Power*, 53.

5. Morris, *Continuance and Change*, 29.

6. English, "Introduction," xv.

7. Burgess, *Novel Now*, 95.

8. Tillyard, *Elizabethan World Picture*, 7.

9. Morris refers to Guy's myopia as both "literal and figurative" ("Olivia Manning," 244).

CHAPTER 4. PAUL SCOTT'S *RAJ QUARTET*

1. Berlin, *Hedgehog and the Fox*, 3.
2. Ibid., 3.
3. Ibid., 4.
4. Ibid., 5.
5. Ibid., 11.
6. Ibid., 15.
7. Ibid. 20.
8. Ibid.
9. Tolstoy, *War and Peace*, 208.
10. Ibid., 21.
11. Ibid., 340.
12. Ibid., 931.
13. Ibid.

14. Ibid., 932.
15. Ibid., 933.
16. Ibid., 717.
17. Ibid.
18. Ibid., 1152.
19. Ibid., 326.
20. Berlin, *Hedgehog and the Fox*, 71.
21. Rao, *Paul Scott*, 145; Mahood, "Paul Scott's Guardians," 244; Petersone, "Concept of History," 228; Weisbaum, *Paul Scott*, 191.
22. All quotations are from Paul Scott, *On Writing and the Novel*, (New York: Morrow, 1987) and *The Raj Quartet* (New York: Morrow, 1976).
23. Spurling, *Paul Scott*, 244.
24. Boyer, "Love, Sex, and History," 64.
25. Parry, "Paul Scott's Raj," 359.
26. Weisbaum, *Paul Scott*, 138.
27. Ibid., 93–94.
28. Scanlan, "Disappearances of History," 153.
29. See Rushdie, "Outside the Whale." As Peter Childs says, "The *Quartet* is undeniably more about the raj and its rule, administration, and treatment of India, than about India's experience under the raj" (*Paul Scott's* Raj Quartet, 33-34).
30. Spurling, *Paul Scott*, 118.
31. I obviously disagree with David Rubin, who says, "The kind of history that most profoundly engages Paul Scott's concern and forms the central theme of the *Quartet* is the spiritual record of individuals for whom 'history,' as we usually think of it—the fate of nations and the end of empires, the sweeping movements and transformations of societies and their institutions—is secondary to their spiritual pilgrimages" (*After the Raj*, 149).
32. Weisbaum, *Paul Scott*, 82; Gorra, *After Empire*, 15.
33. Tolstoy, *War and Peace*, 227.
34. Weisbaum, *Paul Scott*, 33.
35. Spurling, *Paul Scott*, 34.
36. Boyer, "Love, Sex, and History," 73.
37. Weisbaum, *Paul Scott*, 145.
38. Boyer, "Love, Sex, and History," 71.
39. Petersone, "Concept of History," 231.
40. Rao, *Paul Scott*, 130.
41. Childs, *Paul Scott's* Raj Quartet, 118.
42. Tolstoy, *War and Peace*, 717.
43. It is curious that two of the heroes of these epic novels, Guy Pringle and Guy Perron, share the same name.
44. Childs, *Paul Scott's* Raj Quartet, 51.
45. Scanlan, "Disappearances of History," 158.
46. Weisbaum, *Paul Scott*, 45.
47. Forster, *Passage to India*, 322.
48. Other readers, like Weisbaum (*Paul Scott*, 180), Scanlan ("Disappearances of History," 160), and Childs (*Paul Scott's* Raj Quartet, 107) see a parallel between loss of faith in Christianity and in the raj as an institution. Childs (chapter 2) even sees an analogy between all the gardens in the *Quartet* (especially the Bibighar Gardens) and the story of the Fall and exile of Adam and Eve. I argue that Scott would have seen such a loss of faith as not possi-

ble, since the British had never applied the teachings of Christianity in India. They had used it only as another instrument of imperialism.

49. Boyer, "Love, Sex, and History," 65.
50. Parry, "Paul Scott's Raj," 369.
51. Childs, *Paul Scott's* Raj Quartet, 135.
52. Weisbaum, *Paul Scott*, 97
53. Gorra, *After Empire*, 18.
54. Robin Moore, *Paul Scott's Raj*, 116.

Chapter 5. Edward Whittemore's *Jerusalem Quartet*

1. O'Hara, Review of *Sinai* Tapestry, 406.
2. Robertson, *On Christian Doctrine*, xiv–xv.
3. Skow, Review of *Quin's Shanghai Circus*, 92–93.
4. Ishikawa, "Introduction," 14.
5. Keene, *No*, 23.
6. Ibid., 23.
7. Augustine, *On Christian Doctrine*, 37–38.
8. Keene, *No*, 23.
9. All quotations are from *Quin's Shanghai Circus* (New York: Holt Rinehart and Winston, 1974).
10. Creel, *What Is Taoism?*, 2–3.
11. Keene, *No*, 19.
12. All quotations from the *Jerusalem Quartet* are from the following volumes: *Sinai Tapestry*—(NY: Holt Rinehart and Winston, 1977); *Jerusalem Poker*—(NY: Holt Rinehart and Winston, 1978); *Nile Shadows*—(NY: Holt Rinehart and Winston, 1983); *Jericho Mosaic*—(NY: W. W. Norton & Co., 1987).
13. Sonyel, *Turkish Diplomacy*, 173.
14. Dakin, *Unification of Greece*, 236.
15. Sonyel, *Turkish Diplomacy*, xi.
16. Owen, *Collected Poems*, 42.

Chapter 6. Lawrence Durrell's *Alexandria Quartet*

1. Rowland, "Way to the Light," 39.
2. Curtius, *European Literature*, 361–62.
3. Ibid., 120.
4. Yunck, "Introduction," 16.
5. Dante, *Epistle to Can Grande della Scala*, 460.
6. Dante, *Paradise*, 23: 133–45.
7. Friedman, *Lawrence Durrell*, 62.
8. Friedman, *Critical Essays*, 3.
9. Bode, "Guide to Alexandria," 206.
10. "Lawrence Durrell Answers," 151.
11. Pine says, "At the end of *Ulysses* and *A la Recherche* the central figure is satiated, complete; at the end of the *Quartet* he is another man, about to begin writing the book again; Bloom and Marcel are linear creatures, Darley is cyclic" (*Lawrence Durrell*, 208), to

which I would add that Dante, too, is cyclic and can only write the *Comedy* afater being "reborn."

12. Hainsworth, *Idea of Epic*, 140.
13. All quotations from the *Alexandria Quartet* are from the following volumes: *Justine*—(NY: E. P. Dutton, 1957); *Balthazar*—(NY: E. P. Dutton, 1958); *Mountolive*—(NY: E. P. Dutton, 1959); *Clea*—(NY: E. P. Dutton, 1960).
14. Middleton, "Heraldic Universe," 20.
15. Ibid., 21.
16. Wedin, "Artist as Narrator," 179.
17. Peirce, "Fellowship in Time," 76.
18. Ibid., 74.
19. Durrell, *Key*, 68.
20. Hutchens, "Heraldic Universe," 57.
21. Eliot, *The Waste Land* (in *Complete Poems and Plays*), l.60.
22. Durrell, *Key*, 147.
23. Ibid., 154–55.
24. Ibid., 152.
25. Friedman, *Lawrence Durrell*, xv.
26. Pine, *Lawrence Durrell*, 193.
27. Harry T. Moore, *World of Lawrence Durrell*, 162. MacNiven, *Lawrence Durrell*, 527.
28. See Manzaloui, "Curate's Egg."
29. Rexroth, "What Is Wrong with Durrell?" 122.
30. Friedman, *Critical Essays*, 4.
31. Pine, *Lawrence Durrell*, 179.
32. Ibid., 181.
33. Peirce, "That 'one book there, a Plutarch,'" 90. Kermode, "Durrell's *Alexandria Quartet*," 112.
34. Miller, *The Epic Hero*, 361.
35. Friedman, *Lawrence Durrell*, 145.
36. Kermode, "Durrell's *Alexandria Quartet*," 114.
37. Mackworth, "Lawrence Durrell and the New Romanticism," 35.
38. Pine, *Lawrence Durrell*, 172.
39. Weigel, *Lawrence Durrell*, 109.
40. Pursewarden also makes a not terribly flattering reference here to some lines from William Blake, who wrote,

> In a wife I would desire
> What in whores is always found
> The lineaments of Gratified desire

Elsewhere he used the lines a bit differently:

> What is it men in women do require
> The lineaments of Gratified Desire
> What is it women do in men require
> The lineaments of Gratified Desire
>   (*Complete Poetry and Prose of William Blake*, 474–75.

41. Joyce, *Portrait*, 301.
42. "Kneller Tape," 165–66.

43. See Pinchin, "Durrell's Fatal Cleopatra."
44. Trilling, "Quartet," 53.
45. Hollahan, "Who Wrote *Mountolive?*" 116.
46. Wedin ("Artist as Narrator") makes an interesting argument that Darley is also the fictional author of *Mountolive*. See also Hollahan, ibid.
47. Lemon, "Durrell, Derrida, and the Heraldic Universe," 68.
48. Durrell, *Tunc*, 118.
49. Ibid., 183.
50. Durrell, *Key*, 90.
51. Steiner, "Lawrence Durrell," 17.
52. Durrell, *Key*, x.

Works Cited

Adventures of Sayf ben Dhi Yazan: An Arab Folk Epic. Trans. Lena Jayyusi. Bloomington: Indiana University Press, 1996.

Alexandre-Garner, Corinne. "The Triangle of Love, Incest, and Writing." In *On Miracle Ground: Essays on the Fiction of Lawrence* Durrell, ed. Michael H. Begnal, 52–62. Lewisburg, Penn.: Bucknell University Press.

Arlett, Robert. *Epic Voices: Inner and Global Impulse in the Contemporary American and British Novel.* Selinsgrove, Penn.: Susquehanna University Press, 1996.

Asch, Sholem. *The Apostle.* Trans. Maurice Samuel. New York: G. P. Putnam's Sons, 1943.

———. *East River.* Trans. A. H. Gross. New York: G. P. Putnam's Sons, 1946.

———. *Farn Mabul.* 3 volumes. Buenos Aires: Zentral-Farband fun Poylishe Yidn in Argentina, 1949.

———. *Kiddush Ha-Shem and Sabbatai Zevi.* Trans. Rufus Learsi, Florence Whyte, and George Rapall Noyes. New York: Meridian Books, 1959.

———. *Motke the Thief.* Trans. Willa and Edwin Muir. New York: G. P. Putnam's Sons, 1935.

———. *The Nazarene.* Trans. Maurice Samuel. New York: G. P. Putnam's Sons, 1939

———. *Three Cities: A Trilogy.* Trans. Willa and Edwin Muir. New York: G. P. Putnam's Sons, 1933.

Augustine. *On Christian Doctrine.* Trans. and ed. D. W. Robertson. New York: Liberal Arts Press, 1958.

Bakhtin, M. M. "Epic and Novel." In *The Dialogic Imagination,* ed. Michael Holquist, trans. Caryl Emerson and Michael Holquist. Austin: University of Texas Press, 1981.

Begnal, Michael H., ed. *On Miracle Ground: Essays on the Fiction of Lawrence Durrell.* Lewisburg, Penn.: Bucknell University Press, 1990.

Beissinger, Margaret, Jane Tylus, Susanne Wofford, eds. *Epic Traditions in the Contemporary World: The Poetics of Community.* Berkeley: University of California Press, 1999.

Bellamy, Elizabeth. *Translations of Power: Narcissism and the Unconscious in Epic History.* Ithaca: Cornell University Press, 1992.

Beowulf. A New Translation. Trans. E. Talbot Donaldson. New York: Norton, 1966.

Berlin, Isaiah. *The Hedgehog and the Fox.* Chicago: Ivan R. Dee, 1993.

Beye, Charles R. *The Iliad, the Odyssey, and the Epic Tradition.* Gloucester, Mass.: Peter Smith, 1972.

Blake, William. *The Complete Poetry and Prose of William Blake,* ed. David V. Erdman. Rev. ed. Berkeley: University of California Press, 1982.

Bloomfield, Morton W. "Episodic Motivation and Marvels in Epic and Romance." In *Essays and Explorations: Studies in Ideas, Language, and Literature,* 97–128. Cambridge: Harvard University Press, 1970.

Bode, Carl. "A Guide to Alexandria." In *The World of Lawrence Durrell.* Ed. Harry T. Moore, 205–21. Carbondale: Southern Illinois University Press, 1962.

Bowra, C. M. *From Virgil to Milton.* London: Macmillan, 1948.

———. *Heroic Poetry.* London: Macmillan: 1961.

Boyer, Allen. "Love, Sex, and History in *The Raj Quartet.*" *Modern Language Quarterly* 46, no. 1 (1985): 64–80.

Bumke, Joachim. *Courtly Cultures: Literature and Society in the High Middle Ages.* Trans. Thomas Dunlap. Berkeley: University of California Press, 1991.

Burgess, Anthony. *The Novel Now: A Guide to Contemporary Fiction.* New York: W. W. Norton & Co., 1967.

Bynum, Paige Matthey. "The Artist as Shaman: Durrell's *Alexandria Quartet.*" In *Lawrence Durrell, Comprehending the Whole.* Ed. Julius R. Raper, Melody L. Enscore, and Paige Bynum, 82–97. Columbia: University of Missouri Press, 1995.

Calin, William. *A Muse for Heroes: Nine Centuries of the Epic in France.* Toronto: University of Toronto Press, 1983.

Cambridge History of Literary Criticism: Volume 3, The Renaissance. Ed. Glyn P. Norton. Cambridge: Cambridge University Press, 1999.

Childs, Peter. *Paul Scott's* Raj Quartet: *History and Division.* Victoria: English Literary Studies, 1998.

Colie, Rosalie L. *The Resources of Kind: Genre-Theory in the Renaissance.* Ed. Barbara K. Lewalski. Berkeley: University of California Press, 1973.

Creel, Herrlee G. *What Is Taoism? and Other Studies in Chinese Cultural History.* Chicago: University of Chicago Press, 1970.

Cross, Frank Moore. *Canaanite Myth and Hebrew Epic: Essays in the History of the Religion of Israel.* Cambridge: Harvard University Press, 1973.

Curran, Stuart, ed. *Le Bossu and Voltaire on the Epic.* Gainesville, Fla.: Scholars' Press, 1970.

Curtius, Ernst Robert. *European Literature and the Latin Middle Ages.* New York: Pantheon Books, 1953.

Dakin, Douglas. *The Unification of Greece, 1770–1923.* New York: St. Martin's Press, 1972.

Dante. *The Divine Comedy: Paradise.* Trans. Mark Musa. London: Penguin, 1986.

———. *Epistle to Can Grande della Scala.* In *Medieval Literary Theory and Criticism, c.1100–c.1375: The Commentary Tradition,* ed. A. J. Minnis and A. B. Scott. Oxford: Clarendon Press, 1988.

Dasenbrook, Reed Way. "Lawrence Durrell and the Modes of Modernism." *Twentieth-Century Literature* 33, no. 4 (1987): 515–27.

David of Sassoun: The Armenian Folk Epic in Four Cycles. Trans. Artin K. Shalian. Athens: Ohio University Press, 1964.

Degi, Bruce. "Paul Scott's Indian National Army: *The Mark of the Warrior* and *The Raj Quartet.*" *Clio* 18, no. 1 (1988): 41–55.

Delasanta, Rodney. *The Epic Voice.* The Hague: Mouton, 1967.

Derrida, Jacques. "The Law of Genre." Trans. Avital Ronell. *Critical Inquiry* 7 (1980): 55–81.

Dold, Bernard E. *Two Post–1945 British Novelists: Olivia Manning and Tom Sharpe.* Rome: Herder Editore, 1985.

Dubois, Page. *History, Rhetorical Description and the Epic: From Homer to Spenser.* Cambridge: D. S. Brewer, 1982.

Duggan, Joseph J. "The Epic." In *A New History of French Literature.* Ed. Denis Hollier. Cambridge: Harvard University Press, 1989.

Durrell, Lawrence. *Balthazar.* New York: E. P. Dutton, 1958.

———. *Clea.* New York: E. P. Dutton, 1960.

———. *Justine.* New York: E. P. Dutton, 1957.

———. *A Key to Modern British Poetry.* Norman: University of Oklahoma Press, 1952.

———. *Mountolive.* New York: E. P. Dutton, 1959.

———. *Tunc.* New York: E. P. Dutton, 1968.

Eliot, T. S. *The Complete Poems and Plays, 1909–1950.* San Diego: Harcourt Brace Jovanovich, 1971.

English, Isobel. "Introduction." In Olivia Manning, *The Wind Changes.* 1937. New York: Penguin, 1991.

Ercilla, Alonso de. *La Araucana.* Ed. Florencia Grau. Barcelona: Editorial Iberia, 1962.

Erickson, Wayne. *Mapping The Faerie Queene: Quest Structure and the World of the Poem.* New York: Garland, 1996.

Ermolaev, Herman. *Mikhail Sholokhov and his Art.* Princeton: Princeton University Press, 1982.

Fertile, Candace. "The Role of the Writer in Lawrence Durrell's Fiction." In *On Miracle Ground: Essays on the Fiction of Lawrence Durrell*, ed. Michael H. Begnal: 63–76. Lewisburg, Penn.: Bucknell University Press, 1990.

Fielding, Henry. *Joseph Andrews.* Ed. Martin Battestin. Middletown, Conn.: Wesleyan University Press, 1967.

Foerster, Donald M. *The Fortunes of Epic Poetry: A Study in English and American Criticism, 1750–1950.* Washington, D. C.: Catholic University of America Press, 1962.

Forster, E. M. *A Passage to India.* New York: Harcourt, Brace and World, 1952.

Fowler, Alastair. *Kinds of Literature: An Introduction to the Theory of Genres and Modes.* Cambridge: Harvard University Press, 1982.

Friedman, Alan Warren, ed. *Critical Essays on Lawrence Durrell.* Boston: G. K. Hall, 1987.

———. *Lawrence Durrell and* The Alexandria Quartet*: Art for Love's Sake.* Norman: University of Oklahoma Press, 1970.

Frye, Northrop. *Anatomy of Criticism: Four Essays.* Princeton: Princeton University Press, 1957.

Genette, Gérard. *Paliimpsestes: la literature au second degree.* Paris: Seuil, 1982.

Gorra, Michael. *After Empire: Scott, Naipaul, Rushdie.* Chicago: University of Chicago Press, 1997.

Greene, Thomas. *The Descent from Heaven: A Study in Epic Continuity*. New Haven: Yale University Press, 1963.
Hainsworth, J. B. *The Idea of Epic*. Berkeley: University of California Press, 1991.
Hardie, Philip. *The Epic Successors of Virgil: A Study in the Dynamics of a Tradition*. Cambridge: Cambridge University Press, 1993.
Harrison, S. J. "Some Views of the *Aeneid* in the Twentieth Century. In *Oxford Readings in Virgil's Aeneid*, ed. S. J. Harrison, 1–20. Oxford: Oxford University Press, 1990.
Hegel, G. W. F. *Aesthetics*. Trans. T. M. Knox. Oxford: Oxford University Pres, 1975.
Heilbut, Anthony. "History on a Magic Carpet." *Nation*, 10 September 1977, 216–18.
Hollahan, Eugene. "Who Wrote *Mountolive*? The Same One who Wrote 'Swann in Love.'" In *On Miracle Ground: Essays on the Fiction of Lawrence Durrell*, ed. Michael H. Begnal, 113–32. Lewisburg, Penn.: Bucknell University Press, 1990.
Homer. *The Iliad*. Trans. Richmond Lattimore. Chicago: University of Chicago Press, 1951.
———. *The Odyssey*. Trans. Richmond Lattimore. New York: Harper & Row, 1965.
Hougan, Jim. "Catholicism Berserk in the Holy Land." *Harper's*, May 1978, 68–70.
Hutchens. Eleanor N. "The Heraldic Universe in The Alexandria Quartet." *College English* 24 (1962): 56–61.
Ishikawa, Jun. "Introduction." In Donald Keene, *No: The Classical Theatre of Japan*. Tokyo: Kodansha International, 1966.
James, Henry. *The Tragic Muse*. New York: Scribner's, 1908.
Javitch, Daniel. "Italian Epic Theory." In *Cambridge History of Literary Criticism: Volume 3, The Renaissance,* ed. Glyn P. Norton, 205–15. Cambridge: Cambridge University Press, 1999.
Joyce, James. *A Portrait of the Artist as a Young Man*. New York: Viking Press, 1964.
———. *Ulysses*. New York: Modern Library, 1934.
Kaun, Alexander. *Soviet Poets and Poetry*. Berkeley: University of California Press, 1943.
Kazantzakis, Nikos. *The Odyssey: A Modern Sequel*. Trans. Kimon Friar. New York: Simon & Schuster, 1958.
Keene, Donald. *No: The Classical Theatre of Japan*. Tokyo: Kodansha International, 1966.
Keith, A. M. *Engendering Epic: Women In Latin Epic*. Cambridge: Cambridge University Press, 2000.
Keller, Hans-Erich. "Changes in Old French Epic Poetry and Changes in the Taste of its Audience." In *The Epic in Medieval Society: Aesthetic and Moral Values*, ed. Harald Scholler, 150–77. Tübingen: Max Niemeyer, 1977.
Kennedy, Duncan F. "Virgilian Epic." *The Cambridge Companion to Virgil*, ed. Charles Martindale, 145–54. Cambridge: Cambridge University Press, 1997.
Ker, W. P. *Epic and Romance: Essays on Medieval Literature*. 1896. New York: Dover Publications, 1957.
Kermode, Frank. "Durrell's *Alexandria Quartet*." In *Puzzles and Epiphanies: Essays and Reviews, 1958–1961*, 214–27. London: Routledge, 1962. Reprinted in *Critical Essays on Lawrence Durrell*, ed Alan W. Friedman, 110–16. Boston: G. K. Hall, 1987.
Klein, Lisa. *The Exemplary Sidney and the Elizabethan Sonneteer*. Newark: University of Delaware Press, 1998.

"The Kneller Tape." In *The World of Lawrence Durrell*, ed. Harry T. Moore, 160–68. Carbondale: Southern Illinois University Press, 1962.

Kruppa, Joseph E. "Durrell's *Alexandria Quartet* and the 'Implosion' of the Modern Consciousness." *Modern Fiction Studies* 13, no. 3 (1967): 401–16.

Langer, Ullrich. "Invention." In *Cambridge History of Literary Criticism: Volume 3, The Renaissance*, ed. Glyn P. Norton, 136–44. Cambridge: Cambridge University Press, 1999.

Latham, Ernest H., Jr. "Watching from the Window: Olivia Manning in Romania 1939–40." *Journal of the American Romanian Academy of Arts and Sciences* 20 (1995): 92–112.

Lawrence Durrell and Henry Miller: A Private Correspondence. Ed. George Wiches. New York: E. P. Dutton, 1963

"Lawrence Durrell Answers a Few Questions." In *The World of Lawrence Durrell*, ed. Harry T. Moore, 156–60. Carbondale: Southern Illinois University Press, 1962.

Le Bossu. *Treatise of the Epick Poem.* Trans. W. J. London. 1695. In *Le Bossu and Voltaire on the Epic*, ed. Stuart Curran. Gainesville, Fla.: Scholars' Press, 1970.

Lemon, Lee T. "Durrell, Derrida, and the Heraldic Universe." In *Lawrence Durrell: Comprehending the Whole*, ed. Julius R. Raper, Melody L. Enscore, Paige Bynum, 62–69. Columbia: University of Missouri Press, 1995.

Liptzin, Sol. *A History of Yiddish Literature.* Middle Village, N.Y.: Jonathan David, 1972.

Lorenz, Paul H. "Angkor Wat, the Kundalini, and the Quinx: The Human Architecture of Divine Renewal in the *Quincunx*." In *Lawrence Durrell: Comprehending the Whole*, ed Julius R. Raper, Melody L. Enscore, Paige Bynum, 161–71. Columbia: University of Missouri Press, 1995

Lukács, Georg. *The Theory of the Novel: A Historico-philosophical Essay on the Form of Great Epic Literature.* 1920. Trans. Anna Bostock. London: Merlin, 1971.

Lutwack, Leonard. *Heroic Fiction: The Epic Tradition and American Novels of the Twentieth Century.* Carbondale: Southern Illinois University Press, 1971.

Mackworth, Cecily. "Lawrence Durrell and the New Romanticism." In *The World of Lawrence Durrell*, ed. Harry T. Moore, 24–37. Carbondale: Southern Illinois University Press, 1962.

MacNiven, Ian. *Lawrence Durrell: A Biography.* London: Faber & Faber, 1998.

Madison, Charles A. *Yiddish Literature: Its Scope and Major Writers.* New York: Frederick Ungar, 1968.

Mahood, M. M. "Paul Scott's Guardians." *Yearbook of English Studies* 13 (1983): 244–58.

Manning, Olivia. *Artist among the Missing.* 1949. London: Heinemann, 1975.

———. *The Balkan Trilogy.* New York: Penguin, 1981.

———. *A Different Face.* London: Heinemann, 1953.

———. *The Doves of Venus.* 1955. London: Virago, 1984.

———. *The Levant Trilogy.* New York: Penguin, 1982.

———. *The Play Room.* 1969. London: Virago, 1984.

———. *The Rain Forest.* 1974. London: Virago, 1991.

———. *The Wind Changes.* 1937. New York: Penguin, 1991.

Manzaloui, Mahmoud. "Curate's Egg: An Alexandrian Opinion of Durrell's *Quartet*." *Etudes Anglaises* 15 (1962): 248–60. Reprinted in *Critical Essays on Lawrence Durrell*, ed. Alan W. Friedman, 144–57. Boston: G. K. Hall, 1987.

Maresca, Thomas. *Epic to Novel.* Columbus: Ohio State University Press, 1974.

Maskell, David. *The Historical Epic in France, 1500–1700.* Oxford: Oxford University Press, 1973.

McNamee, Maurice B. *Honor and the Epic Hero.* New York: Holt, Rinehart & Winston, 1960.

McWilliams, John P., Jr. *The American Epic: Transforming a Genre, 1770–1860.* Cambridge: Cambridge University Press, 1989.

Merchant, Paul. "Children of Homer: the Epic Strain in Modern Greek Literature." In *Aspects of the Epic,* ed. Tom Winnifrith, Penelope Murray, and K. W. Gransden, 42–108. New York: St. Martin's Press, 1983.

———. *The Epic.* London: Methuen, 1971.

Middleton, Christopher. "The Heraldic Universe." In *Critical Essays on Lawrence Durrell,* ed. Alan W. Friedman, 15–21. Boston: G. K. Hall, 1987.

Miller, Dean. *The Epic Hero.* Baltimore: Johns Hopkins University Press, 2000.

Milton, John. *The Works of John Milton.* New York: Columbia University Press, 1931.

Mooney, Harry J., Jr. "Olivia Manning: Witness to History." In *Twentieth-Century Women Novelists,* ed. Thomas F. Staley, 39–62. London: Macmillan Publishers, 1982.

Moore, Harry T., ed. *The World of Lawrence Durrell.* Carbondale: Southern Illinois University Press, 1962.

Moore, Robin. *Paul Scott's Raj.* London: Heinemann, 1990.

Moorman, Charles. *Kings and Captains: Variations on a Heroic Theme.* Lexington: University Press of Kentucky, 1971.

Moretti, Franco. *Modern Epic: The World-System from Goethe to García Márquez.* Trans. Quintin Hoare. London: Verso, 1996.

Mori, Masaki. *Epic Grandeur: Toward a Comparative Poetics of the Epic.* Albany: SUNY Press, 1997.

Morris, Robert K. *Continuance and Change: The Contemporary British Novel Sequence.* Carbondale: Southern Illinois University Press, 1972.

———. "Olivia Manning's *Fortunes of War:* Breakdown in the Balkans, Love and Death in the Levant." In *British Novelists since 1900,* ed. Jack I. Biles, 233–52. New York: AMS Press, 1987.

Morson, Gary Saul, and Caryl Emerson. *Mikhail Bakhtin: Creation of a Prosaic.* Stanford, Calif.: Stanford University Press, 1990.

Murphy, Brian. "Introduction." In Mikhail Sholokhov, *Quiet Flows the Don,* trans. Robert Daglish, rev. and ed. Brian Murphy. New York: Carrol & Graf, 1996.

Newman, John K. *The Classical Epic Tradition.* Madison: University of Wisconsin Press, 1986.

Niane, D. T., ed. *Sundiata: An Epic of Old Mali.* Essex: Longman, 1965.

Nohrnberg, James. *"The Iliad."* In *Homer to Brecht: The European Epic and Dramatic Traditions,* ed. Michael Seidel and Edward Mendelson, 3–29. New Haven: Yale University Press, 1977.

Norton, Glyn P. "Introduction." In *Cambridge History of Literary Criticism: Volume 3, The Renaissance,* ed. Glyn P. Norton, 1–22. Cambridge: Cambridge University Press, 1999.

O'Hara, J. D. Review of *Sinai Tapestry. Library Journal,* 1 February 1977.

Owen, Wilfred. *The Collected Poems of Wilfred Owen*, ed. C. Day Lewis. London: Chatto & Windus, 1931.

Parker, Patricia A. *Inescapable Romance: Studies in the Poetics of a Mode*. Princeton: Princeton University Press, 1979.

Parry, Benita. "Paul Scott's Raj." *South Asian Review* 8, no. 4 (1975): 359–69.

Peirce, Carol. "A Fellowship in Time: Durrell, Eliot, and the Quest of the Grail." In *Lawrence Durrell: Comprehending the Whole*, ed. Julius R. Raper, Melody L. Enscore, Paige Bynum, 70–81. Columbia: University of Missouri Pres, 1995.

———. "'Intimations of Powers Within': Durrell's Heavenly Game of the Tarot." In *Critical Essays on Lawrence Durrell*, ed. Alan W. Friedman, 200–13. Boston: G. K. Hall, 1987.

———. "That 'one book there, a Plutarch': Of *Isis and Osiris* in *The Alexandria Quartet*. In *On Miracle Ground: Essays on the Fiction of Lawrence Durrell*, ed. Michael H. Begnal, 79–92. Lewisburg, Penn.: Bucknell University Press, 1990.

———. "'Wrinkled Deep in Time': *The Alexandria Quartet* as Many-Layered Palimpsest." *Twentieth-Century Literature* 33, no. 4 (1987): 485–98.

Petersone, Karina. "The Concept of History in Paul Scott's Tetralogy *The Raj Quartet*." *Zeitschrift für Anglistik und Amerikanistik* 37, no. 3 (1989): 228–33.

Pinchin, Jane. "Durrell's Fatal Cleopatra." *Modern Fiction Studies* 28, no. 2 (1982): 229–36.

Pine, Richard. *Lawrence Durrell: The Mindscape*. New York: St. Martin's Pres, 1994.

Pound, Ezra. *An ABC of Reading*. New York: New Directions, 1960.

Quint, David. *Epic and Empire: Politics and Generic Form from Virgil to Milton*. Princeton: Princeton University Press, 1993.

Rao, K. Bhaskara. *Paul Scott*. Boston: Twayne Publishers, 1980.

Raper, Julius R., Melody L. Enscore, Paige Bynum, eds. *Lawrence Durrell: Comprehending the Whole*. Columbia: University of Missouri Press, 1995.

Rexroth, Kenneth. "What Is Wrong with Durrell?" *The Nation*, 4 June 1960.

Robertson, D. W., Trans. and ed. *On Christian Doctrine*. By St. Augustine. New York: Liberal Arts Press, 1958.

Robinson, Lillian S. *Monstrous Regiment: The Lady Knight in Sixteenth-Century Epic*. New York: Garland, 1985.

Routh, H. V. *God, Man, and Epic Poetry: A Study in Comparative Literature*. 1927. New York: Greenwood Press, 1968.

Rowland, Ingrid D. "The Way to the Light." *New Republic*, 30 July 2001, 39–44.

Rubin, David. *After the Raj: British Novels of India Since 1947*. Hanover, N.H.: University Press of New England, 1986.

Rushdie, Salman. "Outside the Whale." *Imagining Homelands: Essays and Criticism, 1981–91*. New York: Granta, 1991.

Safer, Elaine. *The Contemporary American Comic Epic: The Novels of Barth, Pynchon, Gaddis, and Kesey*. Detroit: Wayne State University Press, 1989.

Scanlan, Margaret. "The Disappearances of History: Paul's Scott's Raj Quartet." *Clio* 15, no. 2 (1986): 153–69.

Scholler, Harald, ed. *The Epic in Medieval Society: Aesthetic and Moral Values*. Tübingen: Max Niemeyer, 1977.

Scott, Paul. *On Writing and the Novel.* Ed. Shelley C. Reece. New York: Morrow, 1987.
———. *The Raj Quartet.* New York: Morrow, 1976.
———. *Staying On.* London: Heinemann, 1977.
Sheridan, James, J., trans. *Anticlaudianus or The Good and Perfect Man.* By Alan of Lille. Toronto: Pontifical Institute of Medieval Studies, 1973.
Sholokhov, Mikhail. *Quiet Flows the Don.* Trans. Robert Daglish, rev. and ed. Brian Murphy. New York: Carroll & Graf, 1996.
Sidney, Philip. "An Apology for Poetry." In *Elizabethan Critical Essays*, ed. G. Gregory Smith. Oxford: Oxford University Press, 1904.
Siegel, Ben. *The Controversial Sholem Asch: An Introduction to His Fiction.* Bowling Green, Ohio: Bowling Green University Popular Press, 1976.
Singer, I. B. *The Family Moskat.* Trans. A. H. Gross. New York: Noonday Press, 1950.
Skow, John. Review of *Quin's Shanghai Circus. Time.* June 24, 1974: 92–93
Solzhenitsyn, Aleksandr. *August 1914: The Red Wheel / Knot I.* Trans. H. T. Willetts. 1971. New York: Farrar, Straus and Giroux, 1989.
———. *November 1916: The Red Wheel / Knot II.* Trans. H. T. Willetts. New York: Farrar, Straus and Giroux, 1999.
Sonyel, Salahi Ramsdan. *Turkish Diplomacy, 1918–1923: Mustafa Kemal and the Turkish National Movement.* London: Sage, 1975.
Spencer, Benjamin T. *The Quest for Nationality: An American Literary Campaign.* Syracuse: Syracuse University Press, 1957.
Spurling, Hilary. *Paul Scott: A Life of the Author of* The Raj Quartet. New York: W. W. Norton & Co., 1991.
Steiner, George. "Lawrence Durrell: The Baroque Novel." In *The World of Lawrence Durrell*, ed. Harry T. Moore, 13–23. Carbondale: Southern Illinois University, 1962.
Sundiata: An Epic of Old Mali. Ed. D. T. Niane, trans. G. D. Pickett. 1960. Essex: Longman, 1965.
Suzuki, Mihoko. *Metamorphoses of Helen: Authority, Difference, and the Epic.* Ithaca: Cornell University Press, 1989.
Taylor, Chet. "Dissonance and Digression: The Ill-Fitting Fusion of Philosophy and Form in Lawrence Durrell's *Alexandria Quartet.*" *MFS* 17 (1971): 167–79.
Tedesco, Janis, and Janet Popham. *Introduction to the Raj Quartet.* Lanham, MD: University Press of America, 1985.
Tillyard, E. M. W. *The Elizabethan World Picture.* New York: Macmillan, 1944.
———. *The Epic Strain in the English Novel.* Fair Lawn, N. J.: Essential Books, 1958.
Tolstoy, Leo. *War and Peace.* Trans. Rosemary Edmonds. London: Penguin, 1978.
Trilling, Lionel. "The Quartet: Two Reviews." In *The World of Lawrence Durrell*, ed. Harry T. Moore, 49–65. Carbondale: Southern Illinois University Press, 1962.
Voltaire. *An Essay…upon the Epick Poetry of the European Nations from Homer down to Milton.* 1727. In *Le Bossu and Voltaire on the Epic*, ed. Stuart Curran. Gainesville, Fla.: Scholars' Press, 1970.
Wedin, Warren. "The Artist as Narrator in *The Alexandria Quartet.*" *Twentieth-Century Literature* 18 (1972): 175–80.

Weigel. John. *Lawrence Durrell.* New York: Twayne Publishers, 1965.
Weil, Simone. *The Iliad or The Poem of Force.* Wallingford, Penn.: Pendle Hill, 1945.
Weinberg, Bernard. *A History of Literary Criticism in the Italian Renaissance.* Chicago: University of Chicago Press, 1961.
Weisbaum, Francine S. *Paul Scott: A Critical Study.* Austin: University of Texas Press, 1992.
Whittemore, Edward. *Jericho Mosaic.* New York: W. W. Norton & Co., 1987.
———. *Jerusalem Poker.* New York: Holt Rinehart and Winston, 1978.
———. *Nile Shadows.* New York: Holt Rinehart and Winston, 1983.
———. *Quin's Shanghai Circus.* New York: Holt Rinehart and Winston, 1974.
———. *Sinai Tapestry.* New York: Holt Rinehart and Winston, 1977.
Wilkie, Brian. *Romantic Poets and Epic Tradition.* Madison: University of Wisconsin Press, 1965.
Winnifrith, Tom, Penelope Murray, and K. W. Gransden, eds. *Aspects of the Epic.* New York: St. Martin's Press, 1983.
———. "Postscript." In *Aspects of the Epic,* 109–18.
Wofford, Susanne L. *The Choice of Achilles: The Ideology of Figure in the Epic.* Stanford, Calif.: Stanford University Press, 1992.
Woods, David M. "Love and Meaning in *The Alexandria Quartet:* Some Tantric Perspectives." In *On Miracle Ground: Essays on the Fiction of Lawrence Durrell,* ed. Michael H. Begnal, 93–112. Lewisburg, Penn.: Bucknell University Press, 1990.
Yunck, John. "Introduction." In *Eneas: A Twelfth-Century French Romance.* New York: Columbia University Press, 1974.

Index

Abraham and Isaac, 178
Abramovitsch, Shalom Ya'akov, 59–60, 71
Achilleus, 40–41
Achilleus's shield, 38
Adams, John, on epics, 30
Aeneid (Virgil), 45–46, 49, 100, 191
Alan of Lille, 191
Aleichem, Sholom. *See* Rabinovitz, Shalom
Alexandreis (Walter of Châtillon), 191
Alexandria as allegory, 207
Alexandria as metaphor, 204–5
Alexandria (city), 203, 204, 205–6
Alexandria Quartet, The, 157, 186; and Second World War, 190; structure of, 196–98, 218–19
Alexandria Quartet, The, characters: Balthazar, 208–9; Clea, 206; Darley, 196, 197, 201–2, 205; Justine, 199, 200, 214–15, 216–17; Leila, 209; Lisa Pursewarden, 209; Mahmoud Manzaloui, 206; Mnemjian, 206–7; Mountolive, 209–10; Nessim, 202, 209, 216–17; Pursewarden, 210–13
alien/foreigner, 103, 104–5, 110
Allen, Woody, 53
American Civil War, 123
amoebiasis, 133
Andromache, 34–35, 42–43
Anglo-Egyptian Club, 106
Anna Karenina (Tolstoy), 92
Anticlaudianus (Alan of Lille), 191
anti-Semitism, 109, 144
Apostle, The (Asch), 63–64

Araucana, La (Ercilla), 46–47
Archilochus, 121
Aristotle, 25, 29, 222 n. 19
Arnold, Matthew, 126, 200–201
Artist among the Missing (Manning), 89, 90
Asch, Sholem: career, 63–64; and epic, 192; flaws as writer, 60–61; writing banned, 64
"Astrophel" (Spenser), 20
Ataturk (Mustafa Kemal), 173
Athenian Empire, 108
August 1914 (Solzhenitsyn), 55
Augustine, Saint, 159, 160, 178, 193–94
Avignon Quintet (Durrell), 202, 204

Bakhtin, M. M., 44, 51
Balkan Trilogy, The, 90, 102, 104, 108, 113, 119, 120; and anti-Semitism, 109–11; Phaleron Circle, 99; and Troy, 91, 92, 93
Balthazar, 196
Beatrice, 192–93, 199–200, 214, 216
Bellamy, Elizabeth, 45, 47, 50, 93
Beloff, Max, 127
Beowulf, 36–37, 38–39, 43–44, 100
Berlin, Isaiah, 121, 124, 141
Bible, 174; original manuscript of, 160
Bible: Christian, 49; Sinai, 166–67, 170, 188
Bible as epic, 49
"big form" novel, 125
Blake, William, 229 n. 40
Bloomfield, Morton, 50

Bode, Carl, 195
Bolsheviks, 75–76
boustrophedon, 208
Bowra, Maurice, 27, 28–29, 30, 221 n.16, 223 n. 39, 225 n. 1
Boyer, Allen, 126, 134
Briseis, 42–43
British and Rumanians, 102–4
British and the Indians, 126, 130, 144, 151–52, 155
British Empire, 108, 142–43; dissolution of, 54, 55, 91, 100, 107, 119
Bucharest: British presence in, 102
Burgess, Anthony, 113

Calin, William, 222–23 n. 37
Camperlea Girls, The (Manning), 89
caritas, 193, 199, 201, 216
Catch-22, 174
cathedral analogy, 194–95
Chamberlain, Neville, 93
chaos/order, 168
Childs, Peter, 135, 141, 154, 227 n. 29
Chmielnicki massacres (1648), 62
choice, 170
Chrétien de Troyes, 191
Christianity, 145–47, 227–28 n. 48; Jewish origins of, 64
Cinthio, Giovambattista Giraldi, 23
Clea (Durrell), 195, 197, 202
Clemens, Samuel, 60
Codreanu, Corneliu Zelea, 101
Colie, Rosalie, 20, 21, 224 n. 66
colonialism, 106
Comedy (Dante): and *Alexandria Quartet*, 190–95, 217; structure of, 197
contrasts in *Three Cities:* between Halperin/Hurvitz families, 69, 70–71; between poverty and wealth, 74
Cossacks, 57, 58, 62
Courtier (Castiglione), 21
Cross, Frank, 224 n. 60
Crying of Lot, 49, The (Pynchon), 21, 158
cupiditas, 193, 199
Curtius, Ernst Robert, 190–92, 219

Dance to the Music of Time, A (Powell), 186
Day of the Scorpion, The (Scott), 126

death in war, 31, 32, 42
De bello Troiano (Joseph of Exeter), 191
Derrida, Jacques, 20
deus loci, 204, 205, 225 n. 81
"Deus Loci" (Durrell), 204
dialogic / monologic, 44–45, 91
Dickens, Charles, 142
Different Face, A (Manning), 89
dirges of women, 44
Divine Comedy, The (Dante), 187
Division of the Spoils, A (Scott), 126, 133, 139
Documentary Hypothesis, 167
Dold, Bernard, 90
domination, 109
"Dover Beach" (Arnold), 200–201
Doves of Venus, The (Manning), 89
Dubliners (Joyce), 90
Durrell: alter ego, 210, 211, 214; treatment of women, 214–15, 217
Dyer, General, 132, 133

East River (Asch), 63
Egypt, 157
Egyptian Empire, 108
Einstein, Albert, 203
elegiac form, 125–26
Emerson, Ralph Waldo: essays, 136, 140
English, Isobel, 107
enigma, 189
epic: defining, 24–29, 190, 222 n. 37; evolution in, 44; identifying, 22–23, 188–89; medieval, 26; mock, 22
epic and nationalism, 45
epic / heroic distinction, 30, 37
epic novel, 51–53, 56
epic / romance distinction, 49
Ermolaev, Herman, 56, 57
Exodus, 49

Faerie Queene, The (Spenser), 46, 50, 158, 167, 207
female moon / male sun, 214–15
Fiddler on the Roof, 60
Fielding, Henry, 22–23, 51
Finnegans Wake (Joyce), 186
First World War, 55
Five Books of Moses, 49
foreigner/alien, 104–5, 110

formalists, 21–22
Forsyte Saga, The (Galsworthy), 127, 190
Fortunes of War: brooch incident, 99, 115; "dishonest game," 107; as two trilogies, 90, 91
Fortunes of War, The, characters: Aidan Pratt, 93, 117–18; Angela, 96, 97, 99; Bella, 95, 103–4, 109, 113; Ben Phipps, 99–100; Charles, 99, 114; Clarence, 93, 95, 97, 116; Cookson, 113; David (friend), 92; Doamna Prolopopescu, 109; Dobson, 93, 119; Druckers, 109, 110; Dubedat, 97–98; Gilpin (reporter), 92; Gracey, 98, 106, 114; Guy and Harriet Pringle, 91; Guy Pringle as Hektor, 93–94, 108, 116; Guy Pringle personality, 98, 100, 113–18; Harriet Pringle as Andromache, 93–94; Harriet Pringle as Guy's wife, 94–96, 98–99; Harriet Pringle's personality, 94–95, 100, 104–6, 108, 114–15, 116–17; Inchcape, 97, 103, 114; Iqal, 105–6; Pinkrose, 98, 106, 113; Prince Yakimov, 94, 97, 104, 109, 111–13; Sasha Drucker, 109–12, 113; Sheppy, 93–94; Simon Boulderstone, 97, 106–7, 113, 118–19; Sir Brian Love, 101–2; Sophie, 95, 96–97, 98; Toby, 97–98; Woolley, 94, 97, 103
Four Quartets (Eliot), 204
Fowler, Alastair, 21, 221 n. 16
fox and hedgehog, 141, 155
Freud, 203
Friedman, Alan, 195, 208, 210
"Frost at Midnight" (Coleridge), 201
Frye, Northrop, 19, 222 n. 24

Gandhi, Mahatma, 55, 144–45
gender roles: in Manning novels, 90, 95–96
generational tension, 80–81
Genette, Gérard, 19, 54
genre: evolution in, 23; identifying, 19–22; male, 91; pure example, 50
genres: hierarchy of, 25
Gerusalemme Liberata (Tasso), 25
Goethe, 191
Gorra, Michael, 129, 155
Gravity's Rainbow (Pynchon), 21, 158

Great Fortune, The (Manning), 92
Greek Testament, 49
Greene, Thomas, 29, 214–15, 221 n. 8
Groddeck, 203

Hainsworth, J. B., 197
haj (pilgrimage), 169
Hardie, Philip, 48, 223 n. 37
Harrison, S. J., 39, 224 n. 54
hedgehog and fox, 121–25, 141, 155
Hegel, G. W. F., 49
Heilbut, Anthony, 158
Helen in Egypt (H. D.), 41
heroic code, 36, 37, 39–40
heroic / epic distinction, 30, 37
heroic poem, 38
hero in epic, 40–41
Hindu-Muslim carnage, 143–44, 154
historical novel, 49
history: use of, 48
history as a phenomenon, 135–36
history/historians, 121, 123, 128–29, 132, 173
Hitler, 100, 102, 179
Hollahan, Eugene, 217
Holocaust, 62, 85, 179
Homer, 23, 94, 151, 187–88
homosexuality, 135
Hotel Metropole, 76–77
Hougan, Jim, 158
Hutchens, Eleanor, 203

idealism, 93
Iliad, 27, 29–30; heroes, 41–43; and heroic code, 31–36; and women, 94
imperialism: national, 96, 105, 145; personal, 96, 99, 100, 109
imperialism as rape, 152
Indian National Army, 134
inexpressible, 158–59, 160–61, 180
Inheritors, The (Asch), 67
In the Days of Simon Stern (Cohen), 172
Iron Guard, 101, 109, 116

Jallianwallah Bagh, 132, 133
James, Henry, 53
Japanese tea ceremony, 160
Javitch, Daniel, 25
Jennings, Asa, 177

Jericho (city), 182–83
Jericho Mosaic (Whittemore), 166, 179, 181–82
Jericho Mosaic, characters: Belle, 187, 188–89; Tajar, 166, 179, 184, 187; Yossi/Halim, 184
Jerusalem (city), 166, 182–83
Jerusalem Poker (Whittemore), 158, 166, 177, 180
Jerusalem Quartet, The, characters: baking priest, 169–70; Belle, 187, 188–89; Bernini, 180; Bletchley, 182; Haj Harun, 165; Joe, 169–70, 175–76, 180–81; Munk Szondi, 170; Plantagenet Strongbow, 165, 179–80; Rabbi Lotmann (Baron Kikuchi)i, 170; Skanderberg Wallenstein, 166–67; Stern, 166, 170–72, 173; Stern as gunrunner, 174–75; Stern's death, 180; Stern's killing of little girl, 177–79; Stern's vision, 172; Ya'qub, 170–71
Jerusalem Quartet, The (Whittemore), 157, 165; allusions to epics, 185–88; structure of, 185
Jesus, 95, 181
Jewel in her Crown, The (picture), 156
Jewel in the Crown, The (Scott), 126, 129, 131, 132, 151, 154
Jewish Enlightenment, 59
Jewish/non-Jewish life, 84
Jews: fate of, 78; prejudice against, 109, 144; social status of, 74–75
Joseph of Exeter, 191
Justine (Durrell), 197, 202, 206

Kazantzakis, Nikos, 23, 221 n. 17
Keene, Donald, 160, 163
Keith, A. M., 27, 41
Keller, Hans-Erich, 224 n. 70
Kennedy, Duncan, 222 n. 31
Kermode, Frank, 210, 211
Key to Modern British Poetry, A (Durrell), 203, 204, 216, 218
Krishna, 146
Kryukova, Marfa, 74

Lawrence, D. H., 213
Le Bossu, 21, 25, 28
Lenin, 74, 77

Levant Trilogy, The (Manning): brooch incident, 99, 115; coda, 101; conclusion, 119; imperialism, 104; and *War and Peace*, 91
Liptzin, Sol, 80, 81
literalism, 101
Lodz (city), 225 n. 13; in *Three Cities*, 71–72, 73
Lord Jim (Conrad), 127
love: divine, 193, 200; modern, 200, 201; modern, investigation of, 195–96, 200, 205, 214, 217; sexual, 215
Lukács, Georg, 22, 51–52, 53
Luther, Martin, 133

Mackworth, Cecily, 211
MacNiven, Ian, 205, 226 n. 1
Madison, Charles, 67, 77, 78
MAD (mutually assured destruction), 174
Magic Wishing Ring, The (Abramovitsch), 71
Mahabharata, The 39, 187
Mahood, M. M., 125
male power game, 97–98, 99–100
male sun / female moon, 214–15
male superiority, 148–49
man-bap, 138, 145
Manning, Olivia, 226 n. 1; and Homer, 94; writing career, 89–91, 100
Manning and Scott, comparison of, 91
Maresca, Thomas, 22
Mary (Asch), 63
Maskell, David, 22
Masterpiece Theatre, 90, 120
McWilliams, John, 26
Mendele the Book Peddler, 59
Menippean satire, 21
Merchant, Paul, 28
Meredith, George, 195
Messiah Period, The (Asch), 67
Messianic Age, The (Asch), 80
Middleton, Christopher, 198
Miller, Henry, 210
Milton, 23–24
Modern Love (Meredith), 195
monologic / dialogic, 44–45, 91
Moore, Robin, 156
Moorman, Charles, 223 n. 40
Mori, Masaki, 29

Morris, Robert K, 93, 224 n. 63, 226 n. 3
Moscow (Asch): analysis, 65; and spiritual poverty, 73
Mother Teresa, 147
Mottke the Thief (Asch), 61, 62
Mountolive (Durrell), 197, 202
Mozart's Jupiter Symphony, 137
Musa, Mark, 202
myth, 165, 166, 167, 198–99

narrative, 29
national imperialism, 96, 105, 145
Nazarene, The (Asch), 63–64, 72, 73, 84
New Criticism, 20
Newman, John, 39, 222 n. 19
Nibelungenlied, 50
Nile Shadows (Whittemore), 166, 172, 177, 179, 180
Nō drama, 160–62, 163–64, 165; defined, 160; rituals of, 161
Nohrnberg, James, 223 n. 37
November 1916 (Solzhenitsyn), 55

"Ode on a Grecian Urn" (Keats), 201, 204
Odyssey (Homer), 27, 49–51, 53
O'Hara, J. D., 158
oppression, 106
order/chaos, 168
Orlando Furioso (Ariosto), 20, 24–25, 49
Ottoman Empire, 104, 119, 165, 171
Owen, Wilfred, 178

palimpsests, 19, 54
Paradise Lost (Milton), 22, 23–24
Parker, Patricia, 50
Parry, Benita, 126, 153–54
Passage to India, A (Forster), 144, 155
Peirce, Carol, 199, 210
Peretz, Yitzchak Leib, 60, 72
personal imperialism, 96, 99, 100, 109
Petersburg (Asch), 65, 74
Petersone, Karina, 125
Petrarch, 23, 24
Pinchin, Jane, 214, 215
Pine, Richard, 205, 208, 228 n. 11
pivotal moment in history, 29, 30, 55, 57, 64, 87, 118, 141, 173, 190, 191–92, 219

Play Room, The (Manning), 89
Poem of my Cid, The, 37–38
Poetics (Aristotle), 222 n. 19
political literature, 91
Pope, Alexander, 22
Portrait of the Artist as a Young Man (Joyce), 186, 213
Pound, Ezra, 47
poverty, physical, 73
poverty, spiritual, 73
power, 25, 109
princedoms: Indian, 142–43
Prokofiev, 53, 124
Pynchon, Thomas, 21, 157–58

Quiet Flows the Don (Sholokhov), 55–56, 57, 225 n. 3
Quinn, K., 39
Quin's Shanghai Circus (Whittemore), 158, 160–65, 185; relationships in, 164
Quint, David, 22, 45, 223 nn. 44 and 49
Quit India, 144–45

Rabinovitz, Shalom, 60
racism, 130
Rain Forest, The (Manning), 90, 108
raj: end of, 127, 128, 129, 135, 155
Raj Quartet (Scott): as elegiac, 126–27; as epic, 128; genre of, 127–28; as Scott's view of life, 126, 128, 141, 142
Raj Quartet, characters: Ashok, 147; Aunt Charlotte, 143–44; Barbie Batchelor, 134, 136–37, 140, 146–47; Captain Samuels, 144; County Bronowski, 139; Daphne Manners, 129, 148–50, 151–52; Duleep Kumar, 148; Edwina Crane, 134, 137, 145; General Reid, 131–32, 135; Guy Perron, 128, 139, 143–44, 145–46, 156; Hari Kumar, 128, 130–31, 148; Havildar Karim Muzzafir Khan, 133–34; Jimmy Clark, 150; Lady Manners, 153; Lance-Corporal Pinker, 135; Mabel Layton, 136, 138, 147, 153; Mildred Layton, 152; Mohammed Ali Kasim (MAK), 134, 140; Mr. Chaudhuri, 145; Parvati, 134, 150, 153–54; Ronald Merrick, 128, 130–31, 133, 134–35, 140; Sarah Layton, 141, 150, 154; Sister Ludmila,

129–31, 147; Stranger, 129, 132, 150; Susan Layton, 141; Teddie (Edward), 138–39, 141
Raj Quartet, locations: Bibighar Gardens, 131, 149, 151; Chillianwallah Bagh, 127; Sanctuary, 130–31, 134
Rao, K. Bhaskara, 125
rape as metaphor, 151
rape of Daphne, 129, 131, 134, 151, 152
Red Wheel, The (Solzhenitsyn), 55–56
Reich (as empire), 108
relativity proposition, 196–97
religion, 160, 162
religious/non-religious life, 84
Resurrection (Tolstoy), 56
Rexroth, Kenneth, 207
Ring and the Book, The (Browning), 129
Robertson, D. W., 159
romance, 49–51
romance / epic distinction, 49
Ronsard, 23, 24, 45
Roosevelt, Franklin Delano, 144
Routh, H. V., 48
Rowland, Ingrid, 190
Rubin, David, 227 n. 31
Rumanian Iron Guard, 101, 109, 116
Rumanians: and British, 102–3
Rushdie, Salman, 127
Russian-Japanese War (1905), 55
Russian Revolution, 55, 63, 64, 74, 77–78; identifying enemy, 75

Sade, Marquis de, 213–14, 216
Safer, Elaine, 26
sagas, 30
Salvation (Asch), 63, 73, 80
Sanctification of the Name (Asch), 61–62
satire, 21
Scanlan, Margaret, 127, 128
Scott, Paul: biography of, 127, 142; about *Raj Quartet*, 126, 141; as Tolstoyan, 125–26, 132, 154–55
Scott, Walter, 49
Scott and Manning: comparison of, 91
Second World War, 55, 91, 96, 101, 102
Seforim, Mendele Mocher, 59
Servius, 191
Shakespeare plays, 91–92

Shelley, 142
Sheridan, James, 27
Sholokhov, Mikhail, 55–57, 74
Sidney, Sir Philip, 20–21, 181, 222 n. 32
Siegel, Ben, 78, 87
Sinai Tapestry (Whittemore), 158, 165, 166, 177, 179, 180
Six Days' War, 173, 179, 184
Skow, John, 159
Slaughterhouse-Five (Vonnegut), 21
Smyrna (Izmir), 173–74, 176–78, 185, 187–88
social justice: in *Three Cities*, 72
Solzhenitsyn, Aleksandr, 55, 56–57, 57–58
Spanish Civil War, 93, 107
Spenser, Edmund, 20–21
Spinoza, 70
spiritual poverty, 65
Spurling, Hillary, 126, 127, 135, 142
Stalin, Joseph, 56–57, 74, 124, 142
Statius, 191
Staying On (Scott), 140, 150, 154
Steiner, George, 218
Stern, Avraham, and Stern Gang, 172–73
Strongbowism, 167–69, 180
surrealism, 158
Suzuki, Mihoko, 223 n. 47

Talmud, 162
Taoism, 162
Tao Te Ching, 162
tapestry, 159, 167, 168, 179–80, 183–84, 188–89
Tatars, 62
Tedesco and Popham, 129
Tempest, The (Shakespeare), 21
Thermopylae, 104
Three Cities, (Asch), 55–56, 63; analysis, 87–88; comparison to other novels, 58; soup kitchen incident, 83
Three Cities, characters: Akimov (minister), 75, 78; Anushka (Halperin servant), 67; Baruch Chomsky, 82, 84, 86; Comrade Anatol, 85–86; Comrade Sofia (Sosha), 76, 86; Frau Hurvitz, 68–69; Frau Hurvitz and religion, 70; Gabriel Haimovitch Mirkin, 67, 81, 86; Helene (teacher), 86–87; Hurvitz living condi-

tions, 69; Misha Halperin, 67; Nina Halperin, 67, 68, 78–79, 81; Olga Michailovna Halperin, 68, 72, 79; Solomon Hurvitz, 69; Solomon Hurvitz and religion, 72–73; Solomon Ossipovitch Halperin, 65–68, 70–71, 78, 86; Solomon Ossipovitch Halperin and religion, 81; Vassily Andreyevitch, 68–69; Zachary Mirkin, 65, 67, 68–69, 76, 78–80; Zachary Mirkin and idealism, 84–86; Zachary Mirkin and older women, 79, 83–84; Zachary Mirkin and religion, 70, 71–72, 81–83; Zachary Mirkin as epic hero, 87; Zachary Mirkin in military, 85–86
Tillyard, E. M. W., 116
"Tintern Abbey" (Wordsworth), 201
Tolstoy, Leo, 52–53, 56–57, 91, 121–25, 138; as character in *August 1914*, 56
Towers of Silence, The (Scott), 126, 133, 144, 147
Trilling, Lionel, 216
trinity, 176, 183
Troilus and Cressida (Shakespeare), 92, 98, 112–13, 116, 117
Troy, 91–92, 93
Tunc (Durrell), 218
Twain, Mark, 60

Ulysses (Joyce), 39, 186, 203
Uncle Moses (Asch), 63
unsexing men, 149–50, 151

Victoria (Queen), 171
Virgil, 23, 45–46
Virgil (in *Comedy*), 192
Vita Nuova (Dante), 190, 193

Vives, 223 n. 44
Voltaire, 23, 28, 49, 221 n. 17
V (Pynchon), 158

Wagner's *Ring*, 39
Walter of Châtillon, 191
War and Peace (Tolstoy), 28, 52–53, 56–57, 64–65, 100, 119, 121–24; influence of, 52–53; as model, 91
Warsaw (Asch): analysis, 65, 68–73; and the poor, 74; and spiritual poverty, 73
Warsaw massacre, 76
Waste Land, The (Eliot), 186, 203, 204
wave: society as, 137–41, 144, 152
Wedin, Warren, 198–99
Weigel, John, 212
weight (in epic), 28–29
Weil, Simone, 31
Weinbaum, Francine, 125, 126, 127, 129, 134, 144, 155
White, Robin, 131–32, 133
white superiority, 148–49
Whittemore, Edward: and the inexpressible, 158–59; writing career, 157–58
Wind Changes, The (Manning), 91, 107
Winnifrith, Tom, 28, 46, 222 n. 24, 223 n. 44
Wofford, Susanne, 45, 224 n. 52
women: sorrow of, 42–44; stereotype, 95
women's role, 35, 41–44, 91, 94, 97, 135
World War I. *See* First World War
World War II. *See* Second World War

Yiddish epic, 60
Yiddish language, 59
Yiddish literature, 58–59, 71, 72
Yunck, John, 191